Praise

The Hero Doctrine

"Neal Silvester is one of the best new voices in Mormon literature."

—**Boyd Petersen**, professor of Mormon studies at
Utah Valley University, author of *Hugh Nibley: A Consecrated Life*,
former president of the Association for Mormon Letters

"*The Hero Doctrine: Awakening to Your Eternal Potential* is a fascinating look at the messages hidden in modern popular books and films. From Harry Potter to the dark tales surrounding Batman, gospel messages of awakening and redemption are there for those who have eyes to see. Neal Silvester has uncovered the parables concealed in some of the well-known fiction of our day."

—**Diann Thornley Read**, author of the
Sergey Chronicles and the Seventh Shaman series

"With a perfect mix of pop culture, scriptures, and prophet references, *The Hero Doctrine* is the perfect book for anyone who has quoted Dumbledore in sacrament meeting. Silvester has created a book that appeals to those who enjoy finding gospel parallels in the books and movies we all know and love. He references such works as Star Wars and Harry Potter and, without apology or flippancy, enumerates the gospel principles within them. This book manages to be both a serious spiritual discussion and an entertaining read. It's an inspiring call to spiritual heroism and a great family home evening resource—especially for families with older children."

—**Emily Harris Adams**, author of *For Those with Empty Arms:
A Compassionate Voice for Those Experiencing Infertility*

THE
HERO
DOCTRINE

THE
HERO
DOCTRINE

AWAKENING TO YOUR *Eternal* POTENTIAL

NEAL SILVESTER

CFI
An Imprint of Cedar Fort, Inc.
Springville, Utah

ISBN 13: 978-1-4621-1676-8

Published by CFI, an imprint of Cedar Fort, Inc.
2373 W. 700 S., Springville, UT 84663
Distributed by Cedar Fort, Inc., www.cedarfort.com

LIBRARY OF CONGRESS CATALOGING-IN-PUBLICATION DATA

Silvester, Neal, 1987- author.
The hero doctrine / Neal Silvester.
    pages cm
Includes bibliographical references.
ISBN 978-1-4621-1676-8 (perfect bound : alk. paper)
1. Mormons--Conduct of life. 2. Plan of salvation (Mormon theology) 3. Atonement--Church of Jesus Christ of Latter-day Saints. I. Title.
BX8635.3.S63 2016
248.4'893--dc23

                    2015035048

Cover design by Shawnda T. Craig
Cover design © 2016 Cedar Fort, Inc.
Edited and typeset by Kevin Haws

Printed in the United States of America

10 9 8 7 6 5 4 3 2 1

Printed on acid-free paper

This book is dedicated to Travis Kupp, Stephan Peers, and Joseph Harris.

The Mirror
What are we capable of?
Everything.

The Sword
What do we need to be willing to do?
Anything.

The Shield
What do we have to fear?
Nothing.

Contents

Introduction
A Mirror, a Sword and Shield

*A*re you sleeping through the Restoration?" That is the question President Dieter F. Uchtdorf asked all of us in his talk of the same name during the April 2014 general conference. I think too many of us, if we were honest, would answer yes.

Here's another way of putting it: Some in the world profess a theology of deism, viewing God as the watchmaker who made the world, and then He set it down and walked away, leaving it to tick and fend for itself. When we finally arrive at the throne of God, we will find a note saying, "Gone fishing"—thus explaining why so many bad things happen in the world.

But I suggest a different view. I believe it is more likely *we* have "gone fishing"—that it is we who idle or sleep away our time while the world burns.

President Uchtdorf's penetrating question mirrors the ancient prophet Lehi in his final, dying words to his two oldest sons. Four separate times, Lehi called for his forgetful, rebellious sons to awaken, rise, and cast off their shackles. "O that ye would awake," he cried passionately, even miserably, "awake from a deep sleep . . . and shake off the awful chains by which ye are bound" (2 Nephi 1:13). He knew they had been, at best, lukewarm about the gospel he continually tried to teach them. "Awake! and arise from the dust," he pled desperately, exasperatedly (1 Nephi 1:14). "Arise from the dust, my sons, and be men" (21)—men who do not take for granted the blessings they have been given, men who are no longer spiritually asleep but who are "instrument[s] in the hands of God," like their heroic younger brother Nephi (24). And finally, Lehi issued a call to action, a veritable call to arms: "Awake, my sons; put on the armor of righteousness. Shake off the chains with which ye are bound, and come forth out of obscurity, and arise from the dust" (23).

That is a curious phrase in his final cry: "come forth out of obscurity." It is curious because at the time of Lehi's final sermons, Laman and Lemuel would not have been obscure members of their society. They would have been at the top, even the most visible, given their places as the eldest of that family.

Two possible explanations for this word choice enter my mind. The first aligns with the overarching purpose of the Book of Mormon, which is to be a warning to our day. It is quite possible that in that moment when Lehi lay on his deathbed, giving his final sermons, he was seeing our time and speaking, in part, to us. He could have been seeing the slumber of our generation, how large and expansive our own society is, and how lost we, as individuals, are, as single stars among trillions. His words could very well be, like the angel Moroni's, as one crying from the dust, rousing us to our feet, and calling us to stand up for truth and remove the coverings from over our candles. Now is the time to shine.

The second thought arose when I asked my wife about this particular phrase. She turned it over in her mind, and then explained that the Latin *obscurus* means "dark." She then provided her own theory: that the obscurity Lehi talked about isn't necessarily referring to being unknown or having a lack of fame, but rather is more like an obscurity of mind, a cloud of ignorance that we don't care to wave away. Surely this too would account for Lehi's words. Laman and Lemuel rarely ever sought answers to their complaints and criticisms, never asking the Lord if their father's teachings were true. Instead, they were satisfied with their lifestyle, reacting angrily to what Lehi preached and consistently forgetting the many miracles that had saved their family and delivered them out of the hands of their enemies.

This definition of obscurity is apt for our time as well. Spiritual illiteracy plagues much of our generation, and consequently the importance of the cause is lost on so many of us. Lehi's message, his plea to us, is clear: Let us know truth. Let us be familiar with it and not let the sharp lines and vivid colors of the gospel dull or fade or blur. We need to wake up and clear the haze from our minds. Wake up and cast aside the chains with which we are ignorantly bound. Wake up and remember who we are.

The purpose of this book is to help do that: to rouse the sleeping generation, revitalize the gospel in our lives, and reorient ourselves with a celestial lens. We must all rediscover who we are, what we are here on earth to accomplish, and what we are meant to one day become. To that effect, I offer three symbols: a mirror, a sword and shield.

The mirror symbolizes at once our identity and our destiny, as children of God. We are created in His image, inside and out, though we are now clothed with the clay of the natural man. Understanding what we are capable of achieving makes those achievements all the more possible.

The sword is the work, the war we are called to wage. Our purpose and mission in life. Each of us has a unique place, talents, and skills. Yet we are all called to the same white field and apply our abilities in our own way for the same end: the development of ourselves and the salvation of those around us. As we wage this war, the primary blessings we are responsible for utilizing are the Atonement, the temple, and all our individual gifts and talents.

The shield represents those ways in which we can protect our souls from the weapons of the world—the shield of our faith, of the Atonement, as well as the hopes and reassurances of the Resurrection and all other doctrines of comfort. If we throw up that shield God has provided us, we have no need to fear pain, loss, sin, or even hard doctrines.

The titular *Hero Doctrine*, therefore, is the combination of these artifacts of heroism—how we need to be the Lord's mirror, sword, and shield, and how He is our mirror, sword, and shield in return. These symbolic relationships form the backbone of this book, and, I believe, the gospel itself, at least in how it applies to us and how we apply it to the world. The hero understands who he or she is (mirror), is thus adequately capable (sword), and so lives without fear (shield).

I should disclose the fact that, yes, these words are taken directly from the Coldplay song "Viva la Vida," a song rich in religious imagery. They first struck me in an incredibly private way some time ago, and their attributed meaning was really personal to me at first. However, I recently felt that I shouldn't stay selfish and hold the call found in the lyrics to myself.

> Be my mirror, my sword and shield
> My missionaries in a foreign field.[1]

I don't remember quite when or why those words first jumped out to me. It was probably a gradual realization, honestly. The music of that song is so inspiring and ennobling that I couldn't help but read further into the lyrics. Maybe you will see what I see in those words. Maybe the meaning and message, whether from Chris Martin or from God, will grip you as much as it gripped me.

In a similar vein, throughout the book I frequently analyze popular culture for a gospel end. Much of the doctrine taught in this book will be shared first with stories from film and literature (and another Coldplay song). Orson Scott Card has remarked how some of the most memorable lessons Christ taught during His earthly ministry—and consequently, the ones that have lasted two millennia in our cultural consciousness—are those delivered through parables. Stories. Christ's parables were concrete literary applications of what might have otherwise been merely vague, abstract theological ideas. When we see the love the father has for his wayward prodigal son, we see with new eyes the love God has for us. When we read the parable of the talents, we understand exactly why God has granted us blessings, gifts, and skills. When we read about the Good Samaritan, we feel in our hearts precisely what it means to be a neighbor and love our fellow man. All of Christ's parables were painted with the common things of life in that time period so that they made sense to those willing to listen. They understood.

So it is easy to see how fiction of our modern day has more to offer to the table of truth than we generally give it credit for. When we look more deeply at the greatest of stories, we can often find reflections of truth staring right back at us.

Thus I begin most of these chapters with little allegories from stories you might have seen in books, movies, or even through general knowledge. After all, if I can get spiritual instruction from a Coldplay song, you might find similar revelation in the tales of Star Wars, Harry Potter, Batman, *Ender's Game*, and more. These timeless archetypes of heroes, of good and evil, are ripe for reinterpretation from pop culture to profound parable. Thus I chose the stories I did, not just because they will speak to youth and the rising generation, but also because they in particular are richly woven with truth, whether the given author is aware of it or not.

And how much truth does the gospel embrace? Brigham Young said extensively, "All the truth that there is in the heavens, on the earth, under the earth; and if there is any truth in hell, this doctrine claims it. It is all the truth of heaven, the truth of God, the life of those that live forever, the law by which worlds were, are, and will be brought into existence, and pass from one degree or one state of being to another, pertaining to the exaltation of intelligence from the lowest to the highest state."[2]

Truth is everywhere. If we are on the lookout, we can see how the Lord leads us to whatever is relevant to our lives, no matter the medium of communication. The particular stories I share in this book in my opinion not only teach of the need our world has for heroes but also exactly what goes into creating such a being, the transformational process that can help seemingly ordinary souls become like Christ and our Heavenly Father. In the eternal perspective, Batman really has got nothing on you.

That message is the real impetus of this book. It is a rousing reminder of the stakes of this world, written in the hopes that we do not sleep through the Restoration and let our truly eternal potential go unfilled. I want you to catch the vision of not just your potential, but also the plan: *why* you have that potential and what to do with it. I want you to see the context of it all, the grand vision of our unending journey, our eternal arc.

Therefore, some of the encouragement contained herein prods forward like a spur—the sword. Other messages are meant to soothe and comfort like a feather—the shield. All of it is written with the intent of awakening our generation to the conflict of justice, echoing the cry that opens and closes the Book of Mormon: to rise from the dust and come out of obscurity into the light, where we can stand, be counted, and not waste the time or the blessings God has given us. The Lord needs heroes, just as when Captain Moroni raised the title of liberty all those many centuries ago.

Chapter 1
The Eternal Arc

*Y*ou all know of our first mirror. In the story of *Star Wars* (the original movie), Luke Skywalker started out as a moisture farmer on the barren planet of Tatooine and ended as a key player in the rebellion against the evil Empire, gradually transforming from an ordinary soul into the epitome of a classical hero. The general arc of this transformation is called the Hero's Cycle, a literary and mythological concept first formed by Joseph Campbell, author of *The Hero with a Thousand Faces*. In the book, Campbell detailed the various trials and stages a would-be hero has to go through to obtain that status. This cycle is based on myths and legends of old, the stories of heroes; Campbell discovered that all these otherwise disparate myths agree remarkably on the precise situations and experiences that ultimately change an ordinary Joe into a hero. George Lucas, the creator of the Star Wars saga, followed this cycle purposefully and nigh perfectly with his protagonist Luke, and the timeless nature of that tale is one of the primary reasons the Star Wars movies are so universally loved.

There's another arc I'd like to talk about that is similar but far more significant. I call it the Eternal Arc. It is about mankind's potential to become like Heavenly Father, and it parallels the Hero's Cycle with startling precision. Just as Luke unknowingly progressed through various stages of character development in his unconscious quest to become a hero, so must we advance through different stages of existence and states of being in our conscious quest to join Heavenly Father in all His glory and domain.

Now, much of what follows may very well feel remedial to you, but bear with me. We're going to cover this doctrine from beginning to end as it must be properly understood in its context—a process that we echo in our own personal paths into eternity.

Paul, in the book of Acts, called us "the offspring of God" (Acts 17:29). In Romans, he wrote, "The Spirit itself beareth witness with our spirit, that we are the children of God," before following logically that "if children, then heirs; heirs of God, and joint-heirs with Christ" (Romans 8:16–17). That state—as joint-heirs with Christ—is the end goal of our existence, that we might inherit the station and glory of our Heavenly Father. First, we must become like Christ in traits and attributes, and then we may become like Heavenly Father in glory and stewardship. That is the grand destination at the end of our journey.

Journeys, of course, need maps. We need to know where we are going to go and which paths we need to take on our way to the end. Luke Skywalker didn't have a map to chart his personal journey, but we do. We call that map the plan of salvation, otherwise called the plan of happiness. The plan takes us from ordinary peasants, busy with the daily doldrums of mortal toil, to spiritual kings and queens, heroes and rulers in our own kingdoms—from blurry-eyed intelligences all the way to exaltation and eternal life as heirs in the presence of God. This plan was presented to us before we were born, when we were mere disembodied spirits. In that state of being, we lived with Heavenly Father as His literal spirit children. He has a spirit as we do, and as it is an essential part of us, so is it an essential part of Him.

But we existed before we were even tabernacles of spirit. Just as we have an eternal future, so too do we have an eternal past, an existence before even Heavenly Father clothed us in spiritual form. As mere intelligences, we had only the most basic of identities, with potential we perhaps didn't understand. This is the state Luke began in, unaware of his destiny but looking up at the stars, wanting to join them and be a part of a higher life, even if he didn't know what that would be.

In Luke Skywalker, we see a mirror of our own potential.

The Call to Adventure

The Hero's Cycle always begins with a rousing cry. The character is figuratively awoken and called upon to put foot to the path for a special mission or duty that will eventually carry him or her away to a transformative adventure.

Luke was roused from his state of mediocrity by a literal call for help. The message came in the form of C-3PO and R2-D2, droids who possessed a recording from Princess Leia asking for help from whoever got the message. This was Luke's "Call to Adventure"—the first opportunity to show his true potential.

Likewise, our first step in the Eternal Arc was our own "Call to Adventure," the love of a God who showed us what we could one day be: a being like Him. He brought us out of our ethereal existence and gave us more sharply defined identity through spirit and gender.[3]

Crossing the Threshold

The stage of "Crossing the Threshold" refers to the moment when, no matter what the decision, the would-be hero can never turn back. It is a bridge burned, a path chosen, a cause to which the protagonist is comprehensively committed. Without this step, the hero could go back to his or her old life at any time. Because all heroes face weakness and peril in the face of strain and pressure, the path to return to the lesser estate cannot be accessed. This compels the hero to stay the course and hold strong against adversity, for the hero has no other place to go except total surrender.

For Luke and many other heroes, the threshold is the moment when the first call to action is refused. Luke felt the initial weight of destiny on his shoulders but responded with fear and uncertainty, and so refused the call. It wasn't until Luke learned that the Empire killed his aunt and uncle that he accepted Obi-Wan's invitation to train as a Jedi. The deaths of Owen and Beru made staying home and declining the journey an impossibility, and so at this point Luke was compelled to journey on and become who he was born to be.

In pre-earth life, we too made certain choices, but unlike Luke, we did not refuse our initial call. We kept our first estate and stewardship, choosing to heed Heavenly Father's call the first time it was offered. This choice allowed us to be sent to earth and be given bodies, the next essential phase of being in our Eternal Arc and our second great stewardship or estate.

The decision to come to earth was a decision we can never take back, in which our eyes were opened to mortality, with all its pains and pleasures, rights and wrongs, and all the mundanity and mediocrity in between. When our spirits obtained a mortal frame, we became a full soul, with body and spirit fused together. This was our point of no return, after which our eyes could never be closed again.

Mentor

The mentor figure is an essential part of the hero's development, for it is through the mentor that the hero perceives the greater goal. The mentor, who could be a normal human being or a supernatural entity, must be there to guide the future hero to his or her path that otherwise would remain unknown. Luke had Obi-Wan Kenobi, who taught him the basics of fighting and revealed to him his true potential—to be a Jedi knight, like his father.

Similarly, we have mentors everywhere in our lives. Ideally, they teach us to navigate the world, make good choices, and, like Obi-Wan, remind us of our true potential to become like our progenitors. These are the prophets, scriptures, priesthood leaders, and, most especially, earthly parents. From them and the gift of the Holy Ghost, we learn our true parentage, and thus our true identity and destiny.

Without guides, without anyone teaching us truth and training us, we would not be responsible for poor choices—we would not know any better, leaving us ignorant and stunted. With guides, with the Holy Ghost, we become responsible and accountable for our actions, therefore becoming full agents, just like Heavenly Father.

The Road of Trials

The mentor is especially important, given the next stage of the Eternal Arc. After we open our eyes to the reality of the world, we face tests, trials, challenges, and temptations. With our new perspective, we are now susceptible to so much and, as a result, we're going to have to confront spiritual and temporal danger just about everywhere. The mentor helps us understand the purpose of this stage—to be shaped and carved by the winds of adversity—and gives us the perspective needed to complete it successfully. In meeting these trials head-on, we begin the transformational process of this life.

Luke faced many a peril in his quest to save the princess. Threatened by death at every turn, Luke learned the dangers of the world firsthand, but he also learned how to react to them. From the adversity provided by the stormtroopers and Darth Vader, and the guidance given by Obi-Wan in learning the Force, he eventually learned to fight on his own—even to become a leader of other heroic warriors.

But though he mastered the physical side of the training quickly enough, the real trials to come were more mental, even spiritual. Against the warnings of his second mentor, Yoda, Luke succumbed to Vader's manipulation of his emotions, leading him into a dangerous trap that could have easily ended up toppling the Rebel Alliance. But however much his mistake set the Alliance back, this experience became a lesson for him too, and he learned from it.

He had yet to face his greatest challenge, though: confronting Darth Vader, who he came to learn was his morally fallen father, and finally the Emperor himself. This was not a test of skill with the lightsaber but rather a spiritual battle, a trial of temptations. The evil Emperor, in his satanic role, sought to corrupt Luke's soul and bring him over to the dark side. After feeling the pressure of evil within him, Luke fought hard and won out, remembering the hero his father once was and wanting to be just as good. In making that choice, Luke took the final step in his journey and became a full-fledged hero.

The hero-in-training must always face temptations, which are more realistic confrontations with evil than a mere test of swordplay. Like Luke, if in the midst of our temptations we remember our Father and our potential to become like Him, the strength of those temptations will lose their sting. Elder Neal A. Maxwell asked rhetorically, "Will we . . . remember our true identity as we move through daily life? How much sin occurs because people momentarily forget who they really are?"[4]

Many of the temptations we receive are directly related to our physical bodies. Receiving a body grants us capabilities we would not have had solely as spirits, thus furthering our potential to be like our Father in Heaven. But at the same time, the natural man, the inherent impulses in the body, can make it a struggle to retain control over those new aspects of ourselves. These pleasures of the flesh and other earthly appetites are not things we immediately have a great deal of command over. When we let them, our bodies may sometimes take control and make decisions in place of our minds and our spirits. This can lead down a dangerous road, especially with Satan's temptations enhancing our already pleasure-prone inclinations.

But what joy bodies can bring us too! When we bridle our passions and use them in a controlled manner, they can lead to so many wonderful things. Having a body is an essential advancement toward becoming like God, for we know from the First Vision and other modern-day revelation that God Himself is as tangible as we are, possessing a body of flesh and bone (see D&C 130:22), and that only with a body and spirit combined can we attain "a fulness of joy" (D&C 93:33). We were created directly in His likeness and image. In other words, at maturity, we look generally how He looks: a fully grown adult human being, with even more potential as stewards over our bodies with the commandment to take care of what we've been given.

We often hear from the pulpit about many other godly attributes that we can apply to our everyday lives—those aspects of Christ that He exemplified in His earthly mission. The reason we hear about them constantly is because we really need to practice them, and do so actively, not passively. Instead of going about our day simply to get through it, we need to actually make a daily concentrated effort to foster those traits in ourselves in how we act and think. Traits like faith, hope, charity, virtue, knowledge, humility, diligence, obedience, and patience all demand devotion and dedication, as surely as trees need water and light. And fortunately in this life, we are continuously given opportunities to practice them so that they may grow up into a tree of life, whose fruit is sweeter to the taste than any other work in this world (see Alma 32).

Learning to recognize these teachable moments is paramount to becoming like Christ. It is what makes our ordinary, mundane lives training grounds for higher living. Brigham Young said that "the gospel . . . causes men and women to reveal that which would have slept in their dispositions until they dropped into their graves. The plan by which the Lord leads this people . . . brings out every trait of disposition lurking in their [beings]. . . . Every fault that a person has will be made manifest, that it may be corrected."[5]

Take the attribute of patience, for example. It can be applied throughout the day with other people and even inanimate objects. Say you're at a stoplight. You're in a hurry to get somewhere and are waiting for the light to change. It's not turning green, and you can feel your blood pressure is rising. Stress is increasing. You become irritable and more liable to curse at that filthy, dumb, stupid *bleepity bleep* red light. Why won't it change? It isn't helping anyone and is actually preventing people who really need to go somewhere from getting there. It's really an inconsiderate thing, with no regard for those in a hurry. Okay, fine, *there* it goes. Finally. Now you can go. Now you can move forward.

However, now you're in a horrible mood, are liable to be angry to others, and are grumpily aware that you could have done better. Whereas if you had shown some patience and accepted that there are some things you cannot change, you could have felt peace and calm. Exercising patience in these kinds of situations prepares you for dealing with other potentially frustrating events. God Himself has to exercise such patience every day with His children—think of the patience He's had to develop!

Now think of the consequences Luke brought about by not heeding Yoda in *The Empire Strikes Back*. Instead of calming himself and exercising patience, Luke acted rashly and fell right into Darth Vader's trap. This set the Rebel Alliance back significantly and necessitated some improvisation to try to recover what was lost, wasting time they could have spent fighting the Empire. Similarly, when we act without patience, we are more likely to fall into Satan's traps and lose spiritual ground, thus losing limited time on reparative repentance.

Of course, that is just one example. We have endless opportunities in our normal lives to exercise traits of godhood so that we cultivate godliness in ourselves. In their masterful theodicy *The God Who Weeps*,

Terryl and Fiona Givens said, "The particular potency of the challenges we face—our bodily weakness, the instincts and passions that consume us, the press of evil all around us—make a life of virtuous aspiration very like a race through quicksand. However, it is just these conditions of mortality . . . that are especially conducive to growth and progress."[6]

The lectures and sermons we hear from the pulpit, repeating the same prescription of prayer and scripture reading and everything else leaders talk about—all of that is preached for a reason. They remind us that it is the ordinary things that will make us extraordinary. It is love and long-suffering for our fellow humans—and all that emanates therefrom—that will take us and make us closer to God. And each and every Christlike attribute we are asked to take on is something we can practice every day on our own metaphysical moisture farms as we endure to the end with patience and long-suffering.

Death and Rebirth—Transformation

But the point of developing these attributes isn't simply to get us to the end of the exam—this journey is all about who we transform into along the way. Elder Dallin H. Oaks said, "The Final Judgment is not just an evaluation of a sum total of good and evil acts—what we have *done.* It is an acknowledgment of the final effect of our acts and thoughts—what we have *become.* It is not enough for anyone just to go through the motions. The commandments, ordinances, and covenants of the gospel are not a list of deposits required to be made in some heavenly account. The gospel of Jesus Christ is a plan that shows us how to become what our Heavenly Father desires us to become."[7]

And what does Heavenly Father want us to become? Christ asked the Nephites this and answered it not only for that ancient people, but for all: "Therefore, what manner of men ought ye to be? Verily I say unto you, even as I am" (3 Nephi 27:27). Even as Christ. We can see the importance of these transformative attributes, for when cultivated within one's soul and when granted an added measure of them through the Atonement, they are the very things that turn us gradually into beings like Christ. Through sincere repentance, supplication for grace, and a willingness to change, our souls are reshaped and reformed, gradually taking on the Savior's countenance. And *that*, my friends, is the purpose of the exam.

Our paradigm shift from pre-earth life to this world calls to mind the Campbellian notion of "The Belly of the Whale," an image representative of a womb-like state in which the hero undergoes a kind of death and rebirthing. It is here that the hero takes on a new, fresh identity with a greater understanding of his or her potential, and then, through the aforementioned trials and temptations, he or she achieves it.

Luke didn't pass through his adventures just to see them done; he went about doing good—rescuing Leia, blowing up the Death Star, fighting off the evil Empire—for a reason. And while his works were good, even great, in defeating his enemies and bringing the galaxy closer to freedom, Luke himself became something great, someone who *fulfilled* his potential. He became like his father, Anakin: a hero, a legend, and an inspiration to many. He even saved his father's soul, wrenching it from the Emperor's grasp and returning it to the side of good. From farm boy to hero to even savior, that is the transformation process of the Hero's Cycle, and it is the essence of the Hero Doctrine.

As we strive toward Christlike behavior, we cast off the natural man and integrate the roots of our divine heritage into our whole soul. We begin to be concerned for the welfare of others, both spiritually and temporally. We begin to see the world, God, and our neighbors with a spiritual lens, or an eternal perspective. And we begin to feel love and become a source of love in a way that is not possible without Christ's influence.

But that is not the end. Being Christlike is only the first half of our transformation. The second is becoming like Heavenly Father.

Atonement with the Father

The transformation process takes the hero to a certain stage that resonates so loudly with our theology that it almost needs no explanation. After all, what else could "Atonement with the Father" really mean?

To Campbell, it meant a confrontation with the being who holds ultimate power in the hero's life, most commonly a father or father figure. This stage is where we internalize that power and discover the truth about our identity and our place in the world.

Christ expressed a similar desire for His people, for His younger brothers and sisters: "Therefore I would that ye should be perfect even as I, or your Father who is in heaven is perfect" (3 Nephi 12:48).

We are like Heavenly Father in so many ways. In his sermon on faith, Alma remarked, "Every seed bringeth forth unto its own likeness" (Alma 32:31). Bear in mind, the seeds themselves don't look anything like the trees that produced them. Not at first, anyway. If we didn't know any better, they would be totally separate things in our mind. Likewise, a human embryo doesn't look much like a human being; in fact, it doesn't look *anything* like it. But nonetheless, that is how we all started out. That was our physical beginning. Taking it a few steps further, we see that an infant doesn't really look like a human being either. But we don't call a baby any less of a human just because he or she has not reached that stage of adulthood and maturity. A baby is a human—just not developed or fully mature yet.

In other words, kittens grow up to be cats and puppies turn into dogs. So what do children of God grow up and turn into?

Recall Luke's ambition to become a Jedi, like his father before him. After becoming a full soul, with spirit and body, we are asked to go about perfecting that fused being and become like the Father by rejecting all ungodliness, denying the carnal nature inherent in mortal bodies, and choosing the divine nature inherent in our spiritual bodies. This is where we open up to our Father in Heaven and let His power perfect us. Oneness with the Father—eternal life in His presence and the eternal life that He Himself lives—is what the Atonement is all about: God granting us power and increase we would not be capable of producing ourselves.

For the power and heritage of God to be expressed in our lives, faith and the lens of the Spirit are required; we must stop depending on our own eyes and strength and start trusting in His. This is what Luke did during the Death Star attack, when he disregarded the computer's targeting system and put his trust in an unseen higher power. The Force, responding to his faith, guided his decisions. His mortal vision lacked the ability to pinpoint exactly where and when he needed to fire the proton torpedoes. Only with the added measure of the Force and the spiritual vision Luke received could he hit that two-meter exhaust port and destroy the Death Star.

Ultimate Boon

That never-ending inheritance and happiness we're promised, is our "Ultimate Boon"—a veritable Holy Grail, what we've been working on and searching for all this time.

For Luke, it was peace within himself—peace as he rejected the dark side and as he saved his father's fallen soul; peace as he grew to his full potential and realized the Jedi he became; peace as he destroyed the evil in the galaxy, ended the war decisively, and set the prisoners free. In the end, Luke fully realized his destiny, potential, and power.

It is after we receive of the ordinances of the gospel, show our faith in Christ and repent of our sins, and live righteously to the ends or mortality and endure to the end—all steps and stages of the Eternal Arc—that we can advance to our highest state of being: exaltation. A station where we, like Luke, understand ourselves in our totality—our destiny, potential, and profound power that we've accumulated, not to mention the role we've presumably played in frustrating the enemies of our Father's plan. This is the attainment of celestial glory; it is a perfected state, an inheritance of all that the Father hath—the powers of creation and of command.

Supreme happiness and love is the true meaning of the word *heaven*. Sealed to your birth family, your companion, and your children "to receive a greater change, and to be received into the kingdom of the Father to go no more out, but to dwell with God eternally in the heavens" (3 Nephi 28:40), where you will learn sacred powers, create worlds, and tell new stories by knowing all things, doing all things, and having all things.

What else could Christ mean by "all that my Father hath" (D&C 84:38)? Nothing less than that it is our privilege to inherit the kingdom of God if we live righteously to the ends of mortality. By the Atonement and power and priesthood of God, we may achieve this state of being, that we may be in the presence of the Father and our own families forever.

Master of Two Worlds

By the end of the journey, the hero holds power over both the spiritual and the material worlds. He or she has mastery over the inner and outer vessel in turn. The hero, at the end of his or her arc, has not only changed himself or herself, but also changed the entire world.

Luke became a full Jedi and dismantled the Galactic Empire. He conquered the inner battle in his spiritual duel with Darth Vader and the Emperor, refusing to choose anger and become evil like them. He also triumphed in the external duel, helping to defeat the Empire in battle and destroy their source of power. He commanded himself morally (internally) and, through the powers of the Force, physically (externally).

We too must become masters of two worlds. The first world we are meant to conquer is the stewardship of our bodies. The ideal end state of the soul is a spirit that maintains total possession over the body, a soul in which the natural man has no sway, and the perfected mind has full agency. And so, like Luke learning the powers and boundaries of the Force, we must learn the powers of our physical bodies and internalize the boundaries God has provided us to keep them under our souls' domain. When we deny ourselves all ungodliness, what then is left? Only godliness.

It is when we manifest all godly attributes that the natural man ceases to have power over us and our spirits have power over the material elements that comprise our bodies. We are, as Lehi instructed, "things to act," not "things to be acted upon" (2 Nephi 2:14). It should be noted that this is the difference between us and the rest of nature, what sets our potential apart. "Nature," remarked Katharine Hepburn's character in *The African Queen*, "is what we are put in this world to rise above."[8] An exalted body will obey our commands, just as God's body obeys Him perfectly. God is not divided like we are, the natural man pulling Him one way and the spirit the other. This perfect unity of body and spirit is the purpose of the stewardship of our souls. It is the first world we are responsible for.

The second world is the world we will create, the world we are right now in training to organize. By obeying the commandments of God, we show that we, like God, are willing to live within law. And in the same way that our own bodies are our first stewardships, and that children—receivers of law—eventually become parents themselves, so too do we as those obedient to law eventually become lawgivers ourselves. "And he that overcometh, and keepeth my works unto the end, to him will I give power over the nations" (Revelation 2:26).

Some see this destiny as too far off to concern ourselves with now. But we are closer to that lawgiving than we might think. We should never forget that the power God uses to create and organize worlds, to command the elements and shape matter at His will, is the power of the priesthood—the same power used in sacrament meetings, in governing our homes, in the administration of the Church, and in sacred temple ceremonies. Through the regulation of priesthood authority via priesthood keys, any man or woman spiritually called to a work by the Lord through His servants can exercise that creative power. What a humbling realization it is to know that in fulfilling our callings, we act to some degree by the literal power of God, the same power that organizes worlds.

Freedom to Live

The last stage of the hero's journey is liberation. With the Death Star destroyed and the Empire in shambles, Luke could now live his life freely, without fear or enemies. Neither his past nor his future was bound. In his book, Campbell even quoted Christ when He said to the Pharisees, "Before Abraham was, I am" (John 8:58).

Similarly, when we have won our own cup of glory, our conception of time will cease to exist. We will recognize our eternal past and our eternal future as one great now. We too will be freed from fear, from the chains of mortality and hell, by the power of the Resurrection and the Atonement. We will be able to live as free beings, having gained all power over ourselves and the world around us. The life of God is a life of true freedom. That agency is, I believe, the absolute definition of godhood.

But agency has a twin that is just as necessary to godhood and just as beautiful. It is the family: men and women, children of God, united by the sealing bond of the Holy Ghost. As His children, we are what gives God goals. Without progeny, the plan is meaningless.

Without parenthood, a god has no purpose, making all that freedom for naught.

So we see in our tests of mundane mortality the great practice grounds of godhood: the work of marriage and raising children. No other work comes close to the essence and duty of God. That is the responsibility we must take most soberly.

Family is what this is all about. To be given the responsibility and "sacred privilege"[9] of having and taking care of a family, one must first prove worthy to enter the temple and be armed with the attributes needed to be worthy of a temple recommend. In the temple, we take more steps into eternity, principally the endowment and, of course, sealing to an eternal companion. Only then are we given permission to take on the same kind of stewardship as Heavenly Father's: the power to create life and the responsibility to raise a new being the same way He is trying to raise us. First, we are stewards over ourselves, our spirits, and our bodies, or in other words our souls. When we have proven ourselves therewith, we are granted that blessing of increase and subsequently receive grace for grace as we advance in the creative work that is eternal progression, the endless generations of gods.

This, in its totality, is the Eternal Arc, a term that, if thought about, seems to be a paradox. After all, an arc is something finite. It culminates in a defined conclusion. But the Eternal Arc does not. It is progress from all eternity to all eternity. Progress through eternal lives, the endless propagation of the race of gods that only builds on its own glory as eternity continues, linked by love and priesthood power—all of which comes back to choices we make here in this temporal trial and the perspective with which we view this life. As we go through our daily routines, we must never forget that we are actually living something far grander, something so bright and glorious that we can currently only see it through the cracks of our fingers, caught up in mortal moments and telestial tempests as we are.

Those moments matter. This world is full of mediocrity, sameness, and often dull shades of gray and brown. The test lies in how we navigate through it and what lessons we can learn from life as we sharpen our eyes, pay attention to what occurs and why, and maintain an awareness of the grand goal at the far end. We, all of God's children, are on this journey together, a truth too easy to forget. When we pass others in the street, do we see them for their potential and preciousness in the eyes of God? Do we even see *ourselves* that way?

C. S. Lewis wrote, "It is a serious thing to live in a society of possible gods and goddesses, to remember that the dullest and most uninteresting person you talk to may one day be a creature which, if you saw it now, you would be strongly tempted to worship."[10]

Think of the beginning of *Star Wars: A New Hope*. When you first see that whiny kid living on a desert planet with Uncle Owen and Aunt Beru, could you believe he would one day give hope to the galaxy and topple the devil's Empire?

Ponder the consequences if Luke had remained with his aunt and uncle, farming moisture out of a barren wasteland of a planet—what a parable for our modern-day distractions! Meandering through apps and further down the Facebook feed, employing ourselves primarily in video games and putting all our resources and time into merely seeking to gain more and more money and more and more things that fall away from us as we rise into the next world—though flashy and colorful, this kind of living leaves our book of life as empty and dull as Tattooine.

We have a destiny far grander than that. It is Satan's victory if we forget it, disregard it, or treat it as dross. We must take absolute and total advantage of this gift given us by Heavenly Father, this gift of salvation and love and this potential for perfection and eternal increase. For right now, it is only potential—none of us have reached it yet. Potential does not entail success or accomplishment. It does not mean that it will, in fact, happen. Just as a car sitting at a stoplight needs the gas pedal to be pressed to make it move, so are exertion and effort required for any journey. Without any input, we will sit there idly, never going anywhere, forsaking our inheritance for a figurative mess of pottage—for worldly pleasures and distractions— a fate our Father never wants us to fulfill.

And fulfilling the potential God has in mind for us is definitely not as easy as putting your foot on the gas pedal. It takes work and significant sacrifice, and you can't make that sacrifice if the reason for it fades from your eyes.

Yes, we must provide for our families, give our children good lives, work hard to improve ourselves, and maybe even help a neighbor fix his roof. But we must not forget to what end we carry out those temporal chores. Not for the sake of our daily bread or daily lives, but for our *eternal* bread and *eternal* lives. Though the work may look mundane from our view on the ground, by exerting effort and sincerely trying to improve the lives of our families and those around us, we indeed advance through our own Hero's Cycle, our own Eternal Arc. We are becoming a society of gods and goddesses.

A Christlike people striving forward together against the shafts of the whirlwind will become a Godlike people, and on a variety of scales—the self, the family, the community, and even the world. We are working to create a place where we grow together, where our individual progress interweaves with our neighbor's, and where our families bloom in divine destiny—happily helping each other in all things, including and especially in the Eternal Arc—*that is Zion.* It is the reason for our more temporal (but still spiritual) callings in this life—as a bishop, Sunday School teacher, ward clerk, or even building cleanup supervisor. Our progress is truly tethered to those around us. We cannot succeed alone, nor should we even want to.

It is indeed telling that the authority to use the priesthood power is only granted for its capacity to bless others and never one's self. For it is all a part of the pattern of stewardship, taught so perfectly by Christ in the parable of the talents. The talents that the worthy servants invested to gain were not for them alone—those invested talents went into the general economy of the society and would have had to bless others as much as it blessed them. That deceptively short parable contains within it the structure of God's plan for us and eternal progression; our Eternal Arc is not one we undertake for ourselves alone, nor is it by our efforts alone, but by the example and grace of Christ to become as He is, with us rising to celestial glory our sealed families.

This end is the goal Heavenly Father wants for us more than anything. He is our Father, and He loves us more than all else He has created in the ocean, earth, or sky. As He declared to Moses, this is His work and His glory, "to bring to pass the immortality and eternal life of man" (Moses 1:39).

Bishop Vaughn J. Featherstone related the following story:

Many years ago I heard the story of the son of King Louis XVI of France. King Louis had been taken from his throne and imprisoned. His young son, the prince, was taken by those who dethroned the king. They thought that inasmuch as the king's son was heir to the throne, if they could destroy him morally, he would never realize the great and grand destiny that life had bestowed upon him.

They took him to a community far away, and there they exposed the lad to every filthy and vile thing that life could offer. . . . For over six months he had this treatment—but not once did the young lad buckle under pressure. Finally, after intensive temptation, they questioned him. Why had he not submitted himself to these things—why had he not partaken? These things would provide pleasure, satisfy his lusts, and were desirable; they were all his. The boy said, "I cannot do what you ask for I was born to be a king."[11]

Brothers and sisters, this is what we were born to be: kings and queens. Rulers. Creators. We are children of the Most High, heirs to a heavenly throne. We must awaken from our slumber, rouse out of our dormancy, and be reminded of our full potential and fondest dream.

Remember this mirror in your daily lives. Remember it when you say the things you say and do the things you do. Remember it as you press forward and endure well to the end. And remember most of all that, unlike Luke Skywalker, in God's kingdom, there is no limit to your arc, no true end to your story.

Chapter 2
A Mirror of God

*T*o *understand our* future, we must understand our present, and to understand our present, we must understand our past. This knowledge can work both as a shield of hope for us in times of self-doubt and crippled confidence and as a sword in casting light on our celestial parentage and the eternal potential to those around us. When we're awakened to the reality of our identities, we must then go rouse others.

For this chapter's parable, I turn to the climax of *Harry Potter and the Prisoner of Azkaban*. (There will, of course, be spoilers. As with every other story I'll relay in this book, if you haven't read it before, put this one down and go read or watch that one.)

Young heroic Harry, with friends Ron and Hermione and teacher Remus Lupin, just discovered that Sirius Black, alleged mass killer and betrayer of Harry's own murdered parents, was framed for his crime (and is, in fact, actually a pretty good guy). They were on their way to the authorities with the truth and the true traitor in tow when disaster struck. Professor Lupin had been previously revealed as a werewolf, and though usually he was able to drink a potion to remain tame and friendly, they realized too late that the full moon was out that night and he was nowhere near the necessary drink. Chaos fell: Lupin transformed against his will, the traitor got away, and Harry and Sirius found themselves separated from the group, left alone by the side of the lake to deal with an onslaught of dementors, the terrifying guards of the wizard prison Azkaban. Deaf to Harry's protestations, the dementors advanced on a weakened Sirius, intending to suck out his soul. The dark and despair-inducing powers of the dementors bore down on Harry, and his attempts to cast the only spell that works against them all failed. He and Sirius were about to be destroyed by the dementors when a seeming miracle occurred.

Harry, his strength spent, witnessed the sudden appearance of a great beast made of shining white light on the other side of the lake. It began to canter across the reflective surface of the water. It was a Patronus, the only thing that can repel a dementor—exactly what Harry had been trying to cast. The dementors were rebuffed and Harry and Sirius were saved. As his consciousness faded, Harry tried to get a look at his savior on the other side of the lake and see just who it was that cast the magnificent Patronus. "For a moment, Harry saw, by its brightness, somebody welcoming it back . . . raising his hand to pat it . . . someone who looked strangely familiar . . . but it couldn't be."[12]

Disbelieving his own eyes and bodily drained from the whole experience, Harry fainted, unable to confirm the identity of the person across the lake. But the image still haunted him, and midway through the next chapter, he confided to Hermione: "'I think—' Harry swallowed, knowing how strange this was going to sound. 'I think it was my dad.' Harry glanced up at Hermione and saw that her mouth was fully open now. She was gazing at him with a mixture of alarm and pity. 'Harry, your dad's—well—*dead*,' she said quietly. 'I know that,' said Harry quickly."[13]

After all, Harry thought to himself, the traitor they unearthed that night was someone the world thought dead for twelve years. Was it so impossible for his father to be alive somehow? "'Maybe I was seeing things,' said Harry. 'But . . . from what I could see . . . it looked like him . . . I've got photos of him.' Hermione was still looking at him as though worried about his sanity. 'I know it sounds crazy,' said Harry flatly."[14]

Yes, it sounded crazy, and Harry knew it. Yet there was some truth to it, as readers of the book can attest. Just what that truth was, and how it relates to the truth of our own existence, will be explained when this parable is finished at the close.

The Quest to Understand God

"I know plenty of people who genuinely seek to go about doing good but who affiliate themselves with no denomination or system of belief and often are not sure of the existence of God. Why? I believe because no one has ever given them a satisfactory description of who He is, what He does, and what our relationship is with Him."—Travis Kupp (my friend)

Plato's allegory of the cave has held a fundamental role in Western philosophy for literally thousands of years. I'd like to make it a fundamental parable of our LDS theology, relative to the concept of the sword.

Plato depicted several people locked away in a cave since childhood. They were bound in such a way that they could only ever face the cave wall opposite the entrance, which was a long way up and back, but it allowed some light in. There was a fire constantly burning at the entrance, and behind it a wall like a puppeteer's screen. Some people were behind the wall, carrying artifacts like statues of animals and other things made out of a variety of materials. The shapes of the people and the things they carried projected various kinds of shadows against the far cave wall because of the fire. Thus the prisoners inside the cave were only able to see those shadows, and that was their entire life experience. They had no knowledge of each other, nor of themselves. The only truth they knew were the two-dimensional images on the wall.

What would it be like for someone to be suddenly freed from the binds? He would "stand up, turn his head, walk, and look up toward the light" and "be pained and dazzled."[15] This freed prisoner, his eyes flooded by light, would see the world anew, as well as the sun, moon, and stars in the heavens. He would make fantastic discoveries and understand the world as it really is.

Plato, through the character of Socrates, then asked rhetorically,

> What about when he reminds himself of his first dwelling place, his fellow prisoners, and what passed for wisdom there? Don't you think that he'd count himself happy for the change and pity the others? . . .

> If this man went down into the cave again and sat down in his same seat . . . while his vision was still dim, if he had to compete again with the perpetual prisoners in recognizing the shadows, wouldn't he invite ridicule? Wouldn't it be said of him that he'd returned from his upward journey with his eyesight ruined and it isn't worthwhile even to try to free them and lead upward?[16]

Does this sound familiar? It should. As Latter-day Saints, we should feel like the man who was freed and shown the true matter of things. We are making that journey upward, and in this world we are surrounded by these "perpetual prisoners." We know the truth concerning the purpose of this life, so we try to share it with those still unaware, yet for our beliefs and for our efforts we are often mocked and scorned. We are made to think that we are the ones still locked down in that cave, seeing shadows of angels and gods on the wall and thinking they're real.

I testify that is the opposite of the case.

Plato's allegory of the cave encapsulates the entire existential situation of this temporary, telestial world—a world filled with shadows and distractions that confuse and distort and lead us away from immortal treasures, the truths of eternal life. Elder Neal A. Maxwell warned us aptly, "To mistake mortal props for the real drama that is underway is a grave error to be avoided."[17]

What, then, is the real drama underway here? English religious thinker Malcolm Muggeridge offered his insightful perspective:

> When I look back on my life nowadays, which I sometimes do, what strikes me most forcibly about it is that what seemed at the time most significant and seductive, seems now most futile and absurd. For instance, success in all its various guises: being known and being praised; ostensible pleasures, like acquiring money or seducing women; or traveling, going to and fro in the world and up and down it like Satan, exploring and experiencing whatever Vanity Fair has to offer.
>
> In retrospect all these experiences in self-gratification seem pure fantasy, what Pascal called "licking the earth." They are diversions designed to distract our attention from the true purpose of our existence in this world.[18]

A glance outside the proverbial window clearly indicates that those in the world are merely "licking the earth," and that is why they also fail to know what the "real drama" is.

Imagine the following scenario: You tell some people, good friends maybe, that Jesus will save them if only they turn to Him. In return, they stare at you blankly. It doesn't mean anything to them. "Save us from what?" they might ask. "From sin," you say. "Oh, sin," they might scoff, followed by something about good and bad meaning different things to different people. They don't see a hero or a villain because they don't see a conflict.

To understand who we are and what the "real drama" is, we must see the eternal conflict for what it is. The world cannot see the conflict, but it is essential that we preserve an eternal perspective in all that we do. In trying to inform the world of the truth, we seek to liberate, but the world thinks that we only wish to brainwash and enslave. The full story behind our presence on this planet remains in their peripheral, and, as a result, the full story of their own existence is never clear to them.

It calls to my mind a line from Billy Joel, singing nostalgically about the lost days of youth. Back then, "We never knew we could want more than that out of life."[19]

The world's perspective is illuminated in another short parable, this one from Elder James E. Talmage. He once found a bee in his office and, knowing it would end up dead if he did nothing, opened up his window so the bee could escape. After it failed to escape on its own, he tried to guide it to freedom from its office prison with his hand. But the bee did not listen, instead stinging Elder Talmage's hand. Consequently, it died.[20]

This behavior is what Christ called "kick[ing] against the pricks" (Acts 9:5)—biting the hand that's trying to feed you, perhaps thinking that it's trying to strike or take hold of you. But would the people of the world fight against God if they know what He was doing? Would they if they understood His ways and how He guides us all out of the cave of bondage and into the open light? Sadly, we witness most of the world reacting to truth the same way the bee reacted to Elder Talmage: with pride, short-sightedness, and often spite and cynicism. In short, the world has declared war on God, either actively or through ambivalence.

The Hero Doctrine

In the Book of Mormon, the prophet Jacob declared, "Wherefore, do not spend money for that which is of no worth, nor your labor for that which cannot satisfy" (2 Nephi 9:51). So many competing priorities occupy our time and attention in this hectic world; it is easy to be distracted by time-consuming daily worries, caught up in laborious experiences that nonetheless leave us strangely wanting in the end. Immersing activities like video games, television, and film can occupy our minds and cause spiritual stagnancy if not kept in check. Even supposedly big-picture issues like politics, the economy, and global warming can turn our minds and spirits away from the true battle being waged in the world. Scholarship, academia, and art are often pursued as finer things in life, while the real finer things are taken for granted, or thought dross.

Elder Maxwell further observed, "One might learn a great deal about the physical characteristics of this planet earth but yet be ignorant of why it was created in the first place."[21] Though interesting, enlightening, and truly worthy of moderated pursuit, these are generally not occupations that Heavenly Father will care much about at the Final Judgment, not if we have instead let our families, ward callings, and life missions—those personal callings only deliverable in quiet moments by the Spirit—fall by the wayside.

Indeed, Satan is busiest when we are most idle. It is his goal in this life to trick us into wasting our time to halt our progress and keep us from achieving growth. However we spend our time, we are always becoming something; it's our choice if we are changing in the direction of something less or something more. Where we go depends upon our priorities, what we think is of worth. Therefore, the better we understand God and His plan, the more we realize that our lives are not about fulfilling selfish temporal desires, "expressing our individuality," or living however we want. In the end, such lives are tragically wasted—a key goal of Satan.

The wicked in the Book of Mormon were generally wicked not because of open rebellion, but rather because "they understood not the dealings of the Lord" (Mosiah 10:14). Misunderstanding the character of God is also the reason why Laman and Lemuel failed where Nephi succeeded: "And they [Laman and Lemuel] did murmur because they knew not the dealings of that God who had created them" (1

Nephi 2:12). With only a surface glance at the teachings of their father and younger brother, they thought they saw meaningless things and, because they did not truly desire any deeper a relationship with God as Nephi did, fought against their younger brother, kicked against the pricks. We can see the tragic fruits of such shallow understanding in the history of their descendants throughout the rest of the Book of Mormon. So many lives wasted because two brothers could not be humble. Thus, to best use the precious time we have on this earth, we must also understand God's priorities and goals.

We talk at great lengths in the Church about becoming Christ-like, with the eventual goal of becoming like Heavenly Father. The means to achieving this end lies in the rough patches that smooth our edges like sandpaper. That said, the process of attaining divine attributes is not just to emulate Christ but also to eventually understand why God gives us problems and trials to solve and endure, and what we can do to overcome them and use them to our eternal advantage. To understand the nature and meaning of this great thing we call "life," the world and its inhabitants must be taught who and what God really is, what His purposes really are, and what methods He uses to attain them. In essence, we must *all* seek to know the mind of God.

To some, it might be overly bold to even think we can know the mind of God. But Joseph Smith taught, "If men do not comprehend the character of God, they do not comprehend themselves."[22] Failing to know ourselves is also exactly what Satan wants: to destroy our potential and bury who we really are—children of a god, heirs to eternity—by telling us we are someone else or even something else. Thus the imperative is to understand God so we can come to know ourselves in addition to Him.

The Prophet Joseph's words point us to the truth that God can be found in our own world, in nature and in ourselves, for in the creation we find the Creator. "Ultimately," wrote Terryl and Fiona Givens, "we understand God's nature, and human salvation, to be the simple amplification of that which is most elemental, and most worthwhile, about our life here on earth."[23]

For instance, in nature, the purpose of every single life form—all of which were designed and planned by God—is to generate more life like itself. All plants, animals, and even bacteria and viruses share this one singular purpose: procreation. Would not the purpose of nature's Creator be the same? Is it overly bold to think that the greatest thing God could accomplish would be to propagate beings like Himself? And yet, why would God give all life the same directive if He did not share it? Like a mirror, creation reflects the Creator; nature reflects God—and thus we can find the grand yet simple truth within our own creation: we are His offspring, His children, made expressly in His image and likeness. He seeks to raise us to become like Him and continue on the endless chain of eternal lives.

If He is our literal Father, then no doubt truth can be found in some of our own traits and attributes and proclivities, those that result in the greatest happiness and progress of soul. Elder Quentin L. Cook taught that "family relationships help us know, love, and understand the Father . . . we can learn many things simply by observing the pattern for righteous families. . . . Carefully observing and conscientiously living in accordance with righteous family patterns on earth is at the core of our quest to know the Father."[24]

With this end in mind, we'll first go over the character of God. To understand His ways, we must first understand who He is and what our relationship is with Him. We'll then discuss His purposes and goals, for when we understand God's purpose we will understand our purpose.

When we understand all of these things—God's characteristics, purposes, priorities, and methods—we may more effectively come to understand our own identities and potential, and thus be dissuaded from kicking against the pricks. Instead, the path to eternal life will be revealed, both the universal journey we all must take and our own personal trails that have been blazed for us individually as unique sons and daughters of our heavenly parents.

God's Characteristics

"Among the first principles lost in the Apostasy was an understanding of God the Father. It is not surprising, then, that among the first principles revealed in the Restoration was an understanding of God the Father."[25]

Essential to the Restoration was the comprehension of who and what Heavenly Father really is. Why? Christ gave the answer in the

Doctrine and Covenants. Echoing His own astonishing words in the Intercessory Prayer, Christ declared, "This is eternal lives—to know the only wise and true God, and Jesus Christ, whom he hath sent" (D&C 132:24). If knowing God is to attain eternal life, then we must seek after that more than anything else. So, like in the previous chapter, we'll start at the basic knowledge.

God is our Father, the begetter of our spirits, so we are His children. We know from latter-day revelation that He has a body of flesh and bones, a body similar to ours. His body, however, is exalted, immortalized, and glorified, while earthly bodies fade, crumble, and pass away in time. His foremost characteristic is our most common reference to Him: Father.

Elder J. Devn Cornish of the Seventy said, "God our Father is not a feeling or an idea or a force. He is a holy person who, as the scriptures teach, has a face and hands and a glorious immortal body. He is real, He knows each of us individually, and He loves us, every one."[26]

Knowing this is the foundation of the gospel. Note that the first topic in the first lesson of *Preach My Gospel* is "God Is Our Loving Heavenly Father."

If it's true that we can learn about God by looking at ourselves, then fathers and mothers receiving this message understand what drives Father in Heaven better than anyone else on earth. Christ demonstrated this allegorical connection between earthly and heavenly parents toward the end of the Sermon on the Mount when He asked, "What man is there of you, whom if his son ask bread, will he give him a stone? Or if he ask a fish, will he give him a serpent? If ye then, being evil, know how to give good gifts unto your children, how much more shall your Father which is in heaven give good things to them that ask him?" (Matthew 7:9–11).

God, then, being the quintessential Father, is first and foremost a God of love. This is perhaps the least understood trait of God in the world today. A missionary friend, Sean Bell, once wrote to me regarding his negative experiences dealing with investigators in France: "I was never aware of how many people believe in a God who does not love us."

Potentially the most prominent reason people do not understand God as a being of love is because He shows that love in many ways the world does not comprehend. They see pain and tragedy as evidence for either the nonexistence of God or that He does not care. Elder Bell told me about one specific man he had spoken to who said that Americans "only believe in God because we come from a country without war. He felt that sufferings he and his country had felt in war have proven there isn't a God."

We as Latter-day Saints, meanwhile, know of the necessity to reconcile the truth that God loves us with the feeling of "I'm in pain right now." We know that it is possible to do so, though it can be difficult at times. Developing the ability to reconcile between seemingly contradictory pieces of information can help us come to a more perfect understanding of ultimate reality. In this particular case, we need to understand that whatever corridors of hell we are called to pass through in this life can actually be a staircase leading up to heaven. Like Nephi, we must understand and accept that, though we do not know the meaning of all things, we know that God "loveth his children" (1 Nephi 11:17).

Elder Neal A. Maxwell wrote, "We cannot always fully or glibly explain everything that is happening to us or around us, but knowing that God loves us is absolutely crucial."[27] It is the knowledge that He will never retreat fully from us. Though there are dark and stormy days, the sun is still there, hidden by the clouds. Elder Maxwell pointed out that, "We—not he—let something come between us, but no lasting eclipse need ensue."[28]

This knowledge of the eternal mercy and love of God is the foundation of all our faith—the knowledge that, as God so beautifully told Joseph Smith in Liberty Jail, whatever happens, it shall be for our good in the end (see D&C 122:7).

God, in turn, feels our love for Him through our expressions of gratitude for all He's done, shown in our devotion to regular prayer, an attitude of thankfulness, and obedience to the commandments He has given us. He asks nothing more of us than to simply remember Him and show that remembrance in our day-to-day actions and behavior.

However, being filled with love doesn't necessarily equate to being filled with happiness. Is God always happy? I don't think that He is. I think it's because He loves us so much and wants the best for us that it is undoubtedly a tearful occasion when we as His children turn away from Him and make choices that drive us in separate, diverging ways down "forbidden paths." The prophet Enoch witnessed God weeping as He looked over His unrighteous children, and Elder Jeffrey R. Holland said that God and the angels of heaven weep with us when we are going through painful, trying, horrible times.[29] In having perfect love, God most certainly has perfect empathy as well, implying that God mourns on a regular basis. So if God can weep, why should we think to demand constant comfort and unhindered happiness? Are we greater than Him?

Though God's love for us is ever present, it should not be interpreted as accepting and tolerating all behaviors and lifestyles. The pernicious doctrine spread so pervasively through our society is that God merely requires allegiance in our mouths, not our hearts and hands—because God loves us all, He approves of whatever lifestyle we choose to live. Rather, it is because God loves us that He asks so much of us. He wants the best for us, so He gives us commandments that shape and mold us into sharper, more refined individuals.

Now to lay down the facts of God as we know Him:

God is all-wise. He knows and is aware of all. He has the divine ability to process an infinite amount of thoughts at once, whereas we often struggle with just one.

God is patient. He takes time to work, and we should learn to be similarly patient with ourselves, others, and even God as He operates on His own timetable.

God has no fear. If we wish to become like Him, we must extinguish our fears, whether they be temporal or spiritual. We should not seek after fear, but if it arises, we are to overcome it by faith.

God is a covenant maker. If we do our part, He will *always* do His. He extends His arm of mercy "towards them that put their trust in Him" (Mosiah 29:20). He is fair and trustworthy and will always do His part.

God abides by perfect justice. He sets forth laws and is Himself governed by them. It is a theological misconception that certain behaviors and actions in this world are moral because God has said they are, or rather that God's ways are moral because they are God's. This is absolutely false. In the words of Alma, "Now the work of justice could not be destroyed; if so, God would cease to be God" (Alma 42:13). He acts within the boundaries of higher law and gives His children lower laws by which they can eventually ascend to His level.

God's law stretches beyond moral boundaries to the physical laws that define and give shape to this world. Without allowances, mercy, and miracles, nature is an extreme capitalistic world—making its inhabitants free to rise or fall—and is built on physical cause and effect, choice and accountability, and cold hard justice—laws without empathy. The strongest survive, the fittest continue on. Those are the hard truths of the natural world, where only justice, never mercy, exists.

Now, because God is also a God of miracles, He is also a God of mercy. Miracles are exceptions to physical law, moments when higher law set forth by God override the lower law He previously gave to govern nature. His mercy is expressed similarly, providing exceptions to spiritual law through the system of repentance and forgiveness (see Mormon 9:21). Heaven's hand, through the Atonement, reaches down to lift us up.

Elder Quentin L. Cook wrote, "One of the great distortions of the Apostasy was that it cast God the Father's plan of salvation as overwhelmingly harsh. Frederic Farrar, the Anglican church leader, classical scholar, believer, and highly regarded author of *Life of Christ*, lamented that most Christian churches view hell and damnation incorrectly as a result of translation errors from Hebrew and Greek to English in the King James Version of the Bible."[30]

Our views of Heavenly Father and His glorious plan are, of course, entirely different. We understand that God's love and mercy have given us everything we have and may give us everything Heavenly Father has too, should we successfully keep His commandments and endure to the end.

Elder Neal A. Maxwell asked, "Where would we be, in fact, without God's long-suffering? Given the divine sorrow each of us here has caused our God and our Savior, what a divine comfort to know that when we 'get it all together,' it will be mercifully said, 'Behold, he who has repented of his sins, the same is forgiven, and I, the Lord, remember them no more' (D&C 58:42). No more reassuring and important words could be said to any of us than these."[31]

To further illustrate this love, Elder Maxwell invoked the story of Christ when, directly after His agonies in Gethsemane, He "who by then might have understandably been so swollen with sorrow and self-concern that there was no time to think of others, nevertheless restored the severed ear of a hostile guard."[32] What a beautiful characterization! We understand that, first and foremost, Heavenly Father and Jesus Christ are beings of love, and everything They do— the plan, the application, the glorious ends they have in mind—is driven by that love for us.

We know from the scriptures that Christ Himself employs no other servant at the gate; it is He who receives us as we enter into His kingdom (see 2 Nephi 9:41), hands clasped together as we pass through the veil, just as His grace complements our efforts in mortal life. He truly is a profoundly personal God. To paraphrase John the Beloved, we love Them because They first loved us (see 1 John 4:19).

God is also a teacher, an essential aspect to His role as Father. His methods of teaching will be discussed later on in detail, for it is by our interactions with Him that we come to know Him. One method that can be discussed here is that He teaches by example—in particular, by the example of Jesus Christ and His embodiment of the essential traits of faith, hope, patience, long-suffering, meekness, mercy, virtuous, soberness, charity, diligence, and so forth. We learn by doing what we know He did. Such are the words of Christ when He tells us to see what He has done and go and do likewise. As God has treated us with so much tenderness, love, and mercy, so should we treat others.

Another integral part of God's character is the first role that He took on: Creator. Our own desire to create is, I believe, our deepest spiritual instinct that we inherited it directly from our Father in Heaven. We create works of art, music, stories, and even whole worlds of imagination. We even possess the power create other people, to embody souls with tabernacles of flesh and raise them up to be full human beings like ourselves. This is no doubt the greatest of our creative powers, and why its sacred processes are so regulated and limited by Heavenly Father's commandments—we should never take procreation lightly.

It is the ultimate divine attribute to create and care for one's creations. Among all God's infinite works—all the worlds and marvels given form by His hand—none are as important to Him as His children, His family. He does not spend time on other pursuits; He is not off fishing on an ocean planet He created. He is constantly, deeply involved in our lives and the state of our souls. We are His children, His sacred stewardship, His first and only concern.

God's Purposes

"For behold, this is my work and my glory—to bring to pass the immortality and eternal life of man" (Moses 1:39).

So what about us is God concerned about? How do we fit into His plan? What is His purpose? What is our purpose? What is the meaning of our existence?

These are broad questions, but they do have specific answers that can't be found in the philosophies of mankind. As Elder Neal A. Maxwell taught, "Secular education wisely does not pretend to give us answers to the great 'Why?' questions—any more than you and I would read a telephone directory in search of a plot."[33]

Instead of looking to the equivalent of a telephone directory, we can turn back to that principle Joseph Smith taught about the parallel between God and ourselves. So we ask another question, one we can understand and answer as human beings: What do you think is the deepest desire a loving father and mother have for their children?

We might know this because of our experiences with our own parents or our own children, or just by way of common knowledge of parents in general. It's not a hard question. A loving parent's deepest desire for his or her children is to make sure they have everything he or she had and have—and, if possible, more.

With this truth in mind, let us again take into account that God is our Father, the paragon of parenthood. Thus we can see exactly what God's goal is: to give us everything He has. That idea is confirmed many places in the scriptures, both the Bible and latter-day revelation: "All that [the] Father hath shall be given unto him" (D&C 84:38) who comes unto Christ, the necessary spiritual fulcrum upon whose Atonement we are brought into God's presence once more.

When we were little, I'm sure many of us wanted to be a "big boy" or "big girl." We wanted to be like our parents or older siblings (admittedly with some exceptions). As we come to know our Father in Heaven and elder brother Jesus Christ, don't we develop a desire to be like Them? That desire isn't born out of nothing. I believe it's in our spiritual DNA, if you will—implicit in every human being who has ever lived on this earth or on any of the planets on which God has placed His children. At the core of our being is a version of God in embryo form. It is up to us to foster that embryo, that spark of eternal life, and develop it in righteous ways; we must walk down correct paths and make choices that bring us closer to God, in both spiritual proximity and metaphysical likeness.

This is God's purpose: to make His children like Himself, spiritually and physically perfect. Could there be a greater work, a greater cause?

This world, this tiny slice of time, is so immensely important. Before we came to earth, we were (eternally existent) intelligences, brought forth into human spirits, in which state we chose wisely in the war of heaven and kept our first estate. This gave us license to come to earth and receive a body, the next of many steps in our quest to be like our heavenly parents. Here, we experience hands-on lessons impossible to learn as mere spirits; we grow and show our faith, partake of the Atonement of Christ, repent, progress, and prove all we've learned by enduring to the end. Success in this, our second estate, combined with the sacrifice of our Savior, allows us to become like God physically, and then we continue to develop our minds and hearts as we started to do in mortality, growing and growing until perfection is reached and God gives us everything that He hath. From there, we continue the generations of gods as Creators of our own worlds and eternal families that stretch forth into everlasting happiness and glory. This is the plan of salvation; this is eternal lives.

President Boyd K. Packer compared our existence to a three-act play. Currently, we are in the middle of the second act. To truly understand what's going on, we must know what happened in the first act and have an awareness of what awaits us in the third act.[34]

Unfortunately, the world is stuck in the second act, locked in the dimension of time and contained within the tight perspectives of this second estate. Some feel an awareness of the other two acts; they have a sense that there is more to life than what they see before them now. Others, however, because they have seen no evidence of the first or the third, refuse to accept that they exist, and so they attempt to find purpose and meaning in the second act alone. Their search for meaning may be sincere, but the conclusions they come to can often twist or distort the truth of "things as they really are" (Jacob 4:13) and simply be a part of the distractions and dead-ends of this world.

Because the world's perspective on life is severely limited, because people see this life only through the lens of mortality, their main goals are to spend their time doing what they like and want to do. The Lord Himself observed of this limited egoistic perspective: "Every man walketh in his own way, and after the image of his own god, whose image is in the likeness of the world" (D&C 1:16). The world believes what the world wants to believe—things that may not be true but give rationale for the behaviors they already live and the passions they already pursue. Sadly, so many of those things turn out to be distractions from our true purposes, masks over our true identities.

Many in the world claim that the natural man is our only identity, that we are essentially animals built to fulfill appetites given by nature. The world would have us believe that we are born a certain way and thus we should embrace our initial natures. This attitude is a destroying lie, sinister as a poisoned apple. It leads to naught but wasted lives and empty eternities.

In our stewardships given us by the Lord, particularly those of family duties as fathers and mothers, we practice, essentially, being like Heavenly Father. Salvation is not an individual attainment; it is a family dynamic. "And when he shall prove himself faithful in all things that shall be entrusted unto his care, yea, even a few things, he shall be made ruler over many" (D&C 124:113).

In a few words, God's purpose is to give everything He has to His children: the roles of Creator and Lawgiver of an eternal family who begets infinite generations of godhood—what is known in the scriptures as eternal lives.

God's Priorities and Perspective

"It is our choices, Harry, that show what we truly are, far more than our abilities."[35]*—Albus Dumbledore*

We've established who God is and what His aims are. In setting out to accomplish these eternal goals, God has certain priorities that frame His perspective on His work. What I submit to be God's highest priority is not, as one may think, our eternal salvation; rather, it is our agency, the freedom we have to choose between good and evil.

My missionary friend who went to France, Sean Bell, pointed out to me in another letter that agency was important enough to Heavenly Father that He lost a massive portion of His children to it. The Lord confirmed that priority in the Doctrine and Covenants when He said, "A third part of the hosts of heaven turned . . . away from me because of their agency" (D&C 29:36). Though He may have been able to, *He didn't stop them.* The agency of His children, their freedom to choose, was more important than their eternal salvation.

Heavenly Father's perspective seems to be that if we are not our own agents, if we cannot choose between good and evil, then there's no real point to it all. Without accountability for our choices, there is no growth, and if there is no growth, there is no godhood. Where agency and will cease, morality and goodness cease with them. Choice adds significance to the happenings of this world, for we were put here to figure out what to choose.

To give it a specific example, this is also why God doesn't just take our tithing from us; it is why He doesn't force us to drop whatever we just shoplifted or stop our mouths right when we're about to yell at somebody. If He just took ten percent of our income away from us—as is technically His right—then the tithing we contribute would be the result of an amoral act, neither good nor evil, insignificant of who we have decided to be, and so there would be no point to it. Heavenly Father wants our wills far more than He wants our possessions.

As was pointed out earlier, choices without consequences are no choices at all, which is why horrible things happen in this world. Without the allowance of evil, there would be no good and no inherent meaning in any of this. That was the lesson of those who, right before the eyes of Alma and Amulek, threw the believing women and children into the fire. God has given us agency "that every man may be accountable for his own sins in the day of judgment" (D&C 101:78). There is no joy or progress without our choice, for a free agent is a god in embryo.

This doctrine of agency explains the necessity of another doctrine: prayer. Elder Cornish pled, "Little children, young people, and adults alike, please believe how very much your loving Heavenly Father wants to bless *you*," and then he followed with the clinching observation that "*because He will not infringe upon our agency*, we must ask for His help."[36] Likewise, we cannot receive the greatest of all the gifts of God if we do not employ our freedom to choose; if we do not ask for the blessings of repentance and ultimately salvation, we will not be given them. God will do anything and everything to help us come back to Him *except* infringe on our agency.

So He lets us be miserable sometimes. He lets us feel the consequences of our choices in the hopes that we'll learn from them. My wife and I once heard the truth that "good parenting doesn't mean your kids are never upset." God lets us be upset sometimes—what is best for us in the short term is usually not what is best for us in the long term. Make no mistake, we are in this for the long term. We are in this for eternity.

With that eternal perspective in mind, we can see a few other truths about God's perspective more clearly that the world only sees in the context of the middle act of this three-act drama. Two of the most serious sins we can commit are those that alter the course of other lives the most drastically from their original path: the sins of murder and fornication. These two sins are directly connected to the destruction and creation of life, respectively, and are actions that put limits on eternal life in ways other sins can't.

However, it is clear that, from God's perspective—and when God is in control—death is not the worst thing that can happen. Through the lens of mortality, we view death as the worst possible consequence, the greatest of evils. But seen with the lens of eternity, death is as necessary and liberating as any other element of the plan of salvation.

That same celestial lens magnifies spiritual death to its true size and shows how that tragic destiny far outweighs physical death. It also reveals that the state of the soul at the time of death is far more important than the fact of death itself. We see this prominently in the heartbreaking but beautiful story of the Anti-Nephi-Lehies, who willfully suffered death instead of returning to their old, violent ways, a decision that ultimately led to the salvation of even more

Lamanites than the number of Anti-Nephi-Lehies who died. Their physical deaths brought about many more spiritual rebirths, fulfilling God's goals and illustrating His priorities.

This, however, does not necessarily mean that it would be better for us to die than sin. This life is about so much more than simply not sinning. Through errors and mistakes, we learn valuable life lessons that cannot be taught any other way. Seeking death rather than sin would nullify the work we are meant to accomplish for the sake of others' salvation. God knew we would sin before putting us on this earth and obviously felt that the experience we would gain and the joy we could spread is worth the imperfect behavior we would display now and again. That's why Christ performed the Atonement, so the sins we commit won't damn us forever and allow us, in the meantime, to accomplish much righteousness in society at large.

Of all His creations, we are God's number one priority. We are His family, for whom He does everything, for whom He exists. The earth is beautiful, full of splendid sights and marvelous moments. But in the end, it's meant merely a context for human beings to move along the path to eternal life. All that God is and does is for the sake of His children. We are His glory, and without us He is as meaningless as anything could be.

In turn, we are expected to learn from that relationship and make our own families *our* highest priority. The family is the unit not just of society but also of eternal life, and we must prepare ourselves for such responsibilities in the coming world. Indeed, the family is the absolute best context for raising a soul in righteousness and leading him or her down that glorious path to God. How far along we are on that path isn't as important to Heavenly Father as the direction we're facing.

Recently, while flipping through an illustrated book about grammar, I found a picture of two glowing parents being presented with a homework assignment from their young son. The assignment had a big A at the top, and the caption read, "These are Jack's parents. Who could be happier?"

Now, why were they happy? The answer may be obvious, but it's also highly significant, for it points to the pattern of God's happiness with His own children. Jack's parents saw that their young son was learning well. He was still far, far behind them in intellectual capacity, but that wasn't the point; the point is his progression. He was learning, and that made his parents happy because they love him and want everything for him—everything they have and more.

Growth is not an immediate process. It takes time, and God understands that. It's why we are taught patience and why we need to thank our Heavenly Father for His patience toward us.

Elder Maxwell offers the following insight:

> The whole process of subtle inspiration and revelation is like this metaphor: an inspired painter working on a large canvas does not report to or ask patrons or friends to react to each brushstroke. Nor does he exclaim after each stroke of his paintbrush well before the canvas reflects any emerging pattern. Yet each stroke the painter registers on the canvas is a part of an inspired whole. Without those cumulative, individual strokes, there would be no painting. But each stroke, if examined by itself, is not likely to be appreciated by itself, least of all by those who stand outside the process, outside of the contextuality.[37]

Though we shouldn't procrastinate the day of our repentance, we should not run faster than we have strength either. Exercising discipline and patience with God and His timing is just as important as doing the same with ourselves; both come easier as we understand His priorities, His ways and methods, and His perspective of us.

God's Ways and Methods

"Draw near unto me and I will draw near unto you; seek me diligently and ye shall find me; ask, and ye shall receive; knock, and it shall be opened unto you" (D&C 88:63).

"Nearer, my God, to thee, / Nearer to thee! / E'en though it be a cross / That raiseth me."[38]

Some of God's ways and methods can seem quite strange to us at times—for instance, the repetitiveness of the temple ordinances, the garments, or other "weird" doctrines. Other ways God teaches and cares are sometimes hard to interpret or even to recognize. So untrained are our mortal eyes to God's methods that many of us miss them entirely, or see them as threats to our autonomy or mere constructs of a frenzied mind. A closer examination, however, reveals just how perfect they can be for this life's test. President Dieter F. Uchtdorf said of God's words to us, "The teachings of our Heavenly

Father are not the ordinary, predictable, run-of-the-mill kind you can pick up in paperback at the local bookstore. They are the wisdom of an all-powerful, all-knowing celestial Being who loves His children."[39] Such is the same with His methods of helping us return to Him and of showing us His love. They are so different, so much higher, and sometimes so difficult to internalize that, even after hearing them, many people choose instead to rebel.

In the Book of Mormon, after the story of the Anti-Nephi-Lehies—who chose to suffer death instead of take up arms against their brethren—Mormon concluded, "Thus we see that the Lord worketh in many ways to the salvation of His people" (Alma 24:27). They are indeed many, and to understand them we must take into account all that He has given us—our blessings, trials, placement in a family, status in a society, and any given trying moment—and sincerely ask, "Why?" To ask a question sincerely is to not merely wait and expect an answer; after our prayers, we must search our minds, study the scriptures, and reflect on any revelation we might think we've received through His Spirit. If we do not ask, we will never receive; if we do not search, we will never find.

If no answer is immediately granted, then we can know that, for now, it's a trial of our faith, and we need to hold out in patience, trusting God and believing that He will reveal exactly what we need to know exactly when we need to know it. And in the meantime, we continue to think, analyze, ponder, study, and meditate. For it is possible to read God's intentions and thoughts correctly, but only if we are aware, if we pay attention, if we approach our questions and complaints with humility and faith. Often, the quest of seeking greater understanding of Him is precisely why He answers with silence. Doing so gives us opportunities to work the matter out for ourselves and gain valuable experience.

Elder Neal A. Maxwell reminded us, "If people misread life, this leads to murmuring, rebellion, and irreligion."[40] So that we don't misread life, let's go over a few of those methods and ways God has of teaching His children.

To start, we can look at one of the most famed of God's mysteries and theological dilemmas: the "Problem of Evil." This seeming contradiction in the concept of God has probably done more to crack the faith of believers worldwide than any other philosophical issue. I have seen the damage this question can do with my own eyes—that is, when it is asked with anger and insincerity, as it too commonly is. But such anger can be totally understandable. Suffering exists in the world, including the seemingly meaningless suffering of innocents. Would a just and all-benevolent God allow that to happen?

Though the following little parable lacks historical credibility, it still represents one of the ways God works with us as His children. It comes from a sermon given several decades ago by Christian minister William Marrion Branham.

> I guess you've heard the story of the shepherd that broke his sheep's leg one time. Many little stories has been told about it. And was asked this shepherd, "Did the sheep fall off of a mountain and do this?"
>
> He said, "No."
>
> Said, "What happened?"
>
> He said, "I broke its leg."
>
> Said, "Why did you break its leg? Are you a cruel shepherd?"
>
> He said, "No, I love the sheep. But the sheep got to running away from me. And he kept straying out to itself. And I know the nature of sheep. And I know if they stray too far away, the wolf will get them. So I had to break the sheep's leg to keep it with me, to draw it to my bosom, to give it a little special food. And I'll be so kind to it, that when its leg gets well, it'll never leave me anymore."[41]

All of us are lambs who are "dear to the heart of the Shepherd."[42] Sometimes we will have to go through pain, suffering, and sorrows. But if it compels us to return, if from that suffering we deepen our relationship with our Father in Heaven, then it is completely worth it. Just as the physical creation of a human being is worth the pain of childbirth and travail (see John 16:21), so is the spiritual rebirth of a human life worth the pains needed for it to happen. Pain will always pass away, but our relationship with Heavenly Father does not. It is an eternal relationship that will outlive and outlast any suffering we are called to bear in this life—virtually anything that brings us closer to Him is worth it in the long run. However, if we do not think about *why* He gives us that lame leg, we may be more inclined to be angry at Him for the pain and murmur and rebel. That shows just how essential it is that we understand what God is doing with and for us at any given time.

This truth is confirmed by the Lord in the book of Ether: "I give unto men weakness that they may be humble" (Ether 12:27), but that weakness is not meant to last forever. He acts with the intention of making weak things strong, so that one day we can stand on our own and run faster than we ever could have on our own power.

A more direct way God teaches us is through repetition. Christ taught the Sermon on the Mount to both the Israelites and the Nephites, almost word for word. His latter-day prophets do similarly at general conference, often going over doctrine we've heard many times before. But they dwell on the basics so extensively because they are the most essential weapons in our spiritual arsenal, reminders of those simple steps like prayer and scripture study, which, if done regularly, can keep us on the path permanently. In grumbling, complaining, or murmuring about the repetitive nature of sermons, we forget how easy it is to forget.

As the hymn "Come, Thou Fount of Every Blessing" suggests, we are *prone* to wander and leave the God we love. Heavenly Father, aware of this potential problem, solves it via the regular reminders and routines He asks us to follow. We may not learn something new every time we pray or read the scriptures, but it gives us, at the very least, the opportunity to feel the Spirit every day, thus keeping us aware of our duty to God and of the real purposes of life. Those things are easy to forget when we're distracted by the rigors and pleasures of daily life.

Everything we are commanded to do on a regular basis—read the scriptures, say our prayers, do work in the temple, attend church weekly—is specifically designed to tether us to God, so we may regularly feel His presence and the love through the Holy Ghost.

From time to time, the Lord shows His love and affection for us through what we call tender mercies. As previously established, God is a God of justice—we see this in the way the physical world works; everything is governed by laws, and most of the time He lets it play out according to those laws. But frequently, God does intervene. We call these moments miracles, effects of the Almighty on our earthly lives that are only performed where there is faith present, even in the smallest degree.

Christ performed miracles during His mortal ministry to show love to those people He came to save; He offered them the daily bread of physical healing as a type of the Bread of Life, the spiritual healing He was ultimately there to do. In His ministry, He healed those with physical injuries, weaknesses, and pains, a perfect precursor to the Atonement through which He heals our spiritual wounds and brings the spiritually dead back to life in God's presence. The Atonement is the quintessential emblem of divine intervention, of mercy overcoming justice, of the saving influence miracles can have on the children of God.

Not only were Christ's miracles a type of the Atonement, they also served another function: Miracles can help galvanize faith by giving us the initial footing we need to begin the climb toward a heavenly life. This is part of the reason Christ performed so many when He was on the earth. However, as has been shown so many times in history, miracles can't be relied upon to replace a personal testimony of the truth, burned in our hearts by the Holy Ghost. And so in our climb, we must rely on surer footholds that will not crumble under too much pressure.

Miracles are not certain foundations, and we cannot let our faith depend on specific answers we demand from God. At times, God acts and intervenes with answers to prayer and sometimes He doesn't. If we don't get the exact help or answer we prayed for, it generally means either we don't need the help and we're strong enough to manage, or that it is God's will that we do not succeed in that endeavor at this time. This opens up a variety of pathways much wider than the proverbial closed door would have led us to.

Another kind of intervention we see often in the scriptures is God softening the hearts of the wicked. For a while, I wondered what exactly that meant and whether or not that constituted an override of an individual's agency. After all, it might seem to some that God is directly changing minds against their will. But I came to realize that the softening of the heart doesn't change the will of the individual, nor does it directly affect a person's choice. It is merely giving the individual an added measure of the Spirit, allowing him or her to see reality and truth with greater clarity than he or she did before. It is like turning on another light in a dim room lit only by a single lamp. All it does is add light. People still have to make their choices.

However, this subject also made me wonder about another truth we often hear: God is in control. Don't worry, we often hear, God is at the helm. The world is His footstool. But how is God in control? What about agency? Don't we control our own destinies, make our own choices? Isn't it all up to us? Isn't that the whole point?

I've found that yes, it is up to us, and yes, it does depend on our own wills. But God *knows our wills* perfectly and acts through the instrumentality of the Spirit, softening hearts and inspiring the minds and giving direct revelation to His faithful and willing children who will recognize that gentle nudge. God does not control us, but He does work with us and never compels us to do something that we would not be willing to do otherwise. It's been said that one plus God is a majority; and so, by knowledge of our wills, desires, and abilities, He can use each of us, even just one, for the maximum possible good without forcing us into anything. Thus, through the influence of His Spirit and the employment of His willing servants, while still allowing us to retain our agency, God can put our wills into a greater work and ensure everything remains in His hands.

Elder Neal A. Maxwell said, "Only by aligning our wills with God's is full happiness to be found. Anything less results in a lesser portion."[43] God's will, the plan He has in mind, is best, always and for all. If we do something contrary to His will, the whole plan instantly becomes less effective. But with the atoning and redemptive power of Christ, those less effective plans can be brought back to maximum in the world to come. The wrongs of this world can be righted in the next.

Personal revelation is one of the key methods God uses to bring about His will, and it is just as pertinent to our salvation today as it was at any given point in history. If someone tries to tell you otherwise, ask him or her whether Adam was told how to build an ark (thank President John Taylor for that one). Noah received his revelation because it applied to Noah, not Adam. Likewise, we have the capacity to receive revelation that is meant for nobody but us. Just as surely as we can communicate with God through prayer, God can communicate to us through the Holy Ghost.

That said, spiritual instruction can be given through many mediums with varying tones. An institute teacher of mine once observed that God sometimes speaks in a soft, soothing voice, like a feather, and then in times of urgency—or to rouse us from our own apathy—He pokes us with something sharp, like a spur. Sometimes we're held tight in His arms and other times we're chastened with a voice of rebuke. Both methods are signs of God's love, for they illustrate how vitally He is interested in our salvation, how especially invested He is in the one He's chastening (see Doctrine and Covenants 101), and how well He knows us as individuals, speaking to us in the voice we'll best hear. Humility and submissiveness lubricate that process, extinguish the sting of chastisement, and help us see it, as C. S. Lewis did: "We are bidden to 'put on Christ,' to become like God. That is, whether we like it or not, God intends to give us what we need, not what we think we want."[44] Sometimes what we need is a spur in our flanks to get us moving.

Heavenly Father is a God of truth and light. Though He does not actively deceive, I personally believe, from experience, that He sometimes lets us think or believe in untrue things. He lets us believe in possible futures we think we are going to have or lets us make plans based on bad information without correction. One possible reason for this lack of immediate intervention is out of respect for our agency, but another, more compelling reason to me is that our inability to see the future in concrete terms is usually part of His plan. It encourages faith and trust in *His* plan, not ours. We may think one thing and then act according to that, but ultimately end up with something else entirely—God having used that lack of knowledge to lead us to a better land.

President Matthew Holland of Utah Valley University wrote of an experience he had with his father, Elder Jeffrey R. Holland, when he was younger. The two went on a father-son hike through some desert canyons and hills. They were on their way home at dusk when they came across a fork in the road. They could not for the life of them remember which would take them back to civilization. Night was falling rapidly, so they prayed about it and felt prompted to go down one particular path. After just a few minutes, they came to a dead end. Young Matt was confused and asked his father why God would have led them down the wrong path. Elder Holland pointed out to his son that going down that wrong path was the quickest way of knowing which path was the right one. If they had gone down the correct path to start with, they would have remained unsure of its rightness for a long while.[45]

God used this method of teaching to lead them safely and surely back home, and sometimes He acts the same way with us. Though He does not lie, He may not necessarily tell us every element of the plan; that, after all, is the point and purpose of faith.

Faith in a heavenly being with unseen power is often compared to stepping out of the light and into a darkened hall. God does not take that first step for us; we have to be willing to put our foot into the darkness ahead. That step might be shaky, but if it is taken, either the path ahead will be lit or we will know that we have touched solid ground. Either way, our faith is rewarded with greater knowledge—and what we know will be enough. So we continue into the darkness, having faith that the light will eventually turn on, and we will understand what we had passed through, gaining surer knowledge with every step. Through this cyclical process, we come to trust His whispers and learn to more willingly submit to His will, which brings us happiness and peace. If we're going to submit to the will of God, we're going to be stepping into the darkness quite a bit.

This is a lesson for our times; these days, it seems God is testing our faith more and more with doctrines that don't seem to fit with the so-called enlightenment of the world's wisdom. In times past, the practice of polygamy and the barring of black male members from holding the priesthood are examples of this kind of test. Many otherwise faithful members in our day see worldly movements as viable directions for the Church to go, such as the Ordain Women organization and the world's push for same-sex marriage. Maintaining steady faith in the face of the world's logic can be difficult at times, but that's what makes submission so essential.

Hugh Nibley wrote about this issue in his book *Temple and Cosmos*:

> As C. S. Lewis used to point out, the test of the Christian is not to conform with the commandments and accept teachings which are perfectly right and sensible to any normal way of thinking; if the gospel consisted only of such convenient and unobjectionable things, we could be quite

sure that we were making it up ourselves. It is the very contrariness and even absurdity of the Christian teachings that provide, for him, the highest proof of their divinity—this is not man's doing. In the efforts of every president of the Church to explain our position to the world . . . we see the admission that this thing is not the invention of those men—they are embarrassed by it, and they all pass the acid test for honesty when they refuse to put their own opinions forth as revelation—which in their case would have been an easy thing to do. They are all sure that the policy is right, but none claims to give definitive rational or scriptural justification for it, though they are not backward in putting forth suggestions and speculations. This put the Mormons in an embarrassing position, and why not? The Lord has often pushed the Saints into the water to make them swim.[46]

The principle of faith demands that we live in the darkness for a season. So after prayer, fasting, temple attendance, and study, attempting to reconcile, if we still fail to understand or something still doesn't fit quite right, the answer is that it's (at least in part) a test of faith. If all these fail, then it is time to throw up that shield of faith and put on that armor of righteousness, and thus stand in readiness against the fiery darts of the adversary. If we are prepared with every article of our spiritual armor, we will not fear (see D&C 38:30).

Yet still another of God's methods in working with His children is portrayed in Nephi's vision of the tree of life and the chapters surrounding it. In this marvelous vision, the angel of the Lord told Nephi at least thirteen times, "Look!" The angel did not turn Nephi's head for him; the angel merely saw something Nephi didn't and pointed to it, but it was entirely Nephi's decision to actually cast his eyes in that direction.

Likewise, God will, through His prophets and the Holy Ghost, point to things, give us experiences, or deliver a message, but it is our responsibility to look, ponder, and listen. More often than not, we have to be the ones to seek after the interpretation. And oftentimes, it is as simple as just plain asking. But we have to choose to. God wants us to become individuals who make right choices without compulsion, so He will show us the path, but always we have to walk down it.

An example of this truth is found (surprisingly) in the film *Evan Almighty*. The character of God, played by Morgan Freeman, gives the doubting and discouraged Steve Carell some words of wisdom: "Let me ask you something. If someone prays for patience, you think God gives them patience? Or does He give them the opportunity to be patient? If he prayed for courage, does God give him courage, or does He give him opportunities to be courageous? If someone prayed for the family to be closer, do you think God zaps them with warm fuzzy feelings, or does He give them opportunities to love each other?"[47]

Again, here we see that our agency as God's highest priority. He'll neither turn our heads to look in the right direction, nor will He simply zap us into being better; we must choose to do it ourselves with the opportunities He has given us and, in so doing, enlarge our souls.

The translation process of the Book of Mormon reveals God's desire for us to learn and work things out for ourselves. Significantly, God didn't magically deliver the necessary revelations to Joseph Smith; even though God needed its truths revealed to bring to pass the marvelous work of the Restoration, He made Joseph work for it, and in the right way. God was not simply using Joseph as a tool or instrument; the whole process with the seer stones and the pains-taking work of dictation led to spiritual insights and development that Joseph may not have received otherwise and may have needed to lead the Church in those early days. God was as interested in cultivating Joseph Smith's character as He was in bringing forth the Book of Mormon. In the allegory of the olive tree in Jacob 5, the Lord of the vineyard labored with the other laborers, and likewise the Lord labors with us—but He does not do it for us, except in special, unique circumstances.

You can see the work of the laborers for yourself. See the libraries, both physical and digital, full of spiritual instruction and religious scholarship surrounding you on all sides. Leaders and lay members alike have written articles and essays, books and talks devoted to helping others understand finer points of doctrine, explaining how to get more out of scripture study and prayer, and showing just how the Lord views and communicates with His children.

So many topics and subjects are explicated for us just about eve-rywhere, from talks in church to talks in general conference, from the First Presidency message in the *Ensign* to blogs written by ordinary Latter-day Saints—all of it for the purpose of clarifying God's messages to us. But see that it isn't God who does the clarifying! It is us. We are all participants in this great project; we are the ones who help each other directly. We are the ones who build Zion, notwithstanding our weaknesses and imperfections. That opportunity is a privilege and a duty, one we must undertake for ourselves if we are to fully understand it.

I'm reminded of a meaningful experience I had during my employment at a hardware store when we were all required to go through a painting workshop. Normally my experiences at that job were far from being meaningful, but this one stood out to me as a kind of parable. One of the workers from the paint desk demonstrated the process of coating a wall so that if the rest of us (who had little experience with paint) were asked a paint question by a customer, we'd know how to answer. That worker taught us for a good fifteen or twenty minutes how to paint a typical wall in a typical home—to this day, I don't remember a thing he said or did, and in fact probably forgot everything he went over within minutes of the workshop ending.

That incident demonstrated to me not *how to paint*, but *how not to teach*. At least for me, it's incredibly difficult to learn without hands-on experience. If I learn something intellectually but never put it into practice, I'm going to forget it quickly.

Likewise, God, as the Master Teacher, did not merely give us theoretical knowledge of good and evil and expect us to be gods like Him. He put us into this world as His children to discover the things of the world for ourselves, while also providing us higher wisdom through scriptures and faithful leaders so we don't have to start with nothing. As young children grow, they learn that every action has a consequence (despite them wanting otherwise); some of these are natural (when they are learning, say, physical laws and how their bodies work) and others are artificial (receiving punishment or losing access to that chocolate cake and ice cream on the counter). Likewise, necessary growth and learning cannot occur in either the first act of life nor the third. It must happen here, in mortality.

The prophet Brigham Young taught, "There is not a single condition of life that is entirely unnecessary; there is not one hour's experience but what is beneficial to all those who make it their study, and aim to improve upon the experience they gain."[48]

Unfortunately, as we mentioned, this experience doesn't guarantee growth. If taken the wrong way, it can actually lead to a devolution of the soul, making one more bitter, more prideful, and more likely to hate. As Elder Neal A. Maxwell lamented, "I wish I could say to you that suffering teaches automatically, but it doesn't. To paraphrase Anne Morrow Lindbergh, if suffering inevitably taught us, the human family would be a very wise family indeed."[49]

Thus to know the mind of God—and what He is trying to do with each and every one of us—is to stop wasting time, life, and the suffering each of us will inevitably go through. There is nothing so precious in life as time, so we cannot spend it frivolously or use it absorbing the wrong lessons and learning cynicism from suffering rather than sainthood.[50]

Mirrors of God

> *"Therefore, hold up your light that it may shine unto the world. Behold I am the light which ye shall hold up— that which ye have seen me do" (3 Nephi 18:24).*

Much of this life is a constant search for self and identity. We struggle and grope to find meaning, to find belonging. This quest of self-discovery parallels our quest to find God—where we find one, we find the other. To understand our Father is to understand ourselves, and to understand His aims and purposes is to understand our own eternal destiny.

But *temporal* destiny matter as well. Our individual purposes in life, placement in this earth's history, and spiritual development—all of these can speak to broader, vaster interpretations. Meaning can be found as we observe the patterns that define our lives, speak to God through prayer, and consequently receive personal revelation in answers to our questions, whether through the scriptures, a priesthood blessing, or just a quiet whisper as we partake of the sacrament.

The sooner we determine why we're here, the sooner we can accomplish our mission to bring souls to Christ. The more we understand, the more powerful our faith and strength to do good will be—and the more we can come to feel the love of our Savior and Heavenly Father.

Turning to Elder Maxwell again, he said, "When striving disciples reflect deeply upon this mortal experience, certain realities become even more clear. This includes a clarifying and particular reality. . . . We are immortal individuals whose constant challenge is to apply immortal principles to life's constantly changing situations. Seen in this way, life's varied situations are more sharply defined. With this perspective we can improve our daily performances because we have fixed our gaze on eternity and its great realities."[51]

Within this veil of tears, we must focus on those things that apply to the time after the veil is lifted. This focus is conveyed in what Christ presented as the two great commandments: love God and love our neighbor. This is further exemplified in our two most sacred relationships, respectively—first, as children of our Heavenly Father and second, as fathers and mothers to our own children and eternal companions to our husbands or wives.

Always remember that to God—and at this crucial juncture in the eternal scheme of things—we are children and He is our Father. The children we bear as parents in this life are a preparation for when we become like God. Over time, children do develop the ability to communicate with their parents, but in the beginning, they just don't understand. Just as children must expend time and effort to learn and master basic speech (only then to move on to the finer nuance of grammar and style), it takes time and effort to master communication with the Lord in His divine interactions. I'm sure the Lord gets frustrated with us, just as much as we get frustrated with our own children. However, His great love quells that—He will never stop trying to guide and teach us. Above all else, we must cultivate that relationship. For when we do, we will feel His embrace as He "encircle[s] [us] in the arms of [His] love" (D&C 6:20).

The second of the great commandments, in its call to care for our neighbor, directs us to "stand in the place of [our] stewardship" (D&C 42:53). To heed this calling, one must recognize which particular stewardships God is concerned most about. President Uchtdorf clarified this duty in a priesthood session of general conference, saying, "Brethren, when we stand before the Lord to be judged, will He look upon the positions we have held in the world or even in the Church? Do you suppose that titles we have had other than 'husband,' 'father,' or 'priesthood holder' will mean much to Him? Do you think He will care how packed our schedule was or how many important meetings we attended? Do you suppose that our success in filling our days with appointments will serve as an excuse for failure to spend time with our wife and family?"[52]

Steve Jobs, the brilliant mastermind behind Apple, shared his regrets about his failures as a parent and said of the times when he was able to embrace that role of father, "It's 10,000 times better than anything I've ever done."[53] If you know about Steve Jobs, you know he did quite a lot. What does that say about parenthood?

Perhaps as Jobs saw the curtains of his own mortality closing and the sun of immortality distantly dawning, his eyes obtained a lens that gave him new sight as to the greater things that the rest of the world sees as only a trifle. Perhaps he began to see what we see, what we as members of the Church are trying desperately to share with the world: the true nature and meaning of this life.

Poet Edwin Markham, though not a Latter-day Saint, caught the vision of this world:

> We are all blind, until we see
> That in the [universal] plan
> Nothing is worth the making if
> It does not make the man.
> Why build these [buildings] glorious,
> If man unbuilded goes?
> In vain we build the [world], unless
> The builder also grows.[54]

I leave you with a symbol I hope you'll remember. It is the symbol of moonlight. If you think about it, the moon is a veritable mirror. When the earth has turned and the sun no longer sits in the sky, rays from the sun, so blinding when seen in the day, hit the moon and reflect off its surface. This light then travels right to us, proving that though we cannot see the sun directly, we can know it's still there.

In this telestial state, we can really only see a shade of God, a mere reflection of His true glory. Paul referred to this dim view of the celestial as looking "through a glass, darkly" (1 Corinthians 13:12). But even in that shadowy reflection, we see a being not unlike ourselves. For we can see ourselves and know that, in the same way we are like God, God is also like us, and we can come to understand Him, His ways, and His perspective. In so doing, we can progress in that crucial way of becoming like Him and help others to do the same.

Now, it's time we finished that Harry Potter parable.

You have probably discerned some of the lesson already, especially if you've read the book and already know the rest of the story. Similar to the secular world's view of the Latter-day Saints, Hermione thought Harry wasn't quite thinking straight in his belief that his father saved him and Sirius. After all, his father is dead, and no magic can bring back the dead.

But magic can, apparently, take two teenagers back through time to follow their past selves from a distance, save a condemned hippogriff named Buckbeak from execution, and rescue new allies from soul-sucking demons. In this context, it seems Hermione might have been a bit ironically close-minded, especially for one who didn't know magic existed a scant three years ago. Granted, she was correct that Harry did not see his father. Who did he really see across that lake who looked so much like his father?

> "Come on!" he muttered, staring about. "Where are you? Dad, come on—"
>
> But no one came. Harry raised his head to look at the circle of dementors across the lake. One of them was lowering its hood. It was time for the rescuer to appear—but no one was coming to help this time—
>
> And then it hit him—he understood. He hadn't seen his father— he had seen *himself*—[55]

The revelation shocked him and seemed to awaken something within him. Harry, realizing he had caught a glimpse of his future and true potential, raised his wand and cast the Patronus spell to fulfill it. Summoned in majesty was that four-legged creature of light, a magnificent achievement for a young teenage wizard. The Patronus galloped forth and bore down on the massive horde of dementors, banishing them from the scene. The shape of the Patronus was not just any generic beast, however. It was a stag—the exact kind of animal Harry's father James was capable of transforming into in life.

You'll notice that Harry had not only seen himself—he had seen his father's image *in* himself. As he had started down that path to becoming a man, he had come to look so much like his father that he almost couldn't tell the difference. Note that this did not mean his father never existed. It meant just the opposite: his father was *alive in him*, and he was growing up to *look* like him and *be* like him. The stag Patronus proved that. In essence, Harry, seeing the image of his father in himself, shined the light of his father into the darkness, and in doing so learned just how much like his father he truly was.

It is our sacred duty, as those who understand Heavenly Father, to take His message to the world and bring souls to Christ so that they of the world may know the Father as we do. We see, in the images of His creations, in the endless generations of life nature strives for, Him and His ways and purposes—and then at last we comprehend ourselves.

Christ told the Nephites, "Therefore, hold up your light that it may shine unto the world. Behold I am the light which ye shall hold up—that which ye have seen me do" (3 Nephi 18:24). And then "the light of his countenance did shine upon them" (3 Nephi 19:25).

We have been outside the cave. We have seen the real light. Let us be, as Christ invited in His rousing cry, mirrors of God. Let us reflect the light of His countenance and attributes back upon the world. Light truly reveals all things; let our souls and persons reveal the nature, character, and love of Heavenly Father to all.

Let us be mirrors of God.

Chapter 3
More Precious than Fine Gold

*T*o **my readers,** *let me preface this chapter by confessing that, though I have endured difficult trials thus far in my life, I am not an authority on dealing with life's hardships. Others, perhaps some of you, have been dealt harder lots in life and are possibly dealing with weighty burdens even now. On the other hand, maybe you are currently enjoying a reprieve from such trials. Though I believe every human being on earth could find this chapter highly relevant at some specific moment in his or her mortality, it is designed for those readers who are in the process of going through those earth-shattering times in life when the sharp and bitter realities of our fallen world not only stab you in the gut but also twist the blade so hard that it seems life is just not worth it anymore.*

If this chapter finds you in such a state, I believe I can say that, though I don't know who you are, I know some of what you're going through.

Following the quest to understand God is the quest to become like Him. As in any hero's journey, this quest is fraught with peril. Our lives are filled with pain and defined by eternal, incredible stakes. Indeed, it is perhaps the greatest heroes among us, those who have ascended to the highest possible heights in this life, who have also been compelled to rise from the deepest depths and had to pass through the hottest flames. There, in the dungeons and furnaces, we come to understand the extremes of this world and come as close as we can to understanding our downcast and downtrodden brothers and sisters as only Christ truly can. In our shadowy places, we can learn to love as He did, see just how far the Atonement reaches, and even assist in its work ourselves.

None of us will ever know just how far down Christ's arm of mercy extends. But many of the trials we will be called to endure can raise us as high as heroes, if we let them. This crazy world was designed for *just such a thing*. Christ, speaking through Isaiah, declared, "I will make a man more precious than fine gold" (2 Nephi 23:12). For metals like gold to be refined and given their true quality, they must be cast into a fire, where their final impurities are removed. Robert Millet and Joseph Fielding McConkie wrote, "It is in the flames of difficulty that the tempered steel of faith is forged. Ease does not call forth greatness."[56] And greatness is, in God's kingdom, what we all aspire to achieve.

To protect ourselves from the fiery darts of this fallen world, we need a shield. Let's begin the discussion of the hero's shield with another parable. Orson Scott Card's science fiction novel *Ender's Game* is the story of Ender Wiggin, a child genius recruited by the world government to enter a training ground for leaders in humanity's war of survival against an imminent alien invasion. Within a few short years, Ender becomes commander of the entire military and ultimately defeats the enemy and saves the entire human race.

But it wasn't mere military prowess that won the battle—it was a perspective. You see, as brilliant as he was at tactics and strategy, Ender learned—through literal blood, sweat, and tears—that to defeat one's enemies, one must know them and be able to see the world through their eyes. That was exactly what he did with the alien invaders, and it was the key to his victory. He saw and felt their pains, their desires—the soul of their collective consciousness. This was not an unearned perspective. He gradually acquired that empathy by enduring pain of his own, inflicted on him sometimes by fellow child soldiers and other times by the adults overseeing the training program. Before he even reached age twelve, Ender was isolated, envied, hated, picked on, beaten, forced to fight fellow children in self-defense, and psychologically broken by the brunt of his load and the impossible tasks laid out for him almost daily. For some, such opposition would have brought them down to the level of the attackers. Ender, however, proved wiser. He gained empathy and with it won humanity's greatest war.

Remarkably, the inner consequence of such violence was . . . love. Just as Christ exhorts us to do, Ender began to love his enemies, child and alien alike. Even as he was forced to destroy the entire alien species, he regretted it, hated himself for it, and devoted the rest of his life to telling their tale because he understood them, because he loved them. The pain and evil he endured proved therefore not meaningless, nor fruitless; rather, it was an essential element of the world he lived in.

We must understand the same for our world, for our trials and tragedies. If we do not attempt to understand and instead kick against the pricks, we may well waste the pain and the many opportunities our Heavenly Father has given us to grow.

What I've begun to address in this chapter is something mentioned previously, what philosophers call the "Problem of Evil," a theological dilemma that has been debated for centuries. Now, I wouldn't be so arrogant here as to attempt a comprehensive and universal solution to this problem once and for all, but I do want to suggest some gospel insights that may help those struggling with the question—which I believe, by the way, is only solvable in one's own heart and through one's unique relationship with Heavenly Father. It is forever a personal question, and thus no single answer will solve it absolutely for every person asking.

The "Problem of Evil" is this: how can an all-powerful, all-knowing, and all-benevolent God exist when there is so much suffering in the world He supposedly created? How could such a being let all that pain and misery happen?

It's a good and fair question. Among the many answers to the "Problem of Evil" that have been developed by theologians over the course of Western civilization, perhaps the most unexpected comes from Christian apologist C. S. Lewis.

In the biopic *Shadowlands*,[57] Lewis described a horrific traffic accident to a gathered assembly. He followed by asking the audience some "simple, but fundamental questions: Where was God on that December night? Why didn't He stop it? Isn't God supposed to be good? Isn't

He supposed to love us? Does God want us to suffer?" He paused for a moment here and then said, "What if the answer to that question is yes?"

Yes? God wants us to suffer?

The instant reaction to such a notion is rebellion, outright refusal to either believe in or worship a God who would want us to feel pain. Put in those terms alone, God sounds cruel, indifferent, and perhaps even sadistic.

But even a purely secular glance at the natural world supplies a simple and entirely understandable concept of the purpose of pain. For instance, we are all familiar with the concept of touching a hot stove. Say a little girl reaches up in curiosity, brushes her fingers against the glowing red ring, and begins to scream and cry until her mother rushes in, puts ice on the burn, and points out the lesson. The child has now learned never to touch a hot stove again, as well as to never put her hand toward fire. She has gained knowledge: what heat is, how it works, and eventually how to use it as a tool to her advantage.

Now, what would be better—that a child knows pain once and never goes near again, or that he or she continues to participate in a damaging, deadening behavior without feeling any pain at all?

Physical pain is built into our biological systems to make us aware that there is a problem somewhere in our bodies that needs to be taken care of. When I broke my leg jumping down a flight of stairs at a seminary party when I was fifteen, the pain was telling me to get to a hospital, get the broken leg mended, and never do such an insane thing ever again. If I had not felt that pain, I would've continued on in life crippled and handicapped—in other words, stagnant and undeveloped.

Continuing his speech to the assembly, Lewis said, "I suggest to you that it is because God loves us that He makes us the gift of suffering. Or to put it another way . . . pain is God's megaphone to rouse a deaf world."[58]

Lewis had the right to speak on this. He and J. R. R. Tolkien, two of the greatest Christian (and not coincidentally fantasy) writers of the twentieth century, both passed firsthand through the horrors of World War I.

Are you old enough to remember September 11, 2001? How America suddenly united and turned to God in the aftermath? Looking back on it, that tragedy was a message from a megaphone to our whole country. It roused us, woke us up, made us aware, and gave us the desire to love each other, to want to do good.

Moments like those do not come to a society often, but they come to individuals all the time. Our lives are full of problems, challenges, and opposition of infinite varieties. That can be physical pain, emotional, and, in a way all too often ignored, spiritual.

Guilt is that great corrector of spiritual imbalance, and our society has done its darnedest to do away with it and become comfortable with sin. Alma said to his son Corianton, "Now, there was a punishment affixed, and a just law given, which brought remorse of conscience unto man . . . if there was no law given against sin men would not be afraid to sin" (Alma 42:18, 20). Like with physical pain, if guilt did not plague our souls, then we'd have no reason to change, no reason to do anything other than what the carnal man would desire—no reason to repent. That is always the purpose of God's punishments, as it is the purpose of much suffering in the world: change.

Elder Jeffrey R. Holland wrote of the consequences of wrong choices, "Of course sinfulness does bring suffering, and the only answer to that behavior is repentance."[59] When that repentance, that change has taken place, there is no need for further spiritual suffering. We are free to go our way and sin no more. This is the beauty of the plan of happiness: that spiritual suffering can be swallowed up; as we repent, God can erase those moments from the book of life, to be remembered no longer.

But perhaps the pain we suffer most strikingly is not physical or spiritual, for both of those are mere symptoms of other problems that can be corrected. In the same address, Elder Holland pointed out that "sometimes suffering comes to the righteous, too,"[60] regardless of cause. While guilt won't come to a perfect man, *sorrow* certainly will. After all, it came to *the* perfect man and still does. We believe in a God who weeps.

No matter our choices or goodness, all eyes, even God's, will well up from time to time because of things we cannot control. Certainly the prophets throughout the ages can attest to this, as they faced the rejection of their messages—but we ordinary people can too.

Though we strive to do the right thing and may even succeed, our lives are still plagued by loss, heartache, heartbreak, disappointment, injustice, unfairness, rejection, betrayal, financial struggles, and so on. Sometimes we are victims of another's selfishness, indifference, or pride—or even physical disabilities, mental disorders, or emotional frailties we may have been born with. Our lives are rife with all these things, even if we're living the commandments. Why is that?

I'll repeat Lewis's words: "It is because God loves us that He makes us the gift of suffering." Notice those precise words: *because God loves us*.

Lewis went on to say, "You see, we are like blocks of stone out of which the Sculptor carves the forms of men. The blows of His chisel, which hurt us so much . . . are what make us perfect."[61]

This is the principle of adversity, of opposition. It is, in the end, a good thing, a necessary thing, even a kind of blessing. A baby bird, when hatching from its egg, must be allowed to emerge on its own strength. Without the experience of breaking out of its own shell, the bird may not have the ability to survive on its own.

When it comes to our physical bodies, muscles only grow when they experience trauma. Exercise causes the muscles in our limbs to break down and develop tears in the tissue. As we rest, the muscles gradually grow back and actually become stronger than they were before to cope with new and greater burdens.

Agency also has a great deal to do with this. We are here, as youth speaker Brad Wilcox put it, to "learn heaven,"[62] to internalize celestial glory, to become it, to build gods out of mere specks of dust and raw intelligence. To be a god is to be free, an agent who chooses to live a godly life, so there can be no other way of attaining that lofty ambition but by being allowed to make choices freely and let others choose just as freely. The eradication of agency for any reason is the eradication of the reason we are here on earth, hence the destructive nature of Lucifer's plan and desire to do away with consequences to choices, in so doing nullify the choices themselves. Pain, then, coming either from our own choices or the choices of others, has even more implicit meaning than growth. Pain and suffering are the natural byproducts of this necessary experience, this process of cultivating gods.

So yes, there are lessons to be learned from pain, inherent in the process itself. Lessons God feels it is worth it to know, that He teaches us because He loves us. He grants us such lessons because He wants our eternal progression more than our temporal comfort.

Not only will these experiences make us stronger, they will also develop within us a greater and more full appreciation for what joy and happiness can be. Adam and Eve once lived in the Garden of Eden in perfect, simple happiness, never knowing the bitter side of life—the side of death and decay. Consequently, they could not progress. It was only after the Fall, when they were cast into the world, that they were able to have increase, bear and raise children, learn the lessons of life, and discern the bitter from the sweet, the pleasure from the pain, and the good from the evil. One cannot know joy without knowing sadness.

For C. S. Lewis, that "joy" was quite literal; it was the name of his wife, with whom he shared only a tragically short time. In *Shadowlands*, after Joy's unexpected death, he asked bitterly, "Why love, if losing hurts so much?" Thereafter, he received an answer in his own voice but as if from the mouth of God: "The pain now is part of the happiness then. That's the deal."[63]

In other words, the stars are beautiful, but it must be nighttime to even know that they're there.

Sometimes—*many* times—it will feel like it's not worth it. No experience could be worth this much hurt, we may say. No joy is worth the loss. I've been there before. I know what that mindset feels like. I also know that it is a lie.

We must know and understand that God is in control, that He knows what is best for us, and that He will *never* give us something we cannot handle with His help or something that is not worthwhile. If we confront a burden that seems overwhelming, it is because God is giving us the kind of weakness that will ultimately strengthen us if we place our hope and faith in Him. Those crashing waves and billowing winds may attack us as we sail through that storm of suffering and uncertainty. But, as the hymn sings so poetically, "Be still, my soul: The waves and winds still know / His voice who ruled them while he dwelt below."[64]

If it seems too hard, too debilitating to overcome on our own, we must pray, and if we are already praying, pray harder, longer. While it may indeed be insurmountable for you alone, you are not alone if

God is there. Prayer is our chain and channel to Him. It is as easy to access as it was for the Israelites to see the serpent-draped rod Moses raised in the wilderness. Prayer reveals God's presence in a way nothing else can—for true prayer is not a monologue, but a dialogue. He is ever available. The Apostle Peter may have fallen asleep on his watch, but God does not.

This divine presence isn't always easily felt. The Spirit doesn't always work like we want it to. Oftentimes we reject His comfort before it can be offered out of our own willful blindness and bitterness. Elder Jeffrey R. Holland said, "Whenever these moments of our extremity come, we must not succumb to the fear that God has abandoned us or that He does not hear our prayers. He *does* hear us. He *does* see us. He does love us. When we are in dire circumstances and want to cry, 'Where art Thou?' it is imperative that we remember He is right there with us—where He has always been! We must continue to believe, continue to have faith, continue to pray and plead with heaven, even if we feel for a time our prayers are not heard and that God has somehow gone away. He *is* there. Our prayers *are* heard. And when we weep He and the angels of heaven weep with us."[65]

God would not, cannot forget us. We are His work, His purpose. We are His children. Without us, He would be a God alone, and thus no God at all. It is said that over the eons of human existence, of all the names God has been known and could be known as, the one He chooses to go by—the role He chooses to live—is that of Father. Isaiah, speaking messianically, wrote, "For can a woman forget her sucking child, that she should not have compassion on the son of her womb? Yea, they may forget, yet will I not forget thee, O house of Israel. Behold, I have graven thee upon the palms of my hands" (1 Nephi 21:15–16). He has engraved His love for us on the palms of His hands, in the prints of the nails in His hands and feet.

Our Father and our Savior will be there for us always. But because we are agents unto ourselves, we have to make the first move. And though He will not compel us to pray, God does prompt us to make that first move with those needles that cause our regular moments of distress. Without them, we would have little reason to seek God out in the larger scheme of things; if we are content in day-to-day life, what need would we think we had for greater heights? We would remain content to live life and make progress on our own power alone—yet we cannot ascend to higher degrees of existence without Him. And so, even if we are angry or bitter, if we turn to God with any semblance of sincerity, He can wrap us in the "arms of [his] love" (D&C 6:20) and offer access to His saving and exalting power.

So while many in the world endure sadness and sorrow without God or even in defiance of Him, we know that we can't obtain true, lasting salvation by only our own limited vision and capabilities. From the pulpit of general conference, President Thomas S. Monson quoted the words of M. Louise Haskins in April 2009:

> And I said to the man who stood at the gate of the year: "Give me a light that I may tread safely into the unknown!"
>   And he replied:
>   "Go out into the darkness and put your hand into the Hand of God. That shall be to you better than [a] light and safer than a known way."[66]

To successfully face and conquer the darkness of this world, we must put our trust in God and depend on Him. We obviously don't and can't always know why bad things happen to us. Sometimes—most times—we can't see with our mortal, non-spiritual eyes why some horrible thing has happened. In such trying times, we must muster our energy, throw up our shield of faith, and endure the onslaught of life's fiery darts with patience, trusting that either the trial will end or that peace will descend as we put our faith in God.

That trust is important in a trial, for sometimes pain is not a lesson but a test—a test of our obedience, a trial of our faith, those prophesied times in which God "will prove [us] herewith, to see if [we] will do all things whatsoever the Lord their God shall command [us]" (Abraham 3:25). When we are wading through those black waters of adversity on our way to dry land, will we turn to the Lord, keep His commandments, and follow His guiding light, whatever the proximity to the shore? Or will we give up and sink below the surface, submerge in short-sightedness, fall in faithlessness, drown in disbelief?

That test is frequently one of fortitude, to see how long we will bear our suffering patiently. God promises several times in the scriptures that we will receive all the righteous desires of our hearts, but, as with all of God's plans, *that takes time*. We often promise, "I will give [or do] anything" for a certain blessing to be granted. I've said it many times, both to myself and to God in prayer. But one of those times, I was answered pretty directly by the Holy Ghost. The answer was returned in the form of a question: "You say you would give anything. Would you give time?"

That struck me. Well, would I? Would I wait for the Lord to show His hand and remain patient until then? Again, we are promised that we will one day obtain all the righteous desires of our hearts. I say I'd give anything to have them. But would I be willing to wait for them? Sometimes waiting can last a long time, and we can't see where it will end. It is in these particular times that we may doubt God's love for us, or even if He's up there at all.

So often this feeling of despair is attached to our desire for romantic love. I want to make one thing absolutely clear to you, any of you: Whether or not you're in a relationship is *not* an indicator of how much Heavenly Father loves you, nor of your worthiness before Him. I know the despair and loneliness that can be felt in such a state—the perpetual heartbreak one can dwell in because of "the pangs of despised love."[67] Sometimes we look at others who seem to be so happy, so fulfilled, and never lonely, never without help, making us wonder why we can't have that too, why it's easier for them than for us.

Well, Elder Neal A. Maxwell had an answer to that: "Faith in God includes faith in God's timing."[68] As painful, trying, and depressing as that timing might seem, it is, in the end, for our benefit. Almost always, we forego something good now for something great later, even if we might not know it at the time. God sees the future, whereas we cannot. And in the end, I believe we will thank Him for that foresight, for the gift received that is better than the gift desired, and for waiting till dawn to push back the curtains, where before only the black of night reigned.

Is there any temporal trial we've undergone and completed that we were not grateful for later? This kind of perspective is difficult to maintain; in the middle of trials, it's easy to say, "Of course I wish that had never happened." And indeed, some trials last our entire lives, never giving us the proper distance needed to appreciate them. But I believe that when it comes down to it, when we arrive at the end and face our Heavenly Father, we'll be grateful for every ounce of pain that ever marred us because we'll realize that the only way we could have gotten to that end was through those terrible storms.

The Jaredites, in going forth on the great waters to the promised land, "commend[ed] themselves unto the Lord their God." As they set sail, the Lord sent a "furious wind"—a storm that "tossed [them] upon the waves of the sea" and "buried [them] in the depths of the sea," in the midst of "great and terrible tempests." That storm, in fact, "did never cease" (Ether 6:4–6, 8).

Sounds like the pain we've been talking about, doesn't it? But at the conclusion of this passage, we gain a wonderful insight: just as the wind never ceased, neither did it cease "to blow towards the promised land," and despite the crashing "mountain waves which broke upon them," they were protected by being buried so deep in the water. And when "they did cry unto the Lord . . . he did bring them forth again upon the top of the waters" (Ether 6:6–8).

What a profound lesson. The storms of life carried them forward, acted as a constant force pushing them on toward the great blessing at the end of their journey. For most of the time, they probably had absolutely no idea how far they were in their voyage or how long it would be until they reached their destination. But they went anyway, arrived at their salvation, and entered into their promised land.

Like the storm that drove the Jaredites, trials are often the vehicles for unexpected blessings, insights, and soul-growing moments we could not have received any other way. I'll say it boldly: I believe there is almost no needless pain. Lessons can be learned and peace can be achieved in almost any circumstance, if only we pay attention and have in mind the end goal of growth.

But again, easy to say, reasonable to believe, but terribly hard to enact when confronted with those soul-quaking moments that seem impossible to overcome. I think of the example of a woman who battled depression all her life, all the way until it eventually caused her to commit suicide. Such is the sad story of many with mental or emotional illnesses. What is the purpose of their suffering? What had they to gain from such tortured lives? It consumed them in the end; not much room for growth there.

Or so it seems. But do you see, even there, the opportunity for battle? For struggle, for overcoming the imbalance of this mortal world? I would posit that any effort expended in fighting evil, whether that evil be directly from Satan or simply a feature of the Fall, helps us to grow and build toward eternity. This life, after all, is temporary, along with all its pains. And always, at the end of the journey we have the Savior's arms to look forward to, open and waiting for us at the gates. I believe that woman, and all those like her, did indeed arrive at the promised land.

Sometimes pain isn't strictly for learning some moral to the story or growing our souls in some constructive way. Sometimes the point of the trial is to open our minds to the Savior's love for us, the relationship we build with Him. When a loved one dies, for instance, it is generally not a matter of something we did wrong or some flaw we have to correct in ourselves. Rather, it is those times when we're most vulnerable, and thus more open to love, to being loved. Those times are when we can come to know Jesus not just as our Savior but also as our older brother. In those moments of grief—which are actually moments of our deepest love—we can build up our relationship with Him and with Heavenly Father, all to understand the "fellowship of his sufferings" (Philippians 3:10). And all the more joyous our reunions will be with those departed loved ones in the next life. (The next chapter covers this concept in greater detail.)

Any suffering we are called to go through can be lessened as we reach out to the Savior and the peace of His presence. That is an integral part of His Atonement, that He felt pain so He could understand ours, so He could help us endure it—and not only endure it, but endure it *well*. To "endure it well" is to not only suffer but also to grow from that suffering and become more like Him (D&C 121:8). That growth is the other part of the Atonement: fixing our broken hearts, healing all our wounds—spiritual, physical, emotional, mental—and building up our souls over time, grace for grace. When we endure well, and the Savior is present, we learn. If we don't make an effort, if we haven't invited Christ, then we might not.

And that's the danger: we aren't forced to learn from our mistakes, and thus some or all of our suffering goes to waste. Elder Neal A. Maxwell quoted Anne Morrow Lindbergh, wife of famed aviator Charles

Lindbergh, saying, "I do not believe that sheer suffering teaches. If suffering alone taught, all the world would be wise."[69]

Recall the example of September 11 and the love and generosity we felt collectively back then. Now see the state of our society today. In the years since, that unity and love have been splintered and cast aside. Just like the Nephites in their cycle of pride, society at large has forgotten the ideals and values that once bound us together. Clearly we were humbled by the pain, but like many receivers of miracles in early days of the Church, the lessons did not last. Disputes took their toll, and today our nation is divided, just as the Nephites were, by all "manner of -ites" (4 Nephi 1:17).

But in the end, the focus of the Atonement remains centered on individuals, not nations. Our personal journeys carry greater weight with the Lord than those of governments. All nations fade with time, but the individual soul persists forever.

Opportunities for growth come to us personally and uniquely, but they must be faced with the same perspective. Mrs. Lindbergh clarified what is needed to learn from the pain: "To suffering must be added mourning, understanding, patience, love, openness, and the willingness to remain vulnerable."[70] Some of those traits sound to me like many of the attributes of Christ, the One who suffered most and was most aware of what this life is about. It is that awareness and humility that will turn pain into perspective, suffering into salvation.

With such a lens, even dungeons can turn into temples. Such was the case with Joseph Smith in Liberty Jail, a veritable hellhole, where he received some of his most profound and poignant revelation. Hell can be anywhere, but so can heaven. Elder Jeffrey R. Holland wrote of such moments, "When you have to, you can have sacred, revelatory, profoundly instructive experience with the Lord in *any* situation you are in. Indeed, let me say that even a little stronger: You can have sacred, revelatory, profoundly instructive experience with the Lord *in the most miserable experiences of your life*—in the worst settings, while enduring the most painful injustices, when facing the most insurmountable odds and opposition you have ever faced."[71]

I can testify of the truth of Elder Holland's words, that willingly endured trials allow us the greatest communion with God we may ever experience in this life. Consider the life story of Elder Neal A. Maxwell.

As a young man, he volunteered for the army almost immediately after the outbreak of World War II, not delaying his enlistment as some other young men did. In later years, he remarked that if he had waited, he probably would never have seen combat. As it happened, he went on to fight in the horrific Battle of Okinawa, one of the bloodiest battles of the war. There on that island, cornered by the enemy, surrounded by death and brutality, and hidden in as literal a foxhole as you can get, young Neal made the promise so many have in foxholes through the ages: If God would spare his life, he would devote the rest of that life in service to Him. God spared him, and today we can see the fruits of Elder Maxwell's life in that covenant fulfilled. Had he tried to *avoid* or postpone that trial, perhaps he would not have lived the life he did or change the lives he changed. From the influence he has had on my family alone, I can testify that the world would indeed be a darker place without Elder Neal A. Maxwell.

Perhaps the world is darker today for the absence of some other soul, another potentially great man or woman we will never know because they ran from his or her troubles, sought escape from pain, and sidestepped those purging, purifying experiences that define every great man or woman's life. It is in the times we have fallen that we are at our most humble, most willing to be picked up and taught. It is then that we can learn the most about our capabilities, our strength, and ourselves, as well as about God, His love, and our relationship with Him. It can be then, in our most vulnerable moments, that God is able to shape us, form us, and organize us into something profoundly different but superior and stronger than we were before. That's the essence of His work, and it is why this world has such potential for pain.

Of the succor and healing power provided us by Christ, Elder Jeffrey R. Holland wrote, "When what has to be has been and when what lessons to be learned have been learned, it will be for us as it was for the Prophet Joseph. Just at the time he felt most alone and distant from heaven's ear was the very time he received the wonderful ministration of the Spirit and the glorious answers that came from his Father in Heaven: 'My son, peace be unto thy soul; thine adversity and thine afflictions shall be but a small moment; and then, if thou endure it well, God shall exalt thee on high; thou shalt triumph over all thy foes" (D&C 121:7–8).[72]

That is the secret: enduring well. Not just enduring, not just bearing the pain, but, as Anne Morrow Lindbergh so enjoined, learning from it. The fruits of such suffering can be glorious, and in the end we will no longer remember the pain that propelled us to celestial heights. The Savior said to His Apostles, "A woman when she is in travail [childbirth] hath sorrow, because her hour is come: but as soon as she is delivered of the child, she remembereth no more the anguish, for joy that a man is born into the world" (John 16:21).

A man more precious than fine gold. Our adversity and afflictions will be "but a small moment," as the Lord promised Joseph. A small moment in our minds and memories. And then we will no more remember the anguish, but we will have joy in exaltation.

If we can see our lives with that kind of long-term perspective, accept that we don't know everything right now, and trust that the Lord's timing is best, we will triumph all the easier, conquer all the more, and be all the further along our Eternal Arc.

Several years ago, I was at the Oakland Temple for a YSA ward temple night. I came out with an advisor named Jim Mattson, and we stopped to look at the glorious view that temple offers over the entire Bay area. You can see the Bay Bridge, San Francisco across the bay itself, and even the Golden Gate Bridge too. Many cities surround the bay, and the temple, built on the Oakland hills, wears the mantle of a lighthouse—a beacon to both lost souls and temple-worthy Saints, and even literally to airline pilots who use the temple as a reference point and guiding light at night.

Brother Mattson related to me a thought he had while looking out over this marvelous view. He pointed out how the closer we are to something, the worse and more chaotic it seems. In the impoverished and crime-ridden streets, we see up close the misery and hopelessness of the people's lives, with families torn apart, parentless children wandering the streets, and rival gangs in perpetual conflict with each other. There, on the streets, misery is cheap; it is easily come by, and just about everybody has it. But if you take a step back, say to the temple grounds overlooking the city and its myriad lights, nothing is actually as bad as it seems. It is peaceful to look upon, even beautiful. You want to say to these people that it's going to be okay; look at the bigger picture, take a step back, and know that everything is going to work out in the end.

As Brother Mattson pointed out to me, that is also the perspective of Heavenly Father. Think of how far away His view is and how calm and peaceful His outlook must be, how much more knowledgeable and in control of all things He is, and how (of all people) He alone is qualified to tell us that it's going to be okay.

And He tells us exactly that. In fact, He tells us that it's going to be more than okay. If we live the way He asks us to live, we will achieve everlasting happiness, eternal life and eternal love, and all things that He has. But to that end, this sorrow, this sadness, though temporal, is required first.

The oft-unsung fifth verse of "How Firm a Foundation" contain words to truly treasure, both as sublime poetry and as comfort and inspiration:

> When through fiery trials thy pathway shall lie,
>> My grace, all sufficient, shall be thy supply.
>> The flame shall not hurt thee; I only design . . .
>> Thy dross to consume and thy gold to refine.[73]

It is often the best of men who have been called to endure the worst tribulations. All the good that Ender Wiggin did sprang forth from the pain he underwent. The prime lesson of his experience was compassion, the charity that is the pure love of Christ. My friend Stephan Peers once pointed out to me that we see the burdens of others with much more clarity when we've experienced our own. Bearing our own burdens can soften our hearts and open our eyes till our enemies turn to friends, and we consequently become less inclined to add to the load already on their shoulders; instead, we choose to share it, thus taking part in the glorious work of the Atonement. As we are blanketed by heavenly love in the midst of our afflictions, we can in turn share that warmth with others and help them endure what we endured. That's the project of Zion.

Such service is one route to adopting a new attitude and obtaining a different, higher perspective. The power to alter the way we look at the world is one of the greatest tools the Lord has blessed us with in our endeavor to endure. My good friend Joseph Harris, who endured a variety of major health issues the entirety of his life and has since passed away, once declared at a fast and testimony meeting, "Just because I'm in pain doesn't mean I have to be miserable!"

Despite his illness and constant reliance on medication, Joe never really complained, and whenever some bitter word did slip out, he apologized for it immediately. If we try to do likewise, we can discover our will to endure what is necessary to grow closer to God, both in distance and degree, in our hearts and our minds. We can aspire, as the hymn says, to be willing to be lifted up upon our own crosses to be nearer to God.[74]

This fallen world, with its pains and sicknesses, is its own cross on Golgotha. Both the present and the future can be dark and uncertain. We may not know when a given trial will end, or if it ever will. But we will bear it better if we understand that it's not God's intention to remove our trials from us, but rather it is to help us endure them, come off conqueror, and overcome every challenge we face and every problem that comes our way. Christ willingly suffered our pains and afflictions—every single one of them—so He could offer that help, that empathy, that love. If we humbly ask Him for help in bearing our burdens, He will do so. I testify to this personally and echo *Preach My Gospel*, which reminds us, "Everything that is unfair about life can be made right through the Atonement of Jesus Christ."[75]

The Atonement, as broad and epic and encompassing as it is, can be—and very much is—something entirely personal. It can be about solely you and your Savior. He went through it for you. He knows you. He knows your name, your feelings, and the thoughts and intents of your heart. He knows exactly what you are suffering and what help you need to endure it. Ask Him to help bear the load and keep asking in all of your prayers, and you will one day find that trial, that fiery furnace, is over. And thus you have overcome; you have conquered. And you will have become, in the Lord's eyes, more precious than fine gold.

The ugly alternative to this system is a God who keeps us ignorant and overprotected, freezing our souls in a state of smallness. That, I feel compelled to point out, was Lucifer's plan. The key poison of that scheme was that we'd get celestial glory but without celestial growth. Exaltation without transformation is impossible; it's a paradox. It is truly a mark of how much God loves us that He does want us to have these hurtful experiences, that the end of the story might be so much more satisfying, triumphant, and beautiful.

In closing, let me just say that life—our time of testing, the refiner's fire we are meant to go through—can hurt like Hell, literally. Disappointment, grief, pain—the stuff of mortality that attacks our will to go on, perhaps even to the extent that we would rather give up than continue on. But in words often attributed to Winston Churchill, "If you're going through Hell, keep going," and eventually you *will* arrive at those figurative gates of heaven.

For it will all end someday—the pining, the weeping, the wailing, the burning, the carving, the purging. And then it will be as John the Beloved wrote so tenderly in the book of Revelation, "And God shall wipe away all tears from their eyes; and there shall be no more death, neither sorrow, nor crying, neither shall there be any more pain: for the former things are passed away" (Revelation 21:4).

Press on. Have faith. Be patient. Endure it well. Remember, *you are not alone.* Christ is with you. Our Father is with you. And know that you are His child, and to Him—He who knows who and what you'll be someday—you are already more precious than fine gold.

Chapter 4
This Dream Shall End

*M**ortality is fraught** with pain from our own and others' choices, as well as with the grief of inescapable suffering. Yet as we endure, we can look forward with hope to the moment when it will all be swallowed up in the grand, glorious end of our earthly adventure and the beginning of our heavenly one.

At the transition of those two paths, I envision Christ standing in the posture of the *Christus*. He is tall, as high as the heavens. His face looks down in compassion and His arms are held up to expose the prints in His hands and wrists. But as you picture it in your mind's eye, note something else about that stance. Our Savior appears to be ready to envelope all those who approach Him in a tender embrace.

What will it be like, to finally be wrapped physically in His arms? Sometimes I pray to feel that precise sensation, and though I inevitably receive a calming peace as God's answer, I know that even that warmth in my heart cannot compare to what it will be like to be held by Him, to literally weep into His protective shoulder, knowing I've reached my goal and finally achieved my fondest dream.

But of course, the actual "dream" just ended, didn't it?

The end of the film *Inception* is worth discussing in this light. No, not the spinning top, the endless questions of what is real and what is not—I'm talking about the scene in the airplane at the ending of the dream, after Cobb found Saito and all of the crew begin to wake up. If you can remember that scene, focus with me on Cobb as he opens his eyes after a lifetime lived in dreams below; those disconcerted eyes flit madly back and forth, taking in everything he knew before, seeing "things as they really are" (Jacob 4:13). Over just a few seconds' time, he remembers all he once knew—the life he had forgotten, the life that had led him into the dream world in the first place, to the quest to improve his existence and complete it, all so he could ultimately return to the family he had been forced to leave long ago.

Every time I watch that film, I'm struck by those first few seconds of waking, when a lifetime of memory pours back into his mind all at once. I don't think I'm alone in saying I've experienced something similar in waking from my own dreams, things as they really are flying back through my fluttering eyelids.

Now, again in your mind's eye, watch as Cobb's gaze falls onto Saito, the man he made a special promise with—one might call it a covenant. As Saito's eyes lock on Cobb's, more memories flood into their minds, and we can see Saito's near-instantaneous remembrance of their deal, the agreement that gave meaning to the whole dream experience. When Saito wakes and remembers, he makes that precious phone call that would mercifully free Cobb from the constricting binds of justice, honoring the plan that had been agreed to before the dream began.

Do you see it? Do you see the parallel with our own experience of that transition called death? My friend Korance Goodwin pointed out this parable to me. Think of the moment when we leave mortality and awaken back in the spirit world, the realm from which we came. I think it might be like what *Inception* shows us. Would it be so different from waking up in the afterlife, feeling the veil finally brushed aside as we grasp hands with God and enter eternity and return to our true home? I think, as the preponderance of memory comes rushing back into our minds, our faces might look something like the faces of Cobb and Saito, eyes darting back and forth across the halls of heaven, remembering the past eternity we spent in God's household all at once. We would probably think of the people we knew before and what we know of them now; of how many promises we kept and didn't keep; of the things we've done and the words we've uttered that we can never take back; and, more important, of the covenants we made and those we broke. And I think we will remember exactly that deal we made with Heavenly Father before we came to earth, the agreement He is bound to honor if we repented and sincerely tried to follow His path.

Will we look back on that agreement in horror and shame, with weeping and wailing and gnashing of teeth? Will we be filled with regret? Or will we feel joy, that perfect sense of relief and peace as we remember that we gave all we had to give and did all we had to do?

Suppose Cobb had failed in his test. When that plane landed, he would've been instantly arrested and thrown in jail for the rest of his life. Permanent imprisonment. But Cobb didn't fail; he did what he needed to do, and as a result he was blessed with freedom from the chains that once mercilessly held him bound and separated from his home.

The next time you watch that movie (which I hope will be soon), watch with your spiritual eyes. There's a lot there.

But there's another aspect to this parable, and it is what I want to focus on in this chapter. Still bearing in mind that same parallel, in which waking from mortal life will be like waking from a dream, remember the whole sequence of dream levels that comprised most of the movie and recall how much violence there was. Think of the shoot-outs, the fistfights, the explosions, the car chases, the bloodshed. Characters were shot, stabbed, strangled. Think of Saito being wounded in the chest, the hosts of human-like mental projections being extinguished, and the massive scale of destruction being inflicted in each of the dream worlds.

And then remember that they were in fact merely *dream worlds*. None of it was real, or lasting. The bloodshed and carnage ended, and they eventually woke up in that plane perfectly intact, physically speaking. All the suffering and strife were gone, erased, and, frankly, only imagined to begin with. The players in this story were once again whole. The only thing that had truly changed was their minds—or we could say their souls.

We undergo the same kind of violence in this life. Debilitating disorders, broken bones, strokes and starvation, cancers and comas, hunger and heart attacks—all leading to death, for each and every one of us. Truly, it can be said that we live in a sphere of violence and decay. But, just like in *Inception*, all that pain and heartbreak—the scars caused by the inherent suffering of everyday life—is temporary, impermanent. It can and will be wiped away and rendered significant only in how much it changed that part of us that is eternal.

The Second Law of Thermodynamics

What I want to focus on here is *not* those crucial choices we make that affect our eternal destination, but rather those things that fall away, like a snake shedding skin and emerging anew in our next stage of the Eternal Arc.

The Fall introduced death into the world. Death, disorder, decay, and destruction are all a result of Adam and Eve's choice to accept opposition to progress. The fruits of the Fall condemn all that live—humans, animals, plants—to death, sooner or later. All living matter must eventually waste away and crumble back into nonliving dust. All order must turn to chaos, incorruption to corruption. This is the application of what science calls entropy, or the force of mortality and limitation, the law of disorder, the process of going from a more organized state to a less organized one.

It is not purely a physical process; it is also a state of our spiritual being—our own spiritual death, cut off from the presence of the Lord because of sin and the inevitable imperfection. Entropy envelops our physical and spiritual selves. It swallows us up into a state far distant from the glory of God, physically and spiritually speaking.

In his book *The Infinite Atonement*,[76] Tad R. Callister noted the prophet Jacob's words about the effects of this pressing force: "This flesh must have laid down to rot and to crumble to its mother earth" (2 Nephi 9:7). Elder Callister then quoted the masterful scholar Hugh Nibley: "Without the resurrection, entropy—the good old second law of thermodynamics—must take over."[77]

Brother Nibley wrote that entropy "is the second law of nature, but according to Jacob, it is the first to which nature is subjected—the inexorable and irreversible trend toward corruption and disintegration; it can't be reversed. It rises no more, crumbles, rots, and remains that way endlessly, for an endless duration."[78]

As this principle is a law of nature, it affects all, regardless of their place on the globe or time in history. It is a universal problem—all of us know suffering and will know death.

But such is not the end state. The following stories are examples of moments mired in the decay of this world but conclude in the grace and power of Christ, in a glorious, radiant dawn of hope and healing. In that day, physical, emotional, and mental pain will fall away.

Story 1: Physical Pain

Though some in this world are afflicted because of their unrighteousness, still others are afflicted because of their *righteousness*. This was, I believe, the case with my friend Joseph Harris.

For the last few years before his death, Joe's health was in a constant flux, shifting in and out of various medical problems, few of which were even related to each other. He would often call me in the middle of the night, needing to go to the emergency room. There, the nurses would have him rate the level of pain he was feeling at the time on a number scale of one to ten. "Five," he would say to the nurse, or "six" or "seven."

If *I* were the one being treated, I would've have found it difficult to rate my pain the same way; I wouldn't know what to compare it to! But it was simple enough for Joseph to discern between the different levels because he felt all of them so often.

Sometimes he would be discharged later that same night because the doctors, who would continually give him a variety of tests and examinations, couldn't find exactly what was wrong with him. The most they could do was give him some pain medication and send him on his way.

Over his last few years, his body weakened dramatically to the point where he could no longer walk. He and his family were not financially well off, so he always needed rides from friends or ward members to go and do basic things like get groceries, go to the doctor, pick up medicine, and so on. He also dealt with emotional disorders and did not function well in social situations. He never had the chance to marry and was, more often than not, incredibly lonely. He lived his life in both great physical pain and emotional isolation, with genuine hope lying only in the world to come as he endured well to the end.

Story 2: Emotional Pain

Sometimes the grief of this world is so strong it can shift the tectonic plates of the soul, as it did for Alfred Tennyson, master poet. Crushed by the death of his best friend at the tender age of twenty-two, Tennyson began composing a series of grief-stricken, lyric-like poems he eventually titled *In Memoriam*. This stanza illustrates well the classic wrestle of the philosophical issue of trying to find truth and meaning in this world of sorrow.

> O yet we trust that somehow good
>> Will be the final goal of ill,
>> To pangs of nature, sins of will,
>> Defects of doubt, and taints of blood;
>> That nothing walks with aimless feet;
>> That not one life shall be destroyed,
>> Or cast as rubbish to the void,
>> When God hath made the pile complete;
>> That not a worm is cloven in vain;
>> That not a moth with vain desire
>> Is shrivelled in a fruitless fire,
>> Or but subserves another's gain.
>> Behold, we know not anything;
>> I can but trust that good shall fall
>> At last—far off—at last, to all,
>> And every winter change to spring.
>> So runs my dream: but what am I?
>> An infant crying in the night;
>> An infant crying for the light:
>> And with no language but a cry.[79]

Story 3: Mental Pain

About a year ago, I was informed that the mental health of a close family member was gradually breaking down. She'd been long diagnosed as having an emotional disorder and was going through an incredibly stressful and heart-wrenching time in her life. She was waking up in the middle of the night and acting odd, thinking she was still dreaming and remaining mentally stuck in that frame of mind, unable to really awaken.

When I first got that phone call, I felt like I was in a nightmare of my own. I was working an overnight shift at the time, making the moment even more surreal than it already was. It was then that I really had to grasp the hard truth of universal decay for the first time, that it became personal, something very real. With tears in my eyes, I made a decision. I told God I accepted it. I accepted that nightmare, knowing that what she was going through wasn't permanent, that it was only in this life. That night, I felt I was truly living that sacred hymn: "Be still, my soul: The hour is hast'ning on / When we shall be forever with the Lord."[80] That hymn has been a certain comfort in many of my trials, and the verses Tennyson penned in the blackest of ink articulate the despair of the many victims of history's great tragedies: the lives ripped apart unnecessarily by wars and tyrants; the needless horrors of World War I; the destruction on both sides of the globe in the second; the dropping of the atomic bombs; and the attempted extermination of an entire race in the Jewish Holocaust.

So much sadness, suffering, and death.

And yet . . .

Ultimate Realities

And yet. despite these real forms of pain, Elder Neal A. Maxwell wrote of the Latter-day Saints, "We, of all people on this planet, have the best reasons to be of good cheer." Why is that? Because, he said, "We know what the ultimate realities are in terms of the Gospel truths and all the reassurances that those will bring us."[81]

Realities like the one found in Paul's Epistle to the Corinthians: "For as in Adam all die, even so in Christ shall all be made alive" (1 Corinthians 15:22); and in the words of the prophet Jacob (whom Elder Maxwell called the "poet prophet"): "The bodies and the spirits of men will be restored one to the other; and it is by the power of the resurrection of the Holy One of Israel" (2 Nephi 9:12). In Elder Tad R. Callister's book *The Infinite Atonement*, he wrote, "As powerful as is this sinister force that promotes death, chaos, and destruction upon all living things, there is a countervailing, counteracting power that emanates from the Atonement. It is the power of the resurrection."[82]

The true ultimate reality of this world is not death—the grand conclusion and consummation of the universe itself is the reality of the redemption and the resurrection, brought to pass by the Holy Messiah, even Jesus Christ.

For though death may surely claim us in this life, "The grave hath no victory, and the sting of death is swallowed up in Christ. He is the light and the life of the world; yea, a light that is endless, that can never be darkened; yea, and also a life which is endless, that there can be no more death" (Mosiah 16:8–9).

We came to this earth to, among other things, receive bodies. Imperfect, corrupt, and mortal bodies, to be sure, but bodies nonetheless. Obtaining bodies is not only important; it is essential to God's ultimate plan for us. Without bodies, we cannot receive a fulness of joy; we cannot become like God, who has a body of flesh and bone. Obtaining mortal bodies is the first step on that road to exaltation, the second stage of that Eternal Arc. And as with all mortal things, our bodies will die. But our life essence, our eternal spirit, will live on.

We pass into the spirit world, into paradise or prison. Imagine the joy you would feel to wake up in paradise! After all, if that's where you wake, you can be pretty sure you've made it. And now you can rest and cease from all worries (before getting to the real work, I should add).

But on the other hand, imagine finding yourself in the opposite place. For while waking up in spirit prison does not necessarily mean you are damned for all eternity, it does mean there is still a great amount of work to be done. That is, if you hadn't already squandered your many opportunities in this life. But that judgment is up to God, and God alone.

The Principle of Restoration

Either way, we will once more be only spirits, and thus deprived of that fulness of joy promised to us in the scriptures. And we cannot achieve that until the glorious time of the resurrection. We know that all who have lived in this world will be given that blessing of bodily immortality, first to stand once again in God's presence to be judged (fulfilling Jacob's prophecy that "nevertheless, in our bodies we shall see God" [2 Nephi 9:4]) and then, for those who lived righteously, to dwell eternally in His presence and receive all that the Father hath, even the blessings of exaltation and eternal lives.

President Joseph F. Smith saw a vision of the dead awaiting this moment: "Their sleeping dust was to be restored unto its perfect frame, bone to his bone, and the sinews and the flesh upon them, the spirit and the body to be united never again to be divided, that they might receive a fulness of joy" (D&C 138:17). In a later verse, he observes that "the dead had looked upon the long absence of their spirits from their bodies as a bondage" (verse 50). Bodies provide a level of freedom that is impossible to access as mere spirits.

This reunion is another aspect of Christ's atoning power. Hugh Nibley wrote insightfully,

> Without an infinite atonement . . . [w]e could not save ourselves from entropy. Someone else must be there to do it. Notice what atonement means: reversal of the degradative process, a returning to its former state, being integrated or united again—'at-one.' What results when particles break down? They separate. Decay is always from heavier to lighter particles. But 'atonement' brings particles back together again. Bringing anything back to its one original state is at-one-ment.[83]

Alma the Younger told his son Corianton that to return something to its former state—to "bring back again evil for evil, or carnal for carnal, or devilish for devilish—good for that which is good; righteous for that which is righteous; just for that which is just; [and] merciful for that which is merciful"—is "the meaning of the word restoration" (Alma 41:13).

This principle of restoration is another function of the law of the harvest: what we sow, we eventually reap. "That which [we] do send out shall return unto [us] again" (Alma 41:15). It is the reason that all of us here in mortality, both the righteous and the wicked, will be resurrected—because all of us have at least earned this body by passing into the second estate, and "it is requisite and just . . . that the soul of man should be restored to its body, and that every part of the body should be restored to itself" (Alma 41:2).

But it isn't just what we've lost as it pertains to our bodies—we will not simply have our skin free of blemishes, hair grown back, or spine uncurled. Restoration, in the lens of the law of the harvest, is about far more than that. It pertains to Judgment Day, when all our works and the desires of our hearts will be made known, for good or ill. "And if their works were good in this life, and the desires of their hearts were good, . . . they should also, at the last day, be restored unto that which is good" (Alma 41:3).

Alma also explained that at the Judgment, we will be our own judges—our own choices will have already determined our fate. If our works and the desires of our heart were good, then the Atonement will wash away all else through the mercy of Christ; we will be healed and cleansed.

The Coldplay song "Fix You" sings this story:

> [When] the tears come streaming down your face
> When you lose something you can't replace
> When you love someone, but it goes to waste
> Could it be worse?
> Lights will guide you home
> And ignite your bones
> And I will try to fix you."[84]

Now, I don't know whether singer Chris Martin meant to speak from God's point of view, but I like to think he did. In the case of the resurrection and the principle of restoration, however, the Savior won't just try to fix you—He *will*.

All That Lasts

Elder Dallin H. Oaks said, "The assurance of resurrection gives us the strength and perspective to endure the mortal challenges faced by each of us and by those we love, such things as the physical, mental, or emotional deficiencies we bring with us at birth or acquire during mortal life. Because of the resurrection, we know that these mortal deficiencies are only temporary!"[85]

Now, this statement from Elder Oaks raises a pertinent question: What is permanent and what is not? What lasts and what falls away? We take nothing into the next life but . . . what? Obviously no material things. No wealth, no riches—nothing physical that we claimed was ours in mortality.

Rather, we take with us everything we are, everything that we have become. Our spirits, minds, and memories. Ourselves. Elder Neal A. Maxwell said, "If we ponder just what it is that will rise with us in the resurrection, it seems clear that our intelligence will rise with us, meaning not simply our IQ, but also our capacity to receive and apply truth. Our talents, attributes, and skills will rise with us; certainly also our capacity to learn, our degree of self-discipline, and our capacity to work."[86] One could call it the end result of this terrestrial trial.

But that's not all. We take more than that. Consider the two great commandments. The first, as the Savior tells us, is to love the Lord our God with all our heart, soul, and mind. The second is to love our neighbor as ourselves. Can you see why these are the most important, most essential commandments? They correlate to those immaterial possessions we carry into the next life: first, our relationship with God; second, our relationships with other people.

So I ask, what is our relationship to God if not who we've become in His piercing eye, what our minds and souls consist of? This, I believe, can be measured by what we've done with the responsibilities, gifts, and stewardships He has given us. That's who we are; that's how we've loved Him. According to the first great commandment, it is our first purpose. The second purpose is like the first: who we've been to other people. Have we done as the Savior does, helping bear others' loads and ease others' burdens? Have we taken care of our families how Heavenly Father takes care of us? Have we been a friend to all who have crossed our path? Or have we been a negative influence on the world? Have we made others' lives harder, more painful and laden with sin?

What has been our effect upon our spiritual brothers and sisters, upon the world itself?

When we see terrestrial life through this celestial lens, there are indeed many aspects to our earthly journey that are permanent. It is how we react to the *impermanent* challenges that etch the permanent changes into our souls. In this truth, we see the beauty of the Lord's plan: these changes in our souls, in our characters and our intelligences, last forever, but the trials that produce them do not. Pain is temporary, but, as the hymn says, there is no end to wisdom, glory, or light.[87]

And yet it is good and comforting to note some of the impermanence of this world. I'd like to call attention to one in particular: the wicked yet alluring lifestyles of the worldly. The lawless look like they're having fun, like they're even happy as they do things that we, as disciples of Christ, deny ourselves daily. But the draw of the pleasures of the world will end, and the fruitless inanities of lust-driven lives will fade away; true love and affection will continue on eternally. I pray that we can keep that in mind the next time the grass looks greener on the other side.

Escape from the Monster

An old institute teacher of mine named Brother Hansen was particularly fond of a metaphor the prophet Jacob used—"O how great the goodness of our God, who prepareth a way for our escape from the grasp of this awful monster" (2 Nephi 9:10), meaning death and hell. To teach it, he would show us the climactic scene of the film *Jaws.* Brother Hansen would pause it right on the part where the shark clamped down its teeth on Quint's body. It's the most gruesome scene in an already gruesome movie, but it taught a great lesson. Quint couldn't escape from that shark on his own power. Likewise, we cannot escape the grasp of that "awful monster" of death and hell by ourselves (2 Nephi 9:10). We need the redemptive and resurrecting power of Jesus Christ.

It is a two-tiered rescue—escape from death and from hell; escape from physical death and from spiritual death. And thus we see, in parallel, the two-tiered mission of God: "For behold, this is my work and my glory—to bring to pass the immortality and eternal life of man" (Moses 1:39). Immortality is solved by the resurrection; eternal life is granted by Christ's infinite Atonement.

We need our Savior. It is because of His Atonement that all these supreme and everlasting gifts are possible. Resurrection, redemption, restoration—all are given to us free of any price except a broken heart and contrite spirit. And if we pay, He will heal that broken heart and cleanse our earth-stained hands. His lights will guide us home.

Exalted Bodies

The law of the harvest is so much more than a one-to-one ratio. All that's required is a handful of seeds, and you end up with entire fields of grain and stores of bounteous blessings far exceeding the tiny seeds planted in the ground. Likewise, we will not only be given back our bodies, nor will our sins be merely neutralized—our bodies will be glorified and our souls exalted. The reward goes far beyond being just "fixed"—we will be *enhanced.*

We know some of the details of what a resurrected body is and how it works. Alma described the basics of the resurrection: "The soul shall be restored to the body, and the body to the soul; yea, and every limb and joint shall be restored to its body; yea, even a hair of the head shall not be lost; but all things shall be restored to their proper and perfect frame" (Alma 40:23).

I again quote Elder Tad R. Callister: "A resurrected body is not subject to pain or disease or exhaustion. There is no bullet that can harm it, poison that can pollute it, or cancer that can invade it. There is no resurrected being who suffers loss of limb, speech impediment, or failing sight. A resurrected personage has a glorified, immortal body, free from the destructive elements of this temporal world."[88]

What a thrilling concept—a restored, resurrected body will never be exhausted! Joe Harris, for so long bound by his weak and failing legs, will be able to run forever without needing to take a single breath. C. S. Lewis said in his Narnia series, "If one could run without getting tired, I don't think one would often want to do anything else."[89]

One aspect of immortality that our current bodies depart from is blood. The presence of blood in our veins is a key difference between mortal and immortal bodies. In this life, it is what keeps us alive and also what ultimately causes our demise. Elder Callister, in *The Infinite Atonement*, wrote, "The prophets have testified that blood, the mortal element that eventually brings death, will one day be replaced by a spiritual substance in our veins. . . . So spoke the Prophet Joseph, 'When our flesh is quickened by the Spirit, there will be no blood in our tabernacle.'"[90]

As newly whole beings, we will have undergone a total transformation. Elder Callister said, "In such a resurrected state, one's countenance, one's outer glow and beauty will be but a manifestation of one's inner spirituality—thus, the inner and outer beings will be, in essence, mirrors of each other. Celestial bodies will radiate celestial glory; terrestrial bodies, terrestrial glory; and telestial bodies, telestial glory."[91]

Not only will our worldly misconceptions of beauty fall away, but the reflection of our interiors on our exteriors will also be further amplified by the desires of our hearts. Elder Neal A. Maxwell said, "What we insistently desire, over time, is what we will eventually become and what we will receive in eternity."[92] Essentially, we'll become who we always wanted to be, all that is inside us and that we've yearned for. Our inner selves will be reflected in our outer bodies; good will look like good and bad will look like bad.

And that will be who we truly are. In the words of another great (though fictional) religious leader, "Luminous beings are we—not this crude matter."[93]

"Luminous" is exactly the kind of body Joseph Harris will have. Glorious. Perfect. Incorruptible. And now, all those pain ratings of five, six, seven, eight, nine, and even ten—all of them are now and will be one eternal zero. My friend will never feel physical pain again.

When I think of this doctrine, I think of a toy like an Etch-A-Sketch, with a screen you can scribble on and make a mess of things. No matter the mess you've made, you can just slide the erase bar across and it's cleared—a brand new slate on which to draw. This is what the Atonement and Resurrection of the Lord can and will do, respectively: cleanse us spiritually and physically, and then make us whole again.

The Tender Mercies of Restoration

Release from the confinements and discomforts of this world can be a tender mercy, even a comfort. Elder Oaks said, "What a comfort to know that all who have been disadvantaged in life from birth defects, from mortal injuries, from disease, or from the natural deterioration of old age will be resurrected in 'proper and perfect frame.' "[94] Thus, death is a natural part of life should not be mourned over, but rather rejoiced in. It is an emancipation of our woes, a freedom from our fatigues and daily toils. A deadline cannot exist in a timeless world.

And neither can death in an eternal world. What pain can pierce the promise of incomprehensible joy? Of never-ending happiness? Of eternal life?

However, there certainly exist tragedies in this life that seem irreversible. I write now of those faithful members who have had loved ones turn away from the gospel. A mother whose beloved daughter has wandered so far away that it seems impossible she will ever even want to find her way back. The wayward, willfully rebellious child who seems destined for a lower kingdom because that is where she chooses to be, forever separated from God and the rest of her family. Situations in which the heartbroken parent can do nothing but pray, hope ,and have faith that it will all work out in the end, somehow. To such parents and other members, I offer these words from Orson F. Whitney:

> The Prophet Joseph Smith declared—and he never taught a more comforting doctrine—that the eternal sealings of faithful parents and the divine promises made to them for valiant service in the Cause of Truth, would save not only themselves, but likewise their posterity. Though some of the sheep may wander, the eye of the Shepherd is upon them, and sooner or later they will feel the tentacles of Divine Providence reaching out after them and drawing them back to the fold. Either in this life or the life to come, they will return. They will have to pay their debt to justice; they will suffer for their sins; and may tread a thorny path; but if it leads them at last, like the penitent Prodigal, to a loving and forgiving father's heart and home, the painful experience will not have been in vain. Pray for your careless and disobedient children; hold on to them with your faith. Hope on, trust on, till you see the salvation of God.[95]

Along those lines, Brigham Young said, "Let the father and mother, who are members of this Church and Kingdom, take a righteous course, and strive with all their might never to do a wrong, but to do good all their lives; if they have one child or one hundred children, if they conduct themselves towards them as they should, binding them to the Lord by their faith and prayers, I care not where those children go, they are bound up to their parents by an everlasting tie, and no power of earth or hell can separate them from their parents in eternity; they will return again to the fountain from whence they sprang."[96]

That is the sealing power of the temple and the priesthood, another gift from God that no sense of earthly gratitude could ever properly express. No man or woman is beyond the reach of Christ's Atonement, except by his or her own will and choice.

When we appreciate the sealing powers of the temple, we also see more of the principle of restoration at work. Not only will our bodies be restored and glorified, not only will our righteous desires and works be restored to us again, but we will also be restored to the presence of those precious souls with whom we made our strongest connections—our families and our truest friends.

But what about other aspects of this world? For instance, my parents recently had to sell my childhood home, where I lived for the first two decades of my life. I'll probably never enter it again in this life (and that hurts because I'm quite a sentimental guy). Does my old house have to be gone forever? Could it be raised with us in the resurrection and restoration?

This in turn raises all sorts of other related questions. For example, after we die, will it ever be possible to go back and relive old memories, as if rereading a favorite scene in a book? Or are they permanently mere memories? Will we even want to, anyway? Will our minds and spirits have progressed past that stage? Is there any room for nostalgia or sentiment for the past in God's kingdom?

I believe I have an answer—I'll get to that soon enough. But the only thing I know for sure is that as we rely upon the Atonement, we will not be plagued by longings or regrets. I know because the three stories I mentioned earlier have ended in the peace we're promised in this life.

"The Light Which Shineth in Darkness"

The most remarkable part of Joseph Harris's story is that through all of his experiences, sicknesses, and pains, he rarely, if ever, complained. And if he did, he would immediately repent and apologize out loud, saying he knew he shouldn't. His illnesses and disabilities gave him a permanent sense of humility, and never did he feel he was entitled to anything. On so many occasions, he wished out loud that he could be normal, that he could take his health for granted as most of us do, but he knew that the Lord did not see it that way.

The faith Joe showed throughout the years was and is monumental; his example has affected me to this day and will eternally. Perceptive priesthood leaders expressed their feelings to him on multiple occasions. They felt he must surely have been among the upper echelon of even the noble and great ones before the world was. Anyone who knew him and the pain-filled circumstances of his life could not possibly disagree. The kind of faith he possessed proved to me that his whole life had been a test, one of the most searing, frustrating, and heart-wrenching ones that Heavenly Father could give anyone. The way I see it, only a general in the Lord's army could have reacted to life the way Joe did. I am convinced that the Lord gave him so many struggles *because* he was so righteous, in this life and the one before. And I strongly believe that the more pain a person right-eously endures, the greater the blessings the Lord will bestow upon that person in the life to come.

The poet Alfred Tennyson, his soul once shattered, did not end his lament with doubts or anger. Though his best friend had passed away, Tennyson emerged from his grief victorious, with faith and belief all the stronger because it had been tested so viciously. He expressed this victory in one of the last poems of *In Memoriam*:

> That which we dare invoke to bless;
> Our dearest faith; our ghastliest doubt;
> He, They, One, All; within, without;
> The Power in darkness whom we guess;
> I found Him not in world or sun,
> Or eagle's wing, or insect's eye;
> Nor thro' the questions men may try,
> The petty cobwebs we have spun.
> If e'er when faith had fall'n asleep,
> I heard a voice, "believe no more,"
> And heard an ever-breaking shore
> That tumbled in the Godless deep,
> A warmth within the breast would melt
> The freezing reason's colder part,
> And like a man in wrath the heart
> Stood up and answer'd, "I have felt."
> No, like a child in doubt and fear:
> But that blind clamour made me wise;
> Then was I as a child that cries,
> But crying, knows his father near;
> And what I am beheld again
> What is, and no man understands;
> And out of darkness came the hands
> That reach thro' nature, moulding men.[97]

Tennyson knew his Father was near and aware of his pains. And through this misery, he grappled and came to understand God's reasoning, the solution to all the grief and doubt: "the hands / That reach thro' nature, moulding men."

The story of my family member enduring a mental breakdown has its own tender twist—what I see as, at least in part, an unanticipated happy ending. My loved one was taken to the hospital, where she was diagnosed not with a mental disorder, but with pneumonia. Apparently, delirium is sometimes a side effect of that virus. After a few nights in the hospital, she came home, perfectly healthy. The trial was avoided.

But I still believe that incident had meaning. My acceptance of that potential life thread was necessary, perhaps as a test or perhaps as a moment of growth, an opportunity to attain a fuller understanding and testimony of the gospel. Either way, that experience specifically was the origin of this chapter.

As we should be aware, however, the victory claimed in this anecdote is not the ultimate one. It too is temporary, impermanent. Ultimately, death and decay and the symptoms of this fallen world will overcome her. The world will claim all of us, someday.

But fear not—the Savior has overcome the world. He is "the light which shineth in darkness, and the darkness comprehendeth it not" (D&C 6:21).

This Dream Shall End

This dream may at times feel more like a nightmare. Friends may abandon us, our love for another may not be returned, or one who once loved us may now feel indifferent. Sudden unexpected events can leave us reeling and questioning reality "for the thousand natural shocks that flesh is heir to,"[98] as Shakespeare put it. Crumbling relationships can make this life seem more distant and dreamlike than any other part of our mortal life, just as the lives of the prophet Jacob and his people "passed away like as it were unto [them] a dream" (Jacob 7:26).

Most of the emotional wounds acquired in this less-than-holy sphere will heal with time, but it is a cold truth that some leave seemingly permanent scars. It's also true that happiness and pain are not mutually exclusive emotions. God feels sorrow and joy. In the world to come, He promises eternal life and never-ending happiness—what he promises us in this life is the simple presence of peace (see D&C 59:23), even when that never-ending happiness seems to us a will-o'-the-wisp, a phantom, a dream.

But when all the shielding doctrine discussed has failed to adequately reassure, we must remember the simple foundation of this gospel: faith. Blind faith if necessary, and the commandment to cleave unto Him above all else. It may take years, even until after we leave this mortal life, but by our faith, and through the Savior's atoning power, all that is good can and will be restored unto us, with all that is bad being cast away.

The people of Ammon "never did look upon death with any degree of terror, for their hope and views of Christ and the resurrection; therefore, death was swallowed up to them by the victory of Christ over it" (Alma 27:28). *That* is the hope we must maintain inside us. That is the perspective we must hold as we view death and our dearly departed. That is the knowledge in the words of the poet John Donne: "Death, thou shalt die!"[99]

As I near the conclusion of these particular remarks, I'd like to share with you some final thoughts on mortality and its relationship with the concept of time.

Time is, to put it simply, a strange thing. It is also impermanent. Alma wrote that "time only is measured unto men" (Alma 40:8). In *The Last Battle*, the final book in C. S. Lewis's Chronicles of Narnia series, Lewis told the story of the end of the old world, the old Narnia, and the beginning of a new one, the *real* Narnia, as that realm gains what could be called its paradisiacal glory.

In the final chapters, the Pevensie children observed the awakening of a massive giant known as Father Time. Aslan, the Great Lion, said to them, "While he lay dreaming his name was Time. Now that he is awake he will have a new one."[100] Time, wrote Lewis, is only an illusion. A fiction, a dream.

Elder Neal A. Maxwell observed,

> If, on occasion, you notice the strange encapsulation we call time, you'll understand it's not our natural dimension. The birds are at home in the air. They don't think about how to fly. Fish are at home in the water. They don't think about how to swim. It's natural. But you and

I are cocooned, as it were, in this dimension we call time. And it's not our natural dimension. So it is, we're always wishing we could hasten the passage of time or to hold back the dawn. And we can't do either. We're uncomfortable with time because we belong to eternity. If we were comfortable with time, we wouldn't have clocks on the wall and calendars and wristwatches. It is not our natural dimension, so time will whisper to you, in the words of another hymn, that you're a stranger here.[101]

In describing the new Narnia, one character told Lucy Pevensie,

When Aslan said you could never go back to Narnia, he meant the Narnia you were thinking of. But that was not the real Narnia. That had a beginning and an end. It was only a shadow or a copy of the real Narnia which has always been here and always will be here: just as our own world, England and all, is only a shadow or copy of something in Aslan's real world. You need not mourn over Narnia, Lucy. All of the old Narnia that mattered, all the dear creatures, have been drawn into the real Narnia through the Door. And of course it is different; as different as a real thing is from a shadow or as waking life is from a dream.[102]

Perhaps this is the answer to my question about my sentimental feelings for my old home. At least, it suggests one. As another character said, in that heavenly Narnia "no good thing is destroyed."[103] I believe that, in some form, my old home will be raised in the restoration of all good things. And perhaps that celestialized, glorified home is the real thing, not the dream version I hold so much attachment to in this world.

The Pevensie children then came upon a set of great golden gates. Here, they hesitated, wondering if those gates could possibly be meant for them. They then heard a horn, and the gates swung open wide. Out of the gates burst forth all the friends and family they ever had to say goodbye to. The kings and queens of old, the great heroes of Narnia's past, and creatures with whom they once shared adventures but had long since passed away—all at peace and safe at last, never to be lost or bid goodbye to again. In this moment of reunion, "There was greeting and kissing and hand-shaking and old jokes revived."[104]

Might it be like that for us? Might we meet again all those we had known who went before us? Might we reunite with them as tears stream down our faces and we shout and exclaim for joy that we never have to part or suffer again?

In the final spoken line of the story, Aslan declared,

> "The dream is ended: this is the morning." And as He spoke He no longer looked to them like a lion; but the things that began to happen after that were so great and beautiful that I cannot write them. And for us this is the end of all stories, and we can most truly say they all lived happily ever after. But for them it was only the beginning of the real story. All their life in this world and all their adventures in Narnia had only been the cover and the title page: now at last they were beginning Chapter One of the Great Story which no one on earth has read: which goes on forever: in which every chapter is better than the one before.[105]

This dream shall end. This vale of tears, this mortal sphere—all that makes us cry and weep and wail—will end. All that was torn asunder shall be reunited; all that has been lost shall be restored. Everything that we went through—the weights and anchors and crushing gravity of mortality—will be gone, lifted up, vanished. Then we will soar and run forever without fatigue. The slate of physical corruption will be wiped clean, like waking from a dream. And so, just like the players in *Inception*, the only thing that truly will have changed is us.

I testify that this will happen, and that it can only happen because of the Atonement, the redemption and the resurrection brought to pass by Jesus Christ, our Master, our Savior, and our Brother. Let us live our lives so that when we see Him again, it will be with a tearful embrace, and not downcast eyes.

Know that this dream will end. Know that it is nothing compared to what comes next. Know that there is never a true goodbye—only a "see you later." And remember these words from a Bollywood adage: "Life is like a film. It always has a happy ending. If it's not happy, it's not the end."[106]

Chapter 5
Healing in His Wings

*T**he adversary has** many tools to silence our voices, to bind the tongues of the faithful. He and his angels are everywhere, threatening every soul, adding burdens of sin and skewed perspective to weigh down all who seek loftier skies. Darkness drags us down and prevents us from moving forward in the eternal progression God has in mind for us. The stakes of this world are real. Evil is real. Satan and his angels are real. This is a war, plain and simple.

But just as evil is real, so is the Atonement of Jesus Christ. It is there, constantly reaching out to rescue, recover, and heal. It can catch any falling soul, destroy any sin, wipe clean any manner of disease, fill any hole or wound, lift any fallen countenance, and fix any broken heart. I begin this chapter with that testimony. I bear witness to the power of the Atonement.

I know it can do all those things because it's done them to me. I write not out of an intellectual understanding of this doctrine, nor out of some special insight or theory or principle. I know this because Jesus Christ, through the Atonement, redeemed my soul and lifted me up out of darkness into light. He saved me. He healed me.

Allow me another parable, this one found in Christopher Nolan's Batman film *The Dark Knight*. Throughout the film, the satanic villain the Joker has dueled Batman, the hero, in a battle for the soul of

Gotham City. The Joker's primary goal was not to kill or gain power, but rather to corrupt, instigate chaos, and bring everyone down to the moral level of savages to be as wicked and evil as he is. At first, the Joker targeted Batman himself, attempting to destroy his moral standing, but those temptations failed; Batman revealed himself to be unshakeable, even in tragedy. So instead, the Joker targeted another, more vulnerable figure: Harvey Dent, the heroic district attorney who was willing to stand up against corruption in the government—a source of hope that the rampant crime in the city could be stopped the right way.

In the end, the Joker succeeded in bringing down Harvey Dent—representative of the soul of Gotham—and Dent became a fallen man. To avenge his fiancée's death (which was actually the Joker's doing), he killed five people in a spree. This sudden turn forced Batman and Commissioner Jim Gordon into a terrible quandary; if the people of Gotham ever came to know about Dent's corruption, he could no longer be a figure of inspiration to the city, and they would lose all the progress they'd made in saving the city from crime.

It is in Batman's solution to this problem that we see the pieces of the Atonement fall into place: Batman decided to take the blame for Harvey Dent's crimes and take the punishment in his place—this so that the Joker wouldn't win and so the soul of Gotham could be saved. As a result of that sacrifice, Gotham transformed, and evil and criminality were successfully banished for the first time in decades.

Can you see the story with your spiritual eyes? We are Harvey Dent; we are Gotham. The Christ figure takes the sins of fallen mankind, and the punishment thereof, on his own shoulders so that the devil does not win and can lay no claim to the souls of the imperfect. We live and are free to rise up to something greater because Christ took the fall for us. That is the Atonement.

Batman explained his decision to Jim Gordon, saying, "Sometimes people deserve more. Sometimes people deserve to have their faith rewarded."[107] Can't you imagine Christ saying the same thing? That when we even just try to be good, He thinks we deserve mercy? Isn't our faith rewarded with forgiveness when we look to Christ and repent? Though we are prone to wander from the Lord's path, that relationship of faith and love for our Savior can always set us anew on that journey of transformation.

Christ shouldered the weight of justice so we could undergo that transformation and struggle and grow without fear of eternal torment for the sins we've committed. God's whole purpose is to provide us with mercy while operating within the contextual framework of justice so we don't have to suffer permanent punishment, but instead be granted the opportunity to learn from our mistakes. Seen this way, can there be any doubt that, above all, God is love?

Love drove the Savior through the excruciating pain of Gethsemane, "how sore [we] know not, how exquisite [we] know not, yea, how hard to bear [we] know not. . . . Which suffering caused myself, even God, the greatest of all, to tremble because of pain, and to bleed at every pore, and to suffer both body and spirit—and would that I might not drink the bitter cup, and shrink—" (D&C 19:15, 18).

Note that there is a dash there at the end, not a period. I believe that is because it is an unfinished sentence. Stop and reflect on what it might mean. Could our perfect and loving Savior not even bear to finish his sentence because the memory of the pain was too great? What pain could literally halt the speech of God? Whatever it was, in whatever form, He endured it and "suffered [it] for all, that [we] might not suffer if [we] would repent" (D&C 19:16).

Adam Olson pointed out in the September 2012 *Ensign*, "He knew of the depth of iniquity that would be connected with the human family. He understood the awful, inestimable price He would be required to pay. . . . And knowing all, *He still decided [we were] worth it*. No matter how short I think I fall in comparison to others, no matter how little value others see in me, Jesus felt I was worth the price He had to pay."[108]

In *The Dark Knight*, Commissioner Jim Gordon's young son, who Batman had just saved from a murderous, fallen Harvey Dent, asked his father why Batman was running away. The child remarked, insightfully, that Batman "didn't do anything wrong."

Christ too never did anything wrong. So why does He bear the brunt of our sins? Why did He have to go through the tortuous suffering in our stead?

Commissioner Gordon answered his son, "Because he can take it."[109]

Because he can take it. Christ, the Son of God and a god Himself in mortal raiment, is the only Being who could have made an infinite and eternal sacrifice, the sacrifice of a god (Alma 34:10). Knowing that He alone could do it, He did it. He bore our sins, trials and temptations, and torments and tragedies, each and every one of them so He could understand us, see us, be with us, and embrace us. Through Him, we can become clean enough to be with Him again and rejoice in never-ending happiness. It was all for us. None of it was for Him.

He loves you. And I've come to know that He loves me too. "Yea, and as often as my people repent will I forgive them their trespasses against me" (Mosiah 26:30). Think about the magnitude of that compassion. Have you ever held a grudge? Usually such are held over small, petty things, though occasionally they will be for big things. Either way, it's sometimes hard to look past them and forgive. Can you imagine being a perfect being, a being who has never done a wrong thing in life, nor anything hurtful or mean-spirited or cruel, and has given everything possible, even every iota of life and love, to save others and offer them an eternity of everlasting happiness? And can you imagine being mocked, rejected, hated and fought against by those same people? The perfect, incomprehensible love that being has in still reaching out a mighty, saving arm to them, forgiving such people when they realize they were wrong, and again offering them everything offered before? Such are the lengths the Savior would go to and has gone to retrieve all of our souls from darkness and damnation.

His unconditional love expresses itself in grief, mourning, and even a sense of desperation for those whom He might lose. "This human capacity to suffer pain at the distress of a loved one," Terryl and Fiona Givens wrote, "is an imperfect shadow of the unfathomable grief a perfect being feels when His creations put themselves beyond His healing embrace."[110] That He weeps for the pain of the sinner is both awe-inspiring and humbling. Can we understand that level of love? I don't think we can right now. Perhaps only a parent can come close to understanding it. But despite our inability to fully conceive of such love, we can benefit from it. Even though we don't deserve it, even though we are all sinners who fall short of the mark again and again and again—His arm is stretched out still, and we can repent and turn to Him. Even when we're in a state of rebellion and spiritual darkness, we can turn back, look to God, and live.

I testify that you can. You can turn. You can look away and return your gaze to the light and love of Jesus Christ. You can pull your wrists away from the shackles of sin and put your hand in the Savior's, whose arm is always stretched out, reaching toward you. From there, He can pull you up, out of that pit of despair you may languish in. We are commanded to "seek the face of the Lord always, that in patience ye may possess your souls, and ye shall have eternal life" (D&C 101:38). He is offering eternal life—to the entire world, and to you personally—if only you search after Him, though sometimes sweeter than the far-off dream of eternal life is the simple peace He promises to those who seek His face.

If you're at a place in life where you need peace of mind above all, pray. Prayer can bring about so much. It's the most simple and basic of all communication systems, the medium by which repentance and humility trigger the Atonement! It is how you return to the Father and to your true identity and destiny.

During the three days of darkness in the Book of Mormon, the Savior's voice details the drastic consequences of living wickedly, revealing the destruction caused to all the cities who stoned and cast out the prophets and were living in sin. He then pleaded to the survivors of the storms, "O all ye that are spared because ye were more righteous than they, *will ye not now return unto me, and repent of your sins, and be converted, that I may heal you?* Yea, verily I say unto you, if ye will come unto me ye shall have eternal life. Behold, *mine arm of mercy is extended towards you*, and whosoever will come, him will I receive; and blessed are those who come unto me" (3 Nephi 9:13–14; emphasis added).

I testify that now, after the burying torments of Gethsemane, the Lord is truly risen, with healing in His wings.

What a beautiful notion healing is. The knowledge that entropy can be reversed, that chaos and disorder can be deliberately replaced with growth and recovery. That really is the essence of the Atonement: healing and transformation. And with the grace of His wings, we too can soar through celestial skies.

Christ said so tenderly to the weeping Nephites, "Have ye any that are sick among you? Bring them hither. Have ye any that are lame, or blind, or halt, or maimed, or leprous, or that are withered, or that are deaf, or that are *afflicted in any manner*? Bring them hither and *I will heal them*" (3 Nephi 17:7; emphasis added).

If there is *anything* about us that is broken or needs help healing or rejuvenating, and if we merely bring ourselves to Him and knock on the door, He will heal us.

Matthew said, of the healing nature of Christ, that "as many as touched were made perfectly whole" (Matthew 14:36). His three-year ministry of giving sight to the blind and hearing to the deaf was a type of His true, ultimate ministry of healing. And it is this healing, this transformative power and work that I bear testimony of today, with my own story of darkness turned to light.

The above testimony isn't mere empty words. I am no hypocrite when it comes to the Atonement. I am no stranger to the Savior's feet.

There is only one future ahead of us: the future we choose, one choice at a time. There might seem to be other futures, of course—possible but nonexistent; they do not exist literally, and I don't believe we will ever know them. This is why our choices are so important in this life. This is the only chance we get to make them before they're etched into the book of life.

But the Atonement can change the ending of that book, for God is a master novelist. With His majesty and mercy, He can weave—out of a story plagued by failures, doubts, losses, and regrets—a happy ending. True are the words of the hymn, "Thy best, thy heav'nly Friend / Thru thorny ways leads to a joyful end."[111] Such He did with my story.

My dark times began with brief flirtations with pornography in my early teens. It was driven by one simple thing: curiosity. How much other sin occurs in our lives, especially in the lives of our young people, from that feeling of curiosity alone! Over the years, bit by bit, it locked me in its clutches, and I became addicted. My agency was taken away—I'd given it away.

Everything you've heard from other addicts' stories is true. Unbearable guilt soaked my mind constantly, coupled with fear. Of course, no one could know what I was struggling with. Not peers, parents, or priesthood leaders. What shame would it be for others to know. It was something I had to deal with on my own. But I had no idea how to do that. It attacked again and again, and though I knew it was wrong and told myself I'd never do it again—that it was a stupid, stupid problem, and how could I ever indulge in it—it continued, and the guilt and fear mounted. They were so great that I avoided my annual priesthood interview one year by taking sleeping pills so I'd be asleep at the time appointed for the interview. I was able to get out of that one, but the next year I was caught by surprise and ushered in from a mutual activity to the interview to advance in the priesthood. It was finally there, years into my sin, that I confessed to a bishop, simply because there was no way out of it but lying. I'd avoid telling the truth if I could, but I'd never tell someone a direct lie, certainly not a bishop.

But that confession didn't fix anything. In fact, now that I had been specifically told *not* to take the sacrament, I started staying home from church to avoid the public shame. I stayed away from other social events too and became isolated. Loneliness became my game, touched with shame whenever I saw my peers. So I just stayed away.

But despite my inactivity, I never stopped believing. I never turned fully away from God to embrace my sin and go off on my own track. I never accepted my behavior as harmless or normal. I knew exactly where my soul was: in darkness. I just didn't know how to find the light. I was scared of what it would take and certain it was not possible.

Around the time this problem came up in my life, clinical and chemical depression also emerged. My family has a long history of this emotional frailty, and it is no surprise it appeared at the time it did. I had also been gaining a lot of weight, and being a biological late bloomer did not help with my self-image. My spiritual load thus combined with my fragile emotional state to create a near impenetrable sense of self-hatred. I felt myself so worthy of disgust and loathing that I was even ashamed to merely be in the presence of a girl, let alone talk to one or look one in the face. I didn't deserve it; I was beneath them—beneath everyone, but especially girls. Fat, unattractive, unworthy, and in all ways repulsive, especially to myself.

During this time, I discovered that Hell for me was, and is, in comparison. Comparing my own self and situation with those around me (or at least the surface image) destroyed me. It still does from time to time. I would look at everyone else and how successful they were; how those guys had to shave, could talk to girls without looking away, and could not only take but administer the sacrament. They were examples and could go on missions. Seeing all this, I would hate myself all the more. They were the right kind of priesthood holder. They were good in the sight of God. They were men the way I never could be.

The most embarrassing and shameful moment of my life came in a Sunday School class when I was around sixteen. The teacher, for reasons I still cannot fathom, addressed each of the males in the class in turn and asked what office of the priesthood we held. So there, before all of my peers, I had to let out that I still a teacher in the Aaronic priesthood. The implication that I wasn't worthy to advance was left hanging solidly in the air. They knew, by inference, that I was addicted to pornography or something like unto it.

For my senior project in high school, I wrote a novel. Its purpose was penance. A character in the story suffers from a similar compulsion and overcomes it in the end. As a whole, it is a story of symbols, meant as a cautionary tale to society of the problems of sexual and pornographic indulgence, of living without rules or religion and doing whatever one wants to do. I knew how dark and deep I was, and I wanted to tell the world the true consequences to such choices and attitudes. I wanted to warn others away from the path I took.

That was the extent to which I knew what I was doing was wrong and how much I wanted to repent. I just didn't know how to. It is a curious and leveling aspect of chemical depression that it has the power to make it impossible to feel the Spirit, thus one feels spiritually dead, cut off from the Lord. I felt that way for six years, alone.

But I've discovered in the years since that we never truly are. Christ knew what I was going through. He knows what you are going through and have gone through. He knows the problems and, more important, the symptoms of the problems, so He is uniquely qualified to answer your—*our*—prayers. Remember: Christ too suffered solitude; He too was alone, or at least He felt alone. Elder Jeffrey R. Holland said the following in his beautiful April 2009 general conference address:

> That the supreme sacrifice of His Son might be as complete as it was voluntary and solitary, the Father briefly withdrew from Jesus the comfort

of His Spirit, the support of His personal presence. It was required, indeed it was central to the significance of the Atonement, that this perfect Son who had never spoken ill nor done wrong nor touched an unclean thing had to know how the rest of humankind—us, all of us—would feel when we did commit such sins. For His Atonement to be infinite and eternal, He had to feel what it was like to die not only physically but spiritually, to sense what it was like to have the divine Spirit withdraw, leaving one feeling totally, abjectly, hopelessly alone.[112]

That is what those struggling with the powers of darkness must realize: Christ has been in exactly your situations and knows how to comfort you in whatever stupid you've done or whatever unfair thing has been inflicted on you. Consider again the symbol of moonlight: though at night you can't see the sun, you can almost always see the moon shining. And remember that the light of the moon is actually sunlight reflected off the moon's surface, proving the sun's continued existence. Like the sun, God is always there, even if can't see Him or even His hand directly.

But how difficult it was to internalize that truth—partly because of the untreated depression and partly because of my spiritual state. I often considered suicide, but never really seriously. I wanted the pain, the loneliness, the sin, and the repeated attacks from the unbalanced chemistry of my brain to go away. That was all. Two things kept me from ever attempting suicide: one, I *knew* that God was there, and I wasn't supposed to do that; two, it would break my parents' heart forever. I testify that God has a plan for all of us. He had, and has, a plan for me. As a master novelist, He knows the end from the beginning. Elder Neal A. Maxwell reminded us often that having faith in God means having faith in God's timing.[113] And there was indeed a timing to all this, a plan and miracle God had been waiting for just the right time to provide—a "celestial clock," as one particular priesthood blessing called it.

For six years, I struggled and fought and failed and fell, again and again. A never-ending cycle, so it seemed. But there came a certain week in June where, all at once, Christ—through the powers of the Atonement—shattered the shackles with which I was bound and set me free.

For the six or seven months preceding that week in June, things had been getting worse with my depression. It had fully emerged as bipolar disorder, and I was living with a particular type called mixed state bipolar. People with typical bipolar disorder swing back and forth between extreme mania (high energy and optimism) to extreme depression (sadness and despair). But mine did something else: both extremes would hit me at the same time. This meant that at night, my mind raced so fast I couldn't sleep (the manic side), and it raced with horrible, miserable, self-hating thoughts (the depressive side). It was awful. I found ways to cope with it temporarily, but it just got worse. The depression fed the sin, and the sin fed the depression.

But as I said, God had a plan. I first received word of it in church one Sunday in late spring. A voice told me, *Get medication; when you get medication, everything else will fall into place.*

I don't know if the happy and hopeful feeling I felt in church that day was the Spirit or my mania or both, but I finally had a ray of light to follow. Later that week, I called my psychiatrist, whom I had not seen in a long time. (Years ago, I had been on some medication, but in my pride I rejected it because I didn't want to be dependent on something artificial for my health.) Unfortunately, my psychiatrist didn't answer the phone, and I had to leave a message. Weeks went by without word from him, and I returned to my previous state of mind.

But then came the Wednesday of that miraculous week in June, and I got a call. He had an opening that day, within a few hours, and he invited me to come in then. So I did. Miraculously, the first medication we tried turned out to be exactly what I needed. So many poor souls dealing with mental disorders have to try several different medications until they find the right one, and that journey can be stressful and full of unexpected emotions and other issues. But I found the right one on the first try. Getting that medication was miracle number one.

Then that next Sunday, a friend of mine—the only one with whom I'd ever talked about my problems—issued a direct order: "Go talk to the bishop, or I'll beat the crap out of you." The change that was being wrought in my brain at that time made this idea completely possible. Utterly terrifying, yes, but also utterly *necessary*, completely unlike the past six years had been. So I made an appointment with him that day and confessed my sins to him a couple of days later. That caused miracle number two.

Somehow, with those miracles (and a few other small ones I won't go into here), my chains were broken. I can't say why that week was the week after all that time, but the day after getting on medication was the last day of indulgence. The addiction was cut off (though, as with alcoholics and other addicts, I confess it will never leave me totally in this life). I gained control over my life, over my soul. Though some might say I was freed by medication, I know who was responsible for putting me on that path.

After three weeks of worthy living, I took the sacrament again for the first time in years. And because of that fact, I feel I now truly understand the sacrament. It became the most important part of the week; it was the reason I went to church, and still pretty much is. I go to appreciate the sacrifice of Christ and to be grateful for it by always remembering Him.

I began other changes immediately. I started exercising and took pleasure in it, eventually losing about sixty pounds. I also switched from glasses to contact lenses; cosmetic changes, to be sure, but reflective of the change inside me, and I gradually stopped hating myself.

Author and BYU professor Brad Wilcox said in his talk "His Grace Is Sufficient," "The miracle of the Atonement is not just that we can be cleansed and consoled but that we can be transformed."[114] This is what happened to me, inside and out. A friend who left on his mission while I was in my previous state came home and literally did not recognize me for a moment, for my countenance had changed so much. My previous life, defined by self-hatred, stagnation, and failure, was transformed by the power of Christ and His Atonement. I shed the natural man and was reborn spiritually. Christ had healed and transformed me.

Within a few months, I was ordained an elder and received the Melchizedek Priesthood. At that point, I wanted to try to repay the Savior for what He'd done for me, and soon I knew it was finally time to go about preparing to serve a mission.

This I discovered in an unexpectedly concrete way. Related thoughts had been slowly bubbling up in those days, and one day I wrote in my journal the words, "I want to serve . . ." and stopped. For a moment, I pondered what words should follow after; did I want to serve "a mission" or did I want to serve "God"? Both would have worked fine, but as an aspiring writer, I wanted to use just the right words. I ended up scribbling, "I want to serve God and go on a mission." This word choice may seem inconsequential to some, but for me it proved significant. When I looked up Doctrine and Covenants 4—the quintessential missionary scripture—it repeated back to me the phrasing I knew was influenced by the Holy Ghost: "Therefore, if ye have desires to *serve God* ye are called to the work" (D&C 4:3; emphasis added). Reading that verse and taking note of that exact word choice was confirmation to me that I should start working on my missionary papers, so I did.

They were officially submitted by that next May. Like every prospective missionary, I looked forward to finding out where I would go. My guesses were either Canada or Chile, where each of my namesakes were sent. But the weeks passed and the call didn't come. After a few months, my stake president inquired as to what was going on. He discovered what has become one of the greatest ironies of my life: the medication I take for my bipolar disorder, the medication that saved my life and helped put my soul in such a state that I could be worthy to serve a mission, caused a red flag to go up in Salt Lake. Those who take this particular medication are generally not allowed to go on missions because of the conditions they take it for. And so, after months of patience, quiet work, and prayer, my stake president asked me how I felt about not going on a mission and moving on with my life.

Someone else may have taken this news as a wonderful excuse not to take two years out of his life and work his guts out slaving away in some backwoods village for people he didn't know. But I felt something different in my gut. Because of what God had done for me, because of the healing I had received, I took that news and continue to take it in the opposite way: instead of merely serving the Lord for two years, I was filled with resolve that I must serve Him throughout my entire life. He healed me and freed me. What else could I do but help Him heal and free others?

I believe that is the mark of true healing—gratitude that is *shown*, not just told. Joseph Smith once said, "Our Heavenly Father is more liberal in His views, and boundless in His mercies and blessings, than we are ready to believe or receive. God does not look on sin with [the least degree of] allowance, but . . . the nearer we get to our Heavenly Father, the more we are disposed to look with compassion on perishing souls; we feel that we want to take them upon our shoulders, and cast their sins behind our backs."[115] Thus, as the Atonement takes effect and we are gradually brought to be one with Christ, we become more like Him. We see God's children from His point of view and seek to retrieve those eternally important souls back from the abyss and place them in Christ's arms, where they can be healed and transformed.

Stephan Peers elaborated on this point. He told me once, "One of the great aspects of the Atonement is not so much that Jesus takes on our sins. It is why he does and what he asks us to learn from it. Basically, we try to do what he does: lift burdens. As He did, you see the burdens of others which much more clarity when you have experienced your own. . . . When we are in the depths [of pain and despair] and we look up, the Lord says, *This is how it works. Whom do you want to be?* That is when we get bold and strong and learn to lift others, have discernment, and carry burdens, magnificently most of which are not ours."

I understand how hard, awful, and miserable it can be to be locked in a perpetual grapple with sin and how a person struggling with addiction can really and truly be good at heart. I remember how, despite my inner lust, I also could not bear to tell a lie. The fact that a person is struggling and not *complacent* with addiction is proof that they are not inherently bad; we addicts are simply in the devil's hands and so do what he wants us to do. Agency has almost entirely been stripped away and manacles been placed around the wrists. The first choice (even made in ignorance) may have been ours, but the rest, once could say, are not.

And so I ask you, if you do not know this fight firsthand, not to look down on those who are fighting against this enemy. What are needed is love and understanding, and the knowledge that they are not alone and repulsive to you. They need to know, and you need to know, that change is possible. In the mighty words of President Thomas S. Monson, "Men can change."[116]

True, we cannot change alone, but remember that we are never actually alone. Elder Jeffrey R. Holland wrote,

> Brothers and sisters, one of the great consolations of this Easter season is that because Jesus walked such a long, lonely path utterly alone, *we* do not have to do so. His solitary journey brought great company for our little version of that path—the merciful care of our Father in Heaven, the unfailing companionship of this Beloved Son, the consummate gift of the Holy Ghost, angels in heaven, family members on both sides of the veil, prophets and apostles, teachers, leaders, friends. All of these and more have been given as companions for our mortal journey because of the Atonement of Jesus Christ and the Restoration of His gospel. Trumpeted from the summit of Calvary is the truth that we will never be left alone nor unaided, even if sometimes we may feel that we are. Truly the Redeemer of us all said: "I will not leave you comfortless: [My Father and] I will come to you [and abide with you]."[117]

Christ's mercy is all well and good intellectually. But that knowledge of the Savior's love is nothing compared to the actual experience of it. You cannot know Christ by simply reading about Him. To know Him is to feel His eternal love and experience it in all its capacity.

Brad Wilcox said, "The older I get, and the more I understand this wonderful *plan of redemption*, the more I realize that in the final judgment it will *not* be the unrepentant sinner begging Jesus, 'Let me stay.' No, he will probably be saying, 'Get me out of here!' Knowing Christ's character, I believe that if anyone is going to be begging on that occasion, it would probably be Jesus begging the unrepentant sinner, 'Please, choose to stay. Please, use my Atonement—not just to be cleansed but to be changed so that you *want* to stay.' The miracle of the Atonement is not just that we can go home but that—miraculously—we can feel at home there."[118] The Atonement's healing powers can purge those parts of us that are worldly and mortal, those traits of the natural man, and replace them with divinity. For when we deny ourselves of all ungodliness, what then remains?

Though *The Dark Knight* is a dark and violent film about evil's encroaching and pervasive presence, it concludes on a note of *earned* hope. The last image in the movie is Batman, having taken upon himself the burden of the sins of Gotham, riding up an on-ramp with an unseen light up ahead, blocked from view by Batman himself. Though it is night, in the absolutely final frame his cape whips in the wind, allowing just a single ray of light to shine out into the darkness.

That light is hope, an emblem of the Savior, who is "the light which shineth in darkness, and the darkness comprehendeth it not" (D&C 6:21). It's the hope that anyone and everyone can access the power to overcome the darkness that envelops them. Though we all have been sinners, and many of us may currently be puppets in the devil's hands, our strings can be cut. We can become more like Jesus, and even one day a being like Him, perfect in all things—most important, in Christ-like love. That ascension is our great hope and potential.

We owe Him so much—not just a tithe of ten percent, but a consecration of everything we are and possess. Let us show Him our gratitude for His infinite sacrifice and blessings. Though we can never hope to repay Him completely, we can show our appreciation by doing what He did, becoming like Him, and helping others access the freely offered gift of salvation, healing, and heavenly transformation. In Christ, there is hope and help for us all.

Chapter 6
Throw Up That Shield of Faith

*A**s we transition** from talking about the shield to the sword, we return to the story of Harry Potter. This particular lesson is taken from the pinnacle of his journey, the moment he achieved his full transformation into a hero. I offer this example without prelude, asking you to take it briefly on faith and let its deeper meaning sink in as we go on.

In the climax of his seven-book saga, Harry Potter walked, chin up, into the darkness of death, scared but willing. Knowing only that to save the wizarding world he had to face his enemy and let him inflict a fatal blow, Harry entered the Forbidden Forest in a "cold-blooded walk to his own destruction."[119] But Harry wasn't alone. The spirits of his mother, father, godfather, and former mentor walked at his side and supported him, much like angels ministered unto Christ during the Atonement. He received comfort from them, but not reprieve. Death still awaited him, yet Harry walked forward with faith. He didn't know how everything would turn out, but he knew at least that the old Hogwarts Headmaster Dumbledore loved him and that this, presumably his final decision, would open the way for evil to finally be destroyed.

In walking that path, Harry didn't know everything. But he knew enough to make the right choice. He knew enough to go on and make a mortal commitment.

Remarkably, though he didn't know it at the time, his knowledge of his fate was incomplete. The actual big picture eluded him; all he knew and possessed was his own personal piece to the puzzle. That was all he *could* know for the plan to work.

Faith was the key—faith as defined by the willingness to believe and to act on that belief. Harry needed to be willing to die, to look death in the eye and accept his fate. If he had known every iota of Dumbledore's plan, the sacrifice would not have produced the requisite magic to save his friends and loved ones. Like Abraham's near sacrifice of Isaac, Harry only needed to be *willing* to face the end; if he'd had perfect knowledge, the higher plan leading ultimately to evil's downfall would have failed. So it was not perfect knowledge or education that saved the wizarding world—it was perfect faith.

Secular Faith

It is a fascinating thing that the Spirit is something we can only feel and never accurately explain in words or in terms of the senses. This boundary actually serves as a great equalizer. No matter our brain capacity or our physical or mental capabilities, all can feel the Holy Ghost and God's love and know the truth. Indeed, that is the point of Heavenly Father's ways: all are capable of being loved and taught without any kind of training at all.

However, this channel to God also necessitates faith rather than knowledge. There is no consistent empirical way of verifying this sensation, nor any scientific instrument that can measure it, document it, and repeat it. The requirement of this kind of knowledge as a foundation of faith dissuades many from even considering the existence of God. They require satisfaction of the senses before being willing to believe in a higher power, and so say to the gospel, "No thanks" (at the politest), and close their door.

Elder Neal A. Maxwell observed, "The Lord gives more instructions than he gives explanations."[120] Those who have tried to follow those instructions without being granted accompanying explanations know how difficult that can be.

Likewise, Harry's faith was not always so perfect. Midway through the final book, after learning a devastating truth about Dumbledore's past, Harry became despondent. The man he'd looked up to for so long—the symbol of absolute good he had come to know and the mentor who had personally trained him—had flirted with the dark arts and an ideology of tyranny in his youth. This revelation shattered Harry's understanding of Dumbledore and led him to question everything he thought he knew.

In response to this, Hermione tried to buoy up Harry's downtrodden spirits, but Harry parried her every encouragement. Eventually, it comes down to Hermione insisting on the one truth she knew was correct: "'He loved you,' Hermione whispered. 'I know he loved you.' Harry dropped his arms. 'I don't know who he loved, Hermione, but it was never me.'"[121]

Now he was even questioning that.

So if believing in God challenges our minds in such a frustrating way, and if what is asked of us leaves an impression of a distant and indifferent Father, why did God set up the system this particular way? Why make the path so impossible for some people, even good people, to walk down? Why is there a test of faith in the first place?

I'll put it another way. Every other attribute—patience, diligence, humility, and so forth—has obvious merit when it comes to becoming a being like Heavenly Father; they are attributes directly associated with godhood. Faith is too, in a sense—God needs faith for a very different reason: to command the elements.[122] That is faith in a different entity, in a different system. The faith we are meant to hold is in God—faith as defined more by *belief*, or the trust we are willing to have in the salvation of God and in the many uncertain mysteries of the world. Alma said that eventually our knowledge can be perfect in the seed we once planted in faith, and then "your faith is dormant; and this because you know" (Alma 32:34). Belief will be replaced by perfect understanding, so why is willingness to believe so essential to this life? Why institute the veil and blind us to the other two acts of this grand play? Why force faith into the foremost focus of our faculties?

That's a question I've been asking for a long time. Why faith? Why believe when we could make better choices by knowing? Well, I recently found an answer—a few, actually.

The simple answer is that faith, I've discovered, is fundamental to our existence. And here, I don't necessarily mean *faith* as in "faith in God." I mean the general matter of belief and trust in a possible but uncertain future, whatever it is.

For instance, science and natural laws assure us that our planet will continue to rotate, and so the sun will indeed rise in the morning. But is there certainty in that fact? Is there concrete proof that tomorrow will be like today? The laws of physics say so, but those laws are still accepted on faith, on what we think is right based on the knowledge we've accumulated thus far. Scientists must work on that belief to move forward with their work.

We also have faith—by which I mean *trust*—in our physical senses. They are our only method of interacting with the world around us, so we don't have much choice. But our senses can be fooled. We go to the movies and see impossible things on the screen, from dinosaurs and explosions, that convince us for the time we're in that dark theater that they are real, and we feel emotions because of them. After all, in theory, if somehow all our senses were being manipulated at once like a dream, we would have no way of verifying what is real and what is not—other than what is whispered to our spirits, stirring our souls.

So it takes faith to even accept what we see every day. Daily life is a constant matter of belief and trust that things are one way and not another. What we know, whether in religion or science, we know to the best of our knowledge, but we lack a "perfect knowledge." And that is belief. That is faith.

Given that faith and belief are staples in life, what does that say about faith's role in the gospel, in the progression along our Eternal Arc toward certainty and true knowledge?

Faith, which I define as the willingness to believe, is the most necessary part of that progression. It isn't one attribute among many, as I'd previously assumed. It is the guide that coaxes us along that path that makes internalization of godly attributes possible in the first place. Faith is manifested when we trust those teachers of godhood, whether they be wise men and women or just the storms and strife of everyday life. Faith is what catalyzes growth, born when we decide to listen to what they have to say and decide to believe them, even if we don't know absolutely that they will lead us to the right place.

In other words, faith comes before knowledge. You can't know something unless you're willing to learn it first, whatever it may be. And because growth is the core purpose of this life and all existence to come, faith is the first principle and ordinance of the gospel, the foundation of learning. That was the answer to my question.

The same principle applies to worldly learning, does it not? To learn something new about chemistry, you first have to believe in the chemist. Because students know considerably less, or perhaps nothing at all, they must exercise a modicum of belief—even plant a seed in faith, exactly as Alma taught the poor outcasts of Antionum in Alma 32. And because of that faith, they eventually learn enough from their teacher that they can start doing experiments of their own and acquire the same kind of knowledge the chemist possessed.

Do you see how science and religion can contain essentially the same processes? They are both pathways to truth—different kinds of truth, but truth nonetheless. And those pathways, those processes, are the divine way of learning and teaching, which drive the plan of salvation. We are sent here to gain bodies and experiment and learn for ourselves what mortality is like, with all of its aches and pains. That takes time and effort, and it takes faith at first to learn from our parents and families before we go out and discover much of it for ourselves.

It's the same with God, in the end. In this life, we first depend on God, spiritually speaking. We depend on His commandments and directives. But eventually, like Nephi being given the sealing power, we will be able to make choices for ourselves and go to God with our own ideas and plans and receive sanction for them from Him. And someday, when we've learned enough, we can be like Him. We can be gods.

Layers upon layers, all made possible by faith, by a willingness to believe.

Doubts and Hard Doctrines

But like every other attribute, faith cannot grow if it is never tested. Every serious religious believer has, at times, faced doubts. One cannot forge strong faith without fire. Overcoming the fiery darts of the adversary is what reinforces belief and propels that belief toward knowledge. It is only through such a shield that we are able to wield our swords in spiritual combat at all.

Laman and Lemuel never did manage to reconcile their own pride and egos with the hard doctrines Nephi preached to them (see 2 Nephi 5:3). They were never willing to pray about it themselves, thinking that if it was important, the Lord would have already explained it to them in clear language. They didn't know that such spiritual struggles are a part of the growth process—that the Lord, like Dumbledore with Harry, lets us flounder just enough in the surf that we start learning to swim on our own, eventually to brave higher tides.

Indeed, "deep water is what [we are] wont to swim in" (D&C 127:2), and never more so than in these latter days. Faith in the face of these conflicts is more important than ever. Such faith is not exercised by shutting out doubts, suppressing them, or trying to ignore them. No, faith is exercised by facing them and by the process of reconciliation. We can't learn to swim if we only ever reach for the edge of the pool.

Today, doubts come from many places, and our society provides a veritable pantheon of possible gods to worship. These gods can be just about anything and vary from person to person. Yet we each know in our own hearts what deity we kneel to; we see how we devote our time. Time spent proves what our priorities are, after all, and worshipping any god over our Heavenly Father gives Satan an opening to strike against us, cracking our armor (if we are clad in any armor at all). Those cracks are doubts, and they can be good if we treat them as opportunities to gird ourselves in stronger plate rather than an excuse to shed the protection entirely.

In our age, doubts seep from two sources most especially: competing social or political allegiances and the realm of science. We may innocuously join ourselves to certain causes that proclaim otherwise good tidings, but when it comes down to a choice between the causes of the world, which seem to be just, and the gospel, which may diverge on social or political issues from your beliefs, which path will you take? When we use the pronoun *we*, to which organization or cause are we referring?

Satan uses these divergent causes now more than ever to establish disagreements with true but hard doctrine. Though perhaps fighting with good intent, those causes, if not pointed the same direction as the prophets, can rile us up and inflame us with passion that blind us to where our true allegiance should always lie. And make no mistake—there is no worldly cause more pertinent and pressing than the gospel.

We could say that we're all at that moment in Lehi's dream; we're at the tree, those of us who are members of the Church, and have partaken of its fruit. But even after we've been filled with God's love, even after we make covenants and receive the temple ordinances, still the multitudes at the party across the river jeer and mock. Their air of superiority and the public proclamations of their own pride, pleasure, and power draw souls away from the tree of life.

Even after God has given them everything, they still want something else. Perhaps some are ashamed of their religious choices merely because their shallow understanding of the gospel couldn't answer the questions or criticisms shouted from the world. Though a limited, basic understanding is necessary at the start of our testimonies, if that planted seed is never watered or cared for, it will only ever produce a shriveled sapling, and shame will lead them to abandon the responsibility and joy of the gospel to join with the imbibing habits and laughter of Babylon.

Bear in mind—the colors of their clothes and the loudness of their laughs only serve to help them forget, to blind their eyes and dampen their minds to the realities of where their chosen path will ultimately take them. If they ever had a quiet minute to ponder and reflect, they might realize what is really going on. And so they live to forget and avoid facing the hard doctrines and consequences of their choices.

That life of forgetfulness can take multiple forms. For some, like those most vocal and visible in the great and spacious building, it's eat, drink, and be merry, for tomorrow we die. For others, it can be a willful blindness brought on by anger. "Someone offended me at church!" "The Brethren haven't directly answered my question that I posted on Facebook!" "I've received no full answer to the deep doctrinal question I prayed about ten minutes ago!"

At times, we can be met with such obstacles honestly, even fairly—some doctrines can be difficult to swallow with our so-called modern sensibilities. But what matters, what is *really* the test in the face of these minor schisms, is how we respond to them. Confrontations with genuine doubts can torment a soul and break down the supports of the faith they've built their entire lives.

However, if we respond with automatic anger instead of humility and an earnest desire to know, it might indicate unconscious self-deception, an inclination to find an excuse to clothe our desire to leave. At that point, it's not hard to convince ourselves to live a life away from rules and commandments and covenants.

Elder Neal A. Maxwell said, "Lack of intellectual humility is there among those who have deliberately cultivated their doubts in order, they think, to release themselves from their covenants. Some nurture their grievances assiduously. Were their grievances, instead, Alma's seed of faith, they would have long ago nourished a mighty tree of testimony."[123]

It is that tree of testimony that is so essential in our world as insulation against Satan's fiery darts. For God asks us not to forget, but to remember—to remember all that He has done for us, our identities as His children and heirs to His throne, what this life is for, and the tree of life, meaning the love and light of God.

That wonderful vision was given to Nephi in answer to his heartfelt questions. And early in, it is a key admission on his part: that He knew he did "not know the meaning of all things," and yet the one thing Nephi was absolutely sure of was that God "loveth his children" (1 Nephi 11:17). Faith in God's love, in His control and in His servants, is that sure foundation we need build upon. The answers of both Nephi and Hermione—he loves us—can and should be ours when faced with unanswered questions, for it is the foundation of all our knowledge.

The Fruits of Uncertainty

There is something to be said for times of sincere uncertainty. In fact, the Lord *intends* for this life to be just that: a proving ground to see which path we'll choose with our God-given agency. Uncertainty and even doubt can be essential steps to proper learning as we seek out truth and assurances. After all, if we had perfect knowledge and could see God's smile or frown after each step we take, there would be no reason to strive, nor would our choices much matter at all. Elder Neal A. Maxwell wrote, "It seems clear, not only scripturally but logically, that this second estate could not include either the direct memories or the reference experiences of our first estate. If such were to impinge overmuch upon this second estate, our mortality would not be a true proving ground."[124]

Harry, once doubting Dumbledore's leadership, and Hermione, once trying to convince Harry of it, later switched positions. After learning about the mysterious Deathly Hallows themselves, Harry finally caught onto just a glimmer of what he suspected Dumbledore's ultimate plan was, and it excited him. He started to put together clues, see meaning where once he saw void, and connect dots that had appeared to be mere random scatterings. Hermione, alarmed at Harry's reliance on knowledge she believed faulty, essentially tried to talk Harry out of it, to crack his renewed faith in Dumbledore. Driven by logic and reason, she didn't catch the vision Harry had and instead tried to divert his path elsewhere, though she had good intentions.

Nonetheless, Harry reached the conclusion that Dumbledore made the challenge so hard because he was letting Harry try things out for himself. He realized that Dumbledore had worked this way from the beginning—if Dumbledore had swooped in and done all the work for him, Harry would never have had the learning experiences he began to gain all the way back when he first saved the Sorcerer's Stone from Quirrell and Voldemort in the first book. If Harry had never had the chance to be heroic, he could never have become a hero.

So the next time you feel doubt or acknowledge a nagging question, neither of which you have immediate answers to, consider that part of the point. Knowledge is never gained in a day, and it would be unfruitful and untruthful to never admit that a doubt has entered your head. My friend Stephan Peers once wrote me concerning a spiritual question I had, saying, "Aren't doubts great? I mean, they have to be resolved, right? So [if] you find a place for them then they cease to be doubts. If you don't find [them] a place, they become ignorance and end up undermining everything." Indeed, suppressed doubts have a way of bursting out at unfortunate moments designed and planned by the adversary.

Lehi's sons give excellent examples of the two paths of this process. Nephi received his own vision of the tree of life because he wanted to know for himself: "I had desired to know the things that my father had seen, and believing that the Lord was able to make them known unto me, *as I sat pondering in mine heart* I was caught away in the Spirit of the Lord" (1 Nephi 11:1; emphasis added). Nephi only received answers as he tried to work them out in his own mind, while at the same time asking God for help. As we are admonished to frequently in the scriptures, Nephi asked and he received; he knocked, and the Lord gave him what he desired.

Later, Laman and Lemuel were (shockingly) complaining about something their father said to them, and Nephi, overhearing their disputes (probably with a groan and a sigh), sought to know what the matter was this time. They told him that they couldn't understand some particular doctrine; Nephi asked if they had even bothered to pray about it, and they responded no, "for the Lord maketh no such thing known unto us" (1 Nephi 15:9).

Nephi got understandably exasperated and reminded them, after a few critical questions, of the great promise of the Book of Mormon: If you ask in faith, with sincere belief, and exert yourself in trying to do the right thing, then the requested answers will be given unto you. But rays of light will not shine down if your heart is hard and you are unwilling to act on the message delivered (see 1 Nephi 15:6–11.) The examples of Laman and Lemuel, then, are a warning to us that we're not going to get everything by our wits alone; reliance wholly on the arm of flesh will lead to murmuring and perhaps even apostasy. It's the sincere question that is answered, the earnest effort that will be rewarded, as long as the asker maintains the necessary patience and relies on the Lord's timetable, not his or her own, for God's timing is always better.

What's interesting, however, is that Laman and Lemuel did eventually ask questions, and pretty direct ones at that! In fact, just a few verses later, they "were pacified" by Nephi's answers and "did humble themselves before the Lord" (1 Nephi 15:20). But, as the pattern went, they eventually found new causes to complain as they spiritually shrink away from the harder truths, those words of chastisement that they just couldn't bear to hear from their younger brother. It is pride and anger more than the actual doubts that lead down forbidden paths. Thus we can see the imperative of maintaining that attitude of humility and pacification in the face of the next wave of questions or doubts that will inevitably wash over us.

We'll inevitably come across that scary moment where we can only admit we don't know. But though that obstacle might make us stop on the path, it is not just cause for turning around or venturing off on some tangential journey. Such moments drove the great scientists and seekers of truth in more ancient times. Did Newton stop at "I don't know" and turn away from seeking the truth? Did Galileo? Did Darwin?[125] Did fourteen-year-old Joseph Smith?

No. Every revelation to human civilization, terrestrial or celestial, has come because seekers kept seeking. They knew that lack of knowledge about a thing did not extinguish the importance of that thing, nor did they simply label that thing unknowable, dismiss it as a just a contradiction in the laws of the universe, and give up because it didn't make sense. Science and religion, those great bastions of all manner of truths, are driven by the thirst to truly know. Walls do not stop the genuine truth-seeker. Instead, they drive the great thinkers to wonder, *What's behind that wall?*

No serious scientists or theologians have ever demanded every bit of knowledge immediately, but rather have persisted in studying and thinking and working hard until they came across a satisfactory solution. This should be our behavior and perspective as well when we in the Church come across those moments when we don't know. When we hit those walls, we should do some homework: fast, pray, and counsel with your bishop. Go to the temple with an open heart and mind. Look up studies and scholarship being done. Know your religion better, and the factual findings that fill it. And if you truly want to know, to verify what you've been pondering over all that time without being given a direct witness from the Spirit, make a test of obeying the commandments. For Christ said, "If any man will do [God's] will, he shall know of the doctrine, whether it be of God, or whether I speak of myself" (John 7:17).

Live fuller and look deeper, for there are *always* answers.

As we look deeper, however, we may find hard questions answered with equivalently hard doctrines. These are those that test the mettle of our testimonies, whether because they are hard to live or hard to accept that others lived them with the Lord's approval. Such hard doctrines can discourage us and dampen our enthusiasm for the gospel because we might feel betrayed by the Church for seeming to selectively teach certain doctrines and histories and ignore others, as if to hide them. But those truths that lie in the shadows, spiritually speaking, still should not eclipse the effulgent rays of what truth we *have* been given.

In my experience there are many more reasons to believe than to doubt. The tension between the two is, of course, what this is all about. It is why faith is the first and foremost principle of the gospel—why we are to always throw up that shield of faith and are counseled to stay loyal to the Church in all times and situations. I promise it will eventually lead to a brighter enlightenment than you ever could have before, and you will have a deeper, more mature understanding of the inexhaustible gospel than if you'd never asked questions at all.

Though a seemingly unintuitive technique of God, withholding immediate answers from us does assist in the construction of our souls. Elder Neal A. Maxwell wrote, "How often have you and I in our provincialism prayed to see ahead and, mercifully, been refused, lest our view of the present be blurred?"[126] Knowing too much at a given time may dull the edge of this world, and sharpened sensations are necessary to gain all the experience we need here. But the decision to believe that answers are out there, even if we do not know them, should spur us forward—it is what prepares our minds to receive answers when the time is right.

When God doesn't answer our prayers for inspiration, revelation, or confirmation right as we ask them, or even a short time afterward, we should not take this as evidence that there is no God, or that He doesn't care. For if we truly start progressing in attempts to find God—praying more frequently, doubling our scripture study time, gradually discovering more knowledge, and building our minds and spirits block by block—then wasn't that lack of direct answer worth it? Aren't we better, stronger people for it? How far are we willing to go for God? For truth?

Enos was willing to pray all day and all night for his answers. Are we?

Science "Versus" Faith

A few pages ago, I mentioned how science and the gospel take similar paths to truth. Let me explain that point a little further.

The scientific method has been the key to every major technological development and scientific discovery we know of. Every single one. Interestingly enough, the principle at the core of the scientific method is skepticism. It is the necessity to repeat previously done experiments to verify the accuracy of their results. Every completed experiment is an invitation to repeat the experiment and a challenge to find flaws or holes that prove those results wrong.

I wrote that the influence and testimony of the Spirit cannot be empirically proven. That is only half-right—many aspects of our beliefs truly cannot be verified by such methods. But the truthfulness of it *can*.

Moroni's challenge, the rousing cry with which he closed his testimony, parallels the core solicitation of the scientific method as described before: "And when ye shall receive these things, I would exhort you that ye would ask God, the Eternal Father, in the name of Christ, if these things are *not* true; and if ye shall ask with a *sincere heart*, with *real intent*, having faith in Christ, he will manifest the truth of it unto you, by the power of the Holy Ghost" (Moroni 10:4; emphasis added).

Does that not sound like the quintessential mantra of seeking truth? Asking with sincerity, being willing to conform our lives to whatever truth we find at the bottom, and (just as the scientific method goes) attempting to divine if the doctrines and truths found in the text are *not* true.

And again, we see that great equalizer that makes the Spirit superior to science: You don't need to know the ins and outs of chemistry, physics, or biology; you need only to possess a modicum of faith, even a desire for faith, and you can know "by the power of the Holy Ghost . . . the truth of all things" (Moroni 10:5). Like prayer, this experience is extended to all, not just experts—*everyone* is invited to try His words and repeat this experiment for themselves. But there is a warning: Like in science, the conditions of the second experiment must be as identical as possible to the first. It cannot be done for mere intellectual stimulation, for Moroni's promise only applies when we try it with a sincere heart and real intent, graced by a willingness to change our lives to fit the results. Otherwise, there is no use for it, and the Spirit won't act. But millions upon millions have found that such prayers *are* answered, that such faith *is* rewarded.

The Hero Doctrine

All epistemology relies on faith in some form, and science is no exception. Yet we often pit science against faith, so-called reason against religion, facts against truth, when all are merely varied elements that comprise that great sphere we call knowledge. Science is man's way of discovering God's methods and mindset of creation; religion seeks to understand and explain *why* He works—the purpose to it all—and how we may approach the Creator.

But of course, though sometimes we pit them against each other, frequently they pit *themselves* against each other. They can contradict—the scriptural record and the accepted anthropological, geographical, and historical record. This is where the duty to reconcile really begins. This is where we pick a side, where testimonies are born and where they wither away; it is the arena wherein we prove how grounded, rooted, established, and settled we are in the gospel. This is where that shield of faith shines in the sun or falls into the shadow of surrender.

But as important as that choice is, much of the time there is another option: waiting patiently. Science isn't yet finished, is it? New facts are always coming in, and new discoveries are always being made—and all are subject to debate, interpretation, and the continuing process of verification. The scientific community would be foolish to think they possess all the relevant facts at hand; if even experts disagree, how sure is that knowledge? And, like Latter-day Saints attempting to hold fast to faith and endure well in this world, scientists must also act only on what they already have. Tomorrow, they may learn something that changes everything, but for today, they experiment based on the principles that they have. The point of science is that what they have keeps changing—not only changing, but growing. Otherwise, why do more research? Why experiment, if not confronting new problems and new doubts every day?

Just about every major scientific discovery takes us further along an uncertain path, producing knowledge that will allow us to further venture out into the unknown. Confronted with doubts, we can learn something from the practitioners of science, who know there are answers *out there*, somewhere in the darkness—at least, they have faith in that idea. And that faith has always been fulfilled. Answers have always been found that draw us on with promises of even greater facts out there to be discovered.

A Basis for Choosing

And so I ask, what is the rush to decide? Why declare either science or religion as exclusive victors? What is the reason for choosing right now that only one of them is absolutely correct? I doubt many of us have perfectly accurate interpretations of biblical stories, such as how many of them occurred literally and how many are poetic parables. We aren't done evolving yet as a church, as a people, and as we advance, we know higher laws will be declared, while the scaffolding of lower laws will fall away. Some things that puzzle us today will someday be explained at last.[127]

There is time! It is not always necessary to decide if only one side or the other is correct right now. As Latter-day Saints, we seek out *all* truth, wherever it can be found. Brigham Young said, "I want to say to my friends that we believe in all good. If you can find a truth in heaven, earth or hell, it belongs to our doctrine. We believe it; it is ours; we claim it."[128] That is one of the miracles of our theology—we accept all truth, not just what our own scriptures have to say. We are still in that gathering stage, still waiting and working to receive further light and knowledge from on high and from our own experiences.

Elder Neal A. Maxwell advised that Saints obtain a "bilinguality"[129] of truth, achieving fluency in secular and spiritual wisdom. With the right perspective and with enough time, we will see the two holding hands, not locking horns. They are complements that rely on each other, two threads that fill in holes and gaps and weave an eternal tapestry of truth.

But perhaps that time is not yet. The trial will come to us all: that moment in which God gives us the opportunity to choose for ourselves what we believe. When we are poised to lean one way or the other, wavering back and forth on that line—that veritable cliff's edge—what will we choose? When pressed to commit, defend, and align with— which is more important, indeed, more imperative?

I'll cite one scripture: "By their fruits ye shall know them" (Matthew 7:20; 3 Nephi 14:20).

Science and technology built the infrastructure of this modern society, with all its bells, whistles, and HD televisions. But has it made a happier people? Has it made a *better* people? Have we really progressed toward being a Christlike people because of science? What has the atheistic explanation of evolution provided for our civilization? Does knowledge of the layers of the earth's crust purify our hearts and neutralize the natural man? It's a convenient world we live in but also a stunted one. Sin and depression wrack people, and the modern world, perhaps even because of its new god of science, rejects those panaceas that would make us whole.

The gospel, meanwhile, can make a happy and fulfilling society, regardless of what level of technology its people enjoy. The system that builds cell phones can't compare to the system that builds souls. Zion is a place in the heart, not necessarily in the brain. The gospel provides purpose and perspective and reveals the divine design in every corner of the universe. Christ's fruits of goodness, peace, and love transcend a society's level of technology and scientific understanding. Zion can exist anywhere and at any time in a way scientific advancement cannot. Only through our relationship with Heavenly Father do we find meaning and feel the highest order of love. Only God can give us that.

It could be said that science provides the sugary dessert, but religion provides substance, the proteins and vitamins and nutrients necessary for truly higher living. When dessert is eaten first, your appetite for a healthy dinner is often lessened, or "spoiled" as your mother would say. So which is more important? Which is more urgent, more pressing on the mind, more necessary to the well-being of the soul?[130]

The question is, when it comes down to choice—and it inevitably will—which system should you choose to rely on? Your own ability to grope your way in the dark, worshipping the god that is yourself and relying solely on faith in your own abilities? Or will you rely on God, holding His hand as He guides you forward? Critics might mock and ask whose hand are you really holding. How can you be sure it is God's and not that of some evil religious genius? Or how can you be sure you're not led by some psychological effect?

Well, my friends, that is what faith is all about.

We Are All Sheep

In the meantime, are we willing to endure mockery and scorn? Such treatment is common to every age of the Saints, as are the spiteful and unthinking *ad hominem* attacks against those attempting to exercise faith. While such barbs may be hard to take emotionally, especially when received from those we thought friends, they can be laughably easy to parry intellectually.

For instance, many have said of the Church that we "brainwash" our members. I have to say to that, "Really?" Are they aware of the methods by which we are meant to know if it's true or not? Have they not read or heard the myriad scriptures that tell us to *ask God* for answers? Not our parents or bishop—not even the prophet of the Church. No, we are to ask God so that we can know for ourselves. We are commanded to interact with our fellow Saints only "by persuasion, by long-suffering, by gentleness and meekness, and by love unfeigned" (D&C 121:42). There is no brainwashing here—simply Saints and mindful meekness. We are told not to mindlessly accept what the Brethren teach, but rather to *prayerfully* accept it. The Lord wants us to find out for ourselves whether it's right or not; for we answer not to our leaders, but to God, to Jesus Christ, who is the true leader and finisher of our faith.

Another label religious believers are often given is "sheep"—a label handed from contrasting sources. When it is an accusation from the peoples of the world, they mean we are blind, brainless followers who don't think for ourselves. When it is an invitation from the Lord, He means we are *all* sheep—every member of the human race—who are always following somebody, some cause internal or external, and He asks us to instead follow Him, for He will lead us to green pastures, not into the jaws of the wool-draped wolf. So, in fact, it is the world that blindly follows, chasing after passions and pursuing empty lives that lead right over a cliff, right into a fiery maw. We know that only the Shepherd can see the final destination, and so we trust Him, follow Him, and love Him as He coaxes us onward.

That final destination is not a secret, nor has it ever been. The only real unknown is the path He asks us to take. It is that oftentimes rocky, narrow, perilous path that causes dispute between the Church and the world and sows seeds of doubt in otherwise faithful Saints' hearts. Steep climbs dissuade those who aren't quite committed to wander down easier slopes and become lost. Pride convinces others to travel down an unmarked path of their own choosing that only leads to further fruitless wandering and a longer time till we arrive at our destination. Anger at the hurt inflicted by a sharp rock beneath unshod feet prods still others to leave and stay where the grass is soft. These are the sheep that are not, in the words of Elder Neal A. Maxwell, "grounded, rooted, established, and settled"[131] in the gospel—those that have let down their shield of faith, or perhaps never held it up in the first place.

Indeed, we are *all* sheep in the sense that none of us knows everything. Like sheep, we generally can't see much higher than our own heads, nor can we see above the heads of others. Because of that limited vision, we must often accept something in faith, even if we don't know why, so blind faith can be necessary at times. Other times we are encouraged to find out why things have to be the case that we might find out the mind and will of God—but whatever that will is, we must *always* be willing to accept it. And our allegiance in the face of spiritual adversity must always be to the Church; our grasp must, before we face off against doubts, be tightly held on the iron rod. Loyalty to the gospel ensures us that we will reach that tree of life and stay there in the face of mocking crowds.

After all, it is the laughing, riotous crowds in the great and spacious building who should be afraid, not us—and many of them probably are. President Spencer W. Kimball said, "Do not be puzzled if sometimes there are those in the world who mock how you live and what you believe, saying it is all false, but who, deep inside themselves, are really afraid that what you believe is really true."[132] We live with the fruits of that fear: accusations, criticism, mockery, and scorn. So did the prophets before us, and so, I might add, did the Savior.

Hold Fast to Every Good Thing

A reporter once asked Joseph Smith, "Who are you?" He responded, "Noah came before the flood. I have come before the fire."[133] The Savior also spoke of the seed of testimony that grows but cannot withstand the scorching flames of opposition and doubt.

We are indeed living in fiery times, and often only our personal shields of faith and armor of righteousness protect our trees of testimony.

Elder Neal A. Maxwell wrote, "How vital it is to be rooted and grounded in order to take the scorching heat that will be a part of the scorching heat that will be a part of that special summer of circumstances which precedes the second coming of the Son of Man. . . . The unnourished and the shallow will not endure, because they cannot stand the heat."[134] Our level of faith determines how deep we plant that seed, how much water we provide it, and how many rays of sunlight are allowed in to feed it. Faith, really, is the substance by which we endure to the end. Faith is the fertility of the ground in which we plant a seed of testimony.

One possible indication of failing faith and rising pride is when someone starts referring to the Church as "they" rather than "we." This risks being a sin of soft superiority, of casually putting ourselves above the common folk—they who simply believe and don't ask many questions and just try to live plain and ordinary lives doing what they're told. We are better, they might say, because we think about deep and complex things. We are educated and wise, and so we laugh at the little people who just accept everything they're taught, when it obviously is filled with so many flaws, imperfections, and antiquated ideas.

Sometimes such people even claim to still be part of the Church, to still believe in the teachings of the scriptures but worship in their own way and time. This attitude, the apex of vanity and pride, is the reason the Nephite nation fell as often as it did, and it is all too common among our own generation of Saints. Intellectual pursuits both within and outside the gospel can lead to wonderful new understanding and appreciation for just how deep this gospel goes, but as the prophet Jacob declared, with a sense of warning, "to be learned is good *if* [we] hearken unto the counsels of God" (2 Nephi 9:29; emphasis added). If those counsels and commandments are scorned because our "higher" intellect judges it to be foolishness, we are in for something of a surprise when we wake up on the other side and see just who it was that exemplified "the vainness, and the frailties, and the foolishness of men" (2 Nephi 9:28). But frankly, that fact shouldn't be a surprise to any of us.

In the next life, it's not our vast treasures of knowledge that redeem us; it's a sincere and humble heart. Elder Neal A. Maxwell offered the poignant reminder that "Christ does not dominate by his intellect. He leads by example and love."[135] Therefore, it is not what we know, but rather what we do with the knowledge we have, for that is the definition of true wisdom.

As we ask questions and voice our doubts, we must always return to a baseline of what we already know, or at least what we already believe. As he witnessed the gradual fall of his people and the abandonment of their faith in Christ, Mormon counseled a congregation to "lay hold upon every good thing" (Moroni 7:19)—this as he watched the Church in his civilization breathing its last few gasps of air and heard the final fading beats of its heart. While the Church in our day isn't facing a tidal wave of apostasy as his did, we too live in spiritually perilous times, and good Saints fall every day. In this environment, we must do as Mormon instructed, and as Christ told John: "That which ye have already hold fast till I come" (Revelation 2:25). There will be answers and relief, but they will come in the Lord's time, not ours. Until then, we must endure.

Elder Jeffrey R. Holland echoed their counsel:

> In moments of fear or doubt or troubling times, hold the ground you have already won, even if that ground is limited. . . . When those moments come and issues surface, the resolution of which is not immediately forthcoming, *hold fast to what you already know and stand strong until additional knowledge comes.* . . . Be as candid about your questions as you need to be; life is full of them on one subject or another. But if you and your family want to be healed, don't let those questions stand in the way of faith working its miracle.[136]

Let faith be your foundation, and let it be firm. It is the first principle and ordinance of the gospel for that reason. It is meant to be rested on, no matter if our trees of testimony are mighty oaks or just saplings. Always begin your search for answers with the assumption that the Church is true and work on your quest for reconciliation from there. This is not a matter of willful blindness, but logic. The underlying facts of the influence of the Spirit versus the substance of our senses show us that everything we interpret through sight, smell, hearing, and so forth is subject to change, revision, and imperfection, but the love of God and the sensation of the Spirit are not. The world might think that such a feeling is merely the brain tricking itself. But if you're reading this, contemplating the words of the scriptures and of the Apostles, or even just thinking about this subject, you know that there is something to this gospel, something different about this Church. You know that it's a little bit more than belief.

So, if anything, hold to that.

The Substance of Faith

We almost always have at least a few legitimate reasons to which we can fast. We have had experiences that bear what Gerald Lund called "divine signatures."[137] We've seen the direction of our lives changed. We've witnessed miracles and God's tender mercies that could not possibly come from any other source, except maybe nigh-infinite sequences of cosmic coincidence.

It is that last reason that is often the explanation given by dissenters as they leave the faith behind them. Terryl and Fiona Givens described this process as equal and opposite to those who are *finding* their faith:

> Disillusion and readjustment work in both directions. Those who come late on the road to Damascus, and see the light at last, remember all those times they ignored quiet promptings, and their paradigms shift accordingly. The past begins to make new sense, as they reinterpret those annoying doubts and second-guessings as the Lord's gentle proddings. In contrast, those who find their faith unsustainable and so abandon their faith journey, move in the other direction. Those quiet intimations they once took to be God's spirit, those countless minor miracles they took to be answers to prayer, they now interpret as passing moments of self-delusion, wish-fulfillment, and the stuff of mere coincidence.[138]

I have seen this process personally in close friends and family. They are lured away by the strength, expanse, and pull of the philosophies of men, by science and society. It is not the process of science in and of itself that is the enemy, but rather the elevation of science into an artificial god, trusting in the creations rather than the Creator.

Besides the parallel methods, we *can* turn to traditional scientific methods for evidence that verifies much of our faith, in particular the Book of Mormon. Unbeknownst to many, there exists a massive body of Book of Mormon scholarship, informed by the fields of geography, anthropology, history, and even literary analysis. It is all there, researched and written by the hands of great scholars of our faith like Hugh Nibley and Truman Madsen, waiting to be read by people searching for hard facts to support their faith. Over its entire existence, the Book of Mormon has held up to every criticism thrown at it and outlived every single theory as to its origin. Elder Jeffrey R. Holland said so powerfully, "For 179 years this book has been examined and attacked, denied and deconstructed, targeted and torn apart . . . and still it stands."[139]

The book was written over a mere two months, with Joseph Smith dictating straight through, never ceasing to speak from behind that curtain, never verifying where he had stopped the session before—simply continuing on without pause. The writing process of this sacred text is nothing like any other book ever produced. It is filled with Hebrew poetic forms, framed with complex structures, ordered by multiple dating systems that all match up together, and written in the voices of several authors, none of which align with Joseph's own writing voice.

Orson Scott Card, one of the all-time great science fiction writers, has much experience in creating new scientifically valid worlds and dwelling in the fantasy worlds created by others. His essay "The Book of Mormon: Artifact or Artifice?" details how the Book of Mormon transcends any kind of speculative fiction ever written and avoids any and all tropes of world and culture creation in literature. For instance, he showed how the writers of the Book of Mormon composed their historical accounts while only rarely going out of their way to describe the elements of their culture, instead depicting events with an assumed, underlying cultural context they never felt the need to explain. Those details are instead deeply set into the background, as actual historical records are always written.

There is so much there, hidden between the lines, if one only pays attention. The great Hugh Nibley wrote a scholarly account of the world in the time of Lehi after doing an abundance of research. What he found essentially proves the veracity of at least the first forty pages of the Book of Mormon. Those forty pages are teeming with cultural, linguistic, geographical, and historical references, but again, most of it lies in the background, in the assumptions Nephi wrote with as he composed his record.

He did not stop to explain, for instance, why they had to eat raw meat while in the wilderness (see 1 Nephi 17:2). This might seem strange to a casual reader. But even most in-depth readers won't realize that the wilderness they were traveling through is the Arabian peninsula, which, in those days, was a wasteland where thieves lay around every corner, ready to prey on unwitting travelers who made a fire to cook their food at night. Nephi didn't mention this, nor did he mention all the other aspects of their lifestyle he would've take for granted—and there are *many*. Brother Nibley concluded, "There is no point at all to the question: Who wrote the Book of Mormon? It would have been quite as impossible for the most learned man alive in 1830 to have written the book as it was for Joseph Smith."[140]

And none of this even comes close to accounting for the massive and shockingly consistent theological doctrines presented in the text itself. Nothing in the whole book could have been dreamed up by a twenty-five-year-old farmer, nor is belief in it something that could be attributed to a mere "psychological effect." As Elder Jeffrey R. Holland so thunderously testified, if a believer seeks to cast aside his or her membership in the Church, "it must be done by crawling over or under or around the Book of Mormon."[141]

I have seen that there is just as much evidence for the truthfulness of the gospel and the Book of Mormon as there is against it. As President Joseph F. Smith said, those who pursue scientific truth will come to acknowledge new facts as they emerge—facts that will more and more corroborate what we already know to be true. But for now, it comes down to what we choose to believe, whose side we choose to fight for, and which version of reality we are willing to accept. That is the existential dilemma of this life, the great question we are asked. How we answer will prove us herewith to our Father in Heaven.

Why I Believe

As others have said many times before, academic reasons—like those I just mentioned— for believing in the Book of Mormon are not the main propellers of our faith. They are not why we strive to be better people, serve others, go to church, or pay tithing. They are not why we pray to our Heavenly Father, or why we exercise any faith at all. The reason we believe is, again, that great equalizer: the

Holy Ghost. How we have been touched in our hearts and minds is undeniable. Our lives are evidence of that sacred contact.

All three witnesses of the gold plates of the Book of Mormon had, at one time or another, reasons to recant their testimonies. David Whitmer never even came back to the mainstream of the Church, but he never denied the object of his witness. He had seen the plates and an angel. He kept that testimony until the day he died.

There are many ways we know and believe.

My great-great grandmother believed. She was from Sweden, living there at just the time the missionaries made their way into Scandinavia. She and her family had stopped attending their Protestant church because of hypocrisy in the clergy; a friend suggested they go listen to the Mormons who were there preaching. At first, my great-great grandmother declined because she had heard so many awful things about them. But in the end, she gave them a chance, and, according to my great-great grandmother's daughter, "she said that from that very first sermon, she knew that she had come to the right place. She had heard the truth, and after that, of course, she didn't have to find any more churches because the missionaries taught her the gospel."

Soon after that, "they cut a hole in one foot thick ice in the river and were baptized in that icy water. Then they walked a quarter of a mile to their house to change clothes afterwards. They didn't catch cold or freeze, and that was a miracle in itself." But as the influence of the Spirit grew in that area, so did the influence of the adversary. With the arrival of missionaries came also the anti-Mormon literature, and thus began the persecution. But the Lord had a plan. "One night my mother had a dream," said my great grandmother Ranghilde Safsten to my mother. "An angel came to her in the dream and said, 'Don't delay moving to America. Go right now.' From that time, they just sold everything and went, all of them, Grandpa, Grandmother, Erick and Cemoria, Mama and Dad, and us five children, and Emil and Ida and Enes."

I believe because they believed. I believe because of the miracles that took place in their lives and because the Spirit spoke to them the way it speaks to me now. This experience was not unique—my great-great grandfather on the other side of the family survived the winter trek of the Willie Handcart Company when he was only two years old. His parents and family made the same kind of choices, received the same kinds of revelation, and felt the exact same Spirit as my Swedish ancestors did, and they sacrificed everything for it.

All these people, miracles, and pioneers, mirrored over nearly two hundred years—they are why I believe.

I believe because of the testimonies of millions, the miracles in billions, and the divinely inspired life philosophy that produces the greatest peace, understanding, and love for all beings the world has seen or ever will see.

I believe because of the stability of our lives—how consistently rewarding this belief system is and how miraculously abundant it is—and the morality the gospel lives and thrives by that, if followed, can make a near perfect society driven by love, founded in peace, and followed in joy.

I believe because of the inspiration and revelation I receive in the temple every single time I go.

I believe because I see and understand the happiness of the family life that we teach and promote.

I believe because of the miracles in my daily life and the testimonies of others who have felt and seen similar things. So many prayers have been answered as I have turned to external sources like scriptures that cannot be coincidence.

I believe because I see the great movement of the Church, the momentum that has been building up with each successive generation since 1805, and the prophecies of ancient and modern prophets being fulfilled before our eyes.

I believe because of the stunning existence of the Book of Mormon, a book entirely unique in the world's history. It has no peer to match it and is still without a plausible origin other than the one Joseph Smith gave.

I believe because I have felt the shocking reality that there is so much more going on than we as mortal, fallible, and physically limited beings can perceive if we don't care to pay attention or look carefully, which will be missed with a blink of an eye unless we pray with sincerity, pause, meditate, and listen and do as the Spirit directs.

I believe because I have knowledge of the great plan. It gives reason to our lives, purpose to pull us forward, and actual structure to this existence that makes so much sense. The plan is comprised of so much pulchritude that nothing in all the history of civilization has or ever will compare in how complete and all-encompassing it is. It offers answers at every twist and turn, but only if we care to actually learn it and live by and with it.

I believe because of the miracle of my life and my rescue from darkness and despair, with the love of Christ penetrating that darkness and pulling me out and into the light. I know the Church is true because without it, I would be a slave to addiction and my body's desires and appetites. Without the grand goals of the gospel, I would have little reason to fight, to hold myself to a higher standard, to live true freedom.

But of course all that can be dismissed if there is no willingness to believe, no faith, no desire to live as God commands. All knowledge is dormant without faith.

Yet this faith will be dismissed, at least by some as coincidence, brainwashing, or just some psychological effect. Just the brain convincing itself of something it wants to believe, whispering lies in its own ear. Just a trick, a great neurological game, all in a sinister effort to persuade itself that it needs to grow, developed, go through hard things, exercise control over the body instead of letting it do what it wishes, and be washed away in the winds of its desire. The brain, that cunning little con-artist, apparently *wants* hard work to be done and to be denied a steady stream of pleasurable chemicals. That's how the brain works, apparently. Just a series of coincidence and psychological effects adding up to a totally illusory life.

So why isn't the scientific branch of academia—with all its omniscience and intellectual authority, with all its power, reach, and prominence—studying this great psychological effect? Why hasn't it been able to explain this weird trick that has brought happiness and peace and unbelievable amounts of inspiration and ideas to so many people? What is it that makes the Saints themselves so successful in their work and family lives? Why hasn't science figured out that secret, deconstructed it, obtained the valuable brain waves emanating from the skulls of the faithful, and offered whatever wisdom is distilled from that psychological secret to the masses? And why hasn't any avenue of academia or scholarship determined the true origin of the Book of Mormon, if not how Joseph Smith explained it?

We're sometimes told it takes *courage* to break away from our faith, that it is a crutch true men and women do not need. Perhaps it takes courage to leave the institution you have been brought up in all your life, to forge a new identity for yourself and live without commandments and structure. But I would argue that it takes far more courage for an investigator to make the decision to *join* the Church than for a doubting member to leave it and for a believer to stand up to the pressures and mockery and laughter when their beliefs contradict the latest lifestyle trends.

It's easier to live without rules, a life of whims and desires. That's what we call the path of least resistance—let the wind and gravity take you wherever it may. On the other hand, it's much, much harder and takes far more courage to *willingly* live your life according to *new* rules and fight against the wind and stand up against gravitational forces—rules you've never lived by before and in obedience to a god you've never seen. All without artificial constraints without anyone in particular holding you to those new rules or compelling you to keep them if you don't want to. True courage is denying your own will and offering it upon the altar as sacrifice to Heavenly Father, who will then use it to your benefit, if offered in faith.

Our religion is not a crutch. It is a staircase, a mountain to be climbed. We are looked down upon because we have *true* courage—courage to deny ungodly parts of ourselves, live on a higher plane, and have total control over our appetites.

So before you think to cast away the fruit of the tree of life and venture into the mists of darkness to join those in that great and spacious building, realize first that it is not an ascent but a *descent*. And that the wine consumed among those raucous crowds will only deaden your senses, while the fruit of the tree of life does naught but enliven them and sharpen both the joy and pain of this life. *That* is courage.

I have tried the experiment of faith myself. That seed planted has become a tree of life, of whose sacred fruit I have partaken. Now I offer it to you. Take the seeds of the fruit and plant them. Try the experiment yourself. Whether you call the reason for it faith or the scientific method, I invite you to try the same experiment that I did and millions have done. Test it *for yourself*. Verify it again and again, as many times as you need to. Let this be a rousing cry to your soul to wake up and take the gospel seriously, for it is the only thing that truly matters.

A Wider Perspective

Many things—hard doctrines, contradictory evidence, and so on—we just don't understand and won't in this life. To this end, and in closing, I offer you this allegory presented by Elder Neal A. Maxwell.

> I should like, if I may, to share with you on this point the fine writing of your own A. Lester Allen, a dean and scientist on this campus. This is what I have come to call the "Allen Analogy" about time. Let me read you these lines, if I may. Their application will be obvious. Dean Allen writes:
>
> Suppose, for instance, that we imagine a "being" moving onto our earth whose entire life-span is only 1/100 of a second. Ten thousand "years" for him, generation after generation, would be only one second of our time. Suppose this imaginary being comes up to a quiet pond in the forest where you are seated. You have just tossed in a rock and are watching the ripples. A leaf is fluttering from the sky and a bird is swooping over the water. He would find everything absolutely motionless. Looking at you, he would say: "In all recorded history nothing has changed. My father and his father before him have seen that everything is absolutely still. This creature called man has never had a heartbeat and has never breathed. The water is standing in stationary waves as if someone had thrown a rock into it; it seems frozen. A leaf is suspended in the air, and a bird has stopped right over the middle of the pond. There is no movement. Gravity is suspended." The concept of time in this imaginary being, so different from ours, would give him an entirely different perspective of what we call reality.
>
> On the other hand, picture another imaginary creature for whom one "second" of his time is 10,000 years of our time. What would the pond be like to him? By the time he sat down beside it, taking 15,000 of our years to do so, the pond would have vanished. Individual human beings would be invisible, since our entire life-span would be only 1/100 of one of his "seconds." The surface of the earth would be undulating as mountains are built up and worn down. The forest would persist but a few minutes and then disappear. His concept of "reality" would be much different than our own.
>
> That's the most clever way I have seen time and intimations of eternity dealt with. It is very important that we not assume the perspective of mortality in making the decisions that bear on eternity! We need the

perspectives of the gospel to make decisions in the context of eternity. We need to understand we cannot do the Lord's work in the world's way.[142]

If we think about it, we'll realize just how much God has actually been able to tell us, whether directly or by inference, about the realm of the gods—a realm that, in this life, we are blind to. On the other hand, there are so many things we do *not* understand, but is it because God merely likes to be withholding or because the state of existence we're in now precludes our comprehension?

It's good to have questions. It's even good to have questions that are unanswerable in this world because of our mortal limitations. Think of how it will be when, in the next life, we receive direct answers to such ponderings. Perhaps we'll even find that we already know them, that they were veiled with the rest of our memories of our past existence. Whatever the case, at some future day, truth will be known. But until then, we must hold to our faith and the knowledge that we have enough.

Spiritual Evolution

Unanswered or unstudied questions lead to doubts. Doubts not attended to will provide fertile ground for anger. Anger misdirected and fueled by ego and excuses can compel a former Saint to apostasy.

I have seen so many fall away: former home teachers, close friends, and even my own brothers and sisters. Those losses, however heartbreaking, have been prophesied. As we get closer to that great day, the Church will cease to find its purchase in this particular nation and spread out to every corner of the world, becoming a global church and cause.

We are seeing before our eyes the parable of the wheat and the tares. The closer the world comes to the coming of Christ, the more confusing the issue of truth may become in our minds. But as those clouds blur our personal vision, the lines demarcating disciples and dissenters will sharpen. The wheat will be separated from the tares, and the sides will be set more and more in stone. The spiritually strong, those who are "grounded, rooted, established, and settled" in the gospel, will grow ever stronger, developing in the way God wants, while those with infirm foundations, whose seeds of testimony have been cast into shallow, hardened ground, will be scorched by the spiritual fires alight in today's society to be led away down forbidden paths.

The process of our Eternal Arc is almost akin to Darwinian evolution. Those souls with deeper wells of faith will make it and continue on the path toward godhood. Those driven by pride, ego, and defiance—all products of their own choices—will not. And the society that forms from the choices of the righteous will build up greater and greater beings, becoming more spiritually sturdy and powerful in the priesthood than ever.

It is true that some have greater spiritual capacity than others, and many simply seem incompatible with the gospel. But would God give hope and a body to a being He felt was not capable of completing the journey?

Surely none of us can complete the journey on our own anyway. That is why the Atonement is so necessary, why His grace is so amazing. Nature's evolution is cold, cruel, and cutthroat. It declares that might is right. But in our evolution, we are helped along by mercy and compassion. We are transformed by grace into beings we could not ascend to by our own pitiful strength. And with that power, *anyone* can follow the Eternal Arc to its glorious end.

All it takes in the meantime is throwing up a shield of faith—the shield that must come from within. We are all capable of that.

Chapter 7
The Fruits of Repentance

It is much easier to preach the gospel than it is to live it. It is easier to bear a testimony on fast Sunday than it is to bear the burden of the work the Lord requires of us the rest of the week. And it is even easier to type these words on my computer and offer hope to those readers who are struggling than it is to endure the fiery trials in my own life. I am guilty of this dichotomy, even as you turn the pages of this book. With it, I intend to rally the troops while staying safe and snug behind the surging battle line, away from the parries and thrusts of the bloodshed beyond.

But if you are reading this, I hope you feel, as I do about myself, that you owe something to the Lord. Looking at the blessings He has bestowed upon you, knowing the celestial ends He is preparing you for, and feeling the forgiveness of the Savior, a kernel of yearning to contribute to the work grows within; we know we are meant to help out and give back to the Lord by giving to others. You know that some of the change the Atonement promises rests squarely in your own hands. You know that once Christ has lifted you (and me) out of the dust, you are meant to walk with Him and do as He directs, wield the sword of the Spirit, and bring fellow fallen souls unto Him.

That being said, I want to begin this chapter with two stories. One is from literature and the other from history. They are examples of people who I believe recognized the gifts given them and did not waste the chance to change. And as a result, they changed the lives of others.

By "literature," I of course mean Harry Potter, and the character I want to focus on does not get his full focus until the climax of the final book.

The life of Severus Snape is undeniably tragic, and yet, in the rain of tragedy, there often blooms a flower of incomparable beauty. His tale began with loneliness. The only child of constantly bickering parents, young Severus grew up resenting others, insecure about his own identity as a mere half-blooded wizard while being poor and largely friendless at that. He lacked, and this made his little heart cold and hateful.

But a light entered his life in the form of Lily Evans. They became best friends for years, and young Severus was clearly in love with her, but his own prejudices and affinity for dark magic ultimately tore them apart. Severus had to watch as she fell for a rich, handsome, and popular athlete who always teased, taunted, and outright harassed him throughout their years in school. Lily and James went off together, got married, started a family, and received the love and adoration of the wizarding world. Severus, his life lightless, gave in entirely to his fascination with the Dark Arts and joined Lord Voldemort's cult of Death Eaters.

He lived this small and pathetic dark life for a while, in the company of people who generally accepted him and appreciated him but were obviously evil, being devoted to the Dark Lord and the rise of his order. This is the life he could have continued to lead, and he could have brought about the Dark Lord's ascension to immortality and great power but for one single opportunity to change.

Because of information Severus himself unwittingly supplied to his master, Voldemort planned to attack Lily's house and kill her new son, Harry, along with James and Lily herself. In this moment, Snape found himself truly torn between two worlds. It was drastic and stark, but it gave him a clear choice. Would he choose acceptance and fulfillment in the company of Death Eaters and the approval of his onetime hero Voldemort, despite He-Who-Must-Not-Be-Named's intention to murder the only person he ever loved? Or would he sacrifice all that and seek to save Lily's life, even though she didn't love him and had chosen to spend her life with his enemy?

Desperate for hope, Severus sought the aid of Albus Dumbledore. Dumbledore agreed, but Severus then faced his choice when Dumbledore asked him what he would offer in return for his help. In words reminiscent of the prayer of the father of King Lamoni, Severus hesitated, and then whispered, "Anything."[143] And so anything, *everything*, is consequently asked. Attempts to save Lily and James prove in vain, but this moment changed Severus Snape forever. No, he didn't suddenly become kind and loving like Lily. Though his temperament didn't change, his life direction did, and this change in trajectory and his subsequent choices went on to have massive rippling effects across the wizarding world that are too numerous to mention here.

I will say this: Severus is the character upon whom the entire Harry Potter series rests. Without his courage, choices, and change of heart, Harry would not have survived—not at the beginning, when Voldemort attacked his home and family, and not at the end, when Voldemort laid siege to Hogwarts. So it would not be inaccurate or untruthful to say that Voldemort and the Death Eaters were extinguished by an act of repentance.

Now for the other, nonfictional story. You may have heard of this man before, though his name is probably not as well known as Severus Snape's. This man was a member of the Nazi party in Germany in the 1930s and 40s, well-known for his business enterprises and silver tongue. He was also a womanizer who cheated on his wife repeatedly. He was a war profiteer, founding an enamelware factory to capitalize on the conflict of World War II. To save on costs, he employed Jewish laborers in his factory, but because their work was forced, they didn't receive a dime. Once penniless, this man became rich, powerful, and influential, capable of smooth-talking anyone and wealthy enough to bribe officials into ignoring certain of his side endeavors. Perhaps you've heard of this man or seen the film about him. His name was Oskar Schindler, who, in the midst of that hellish war and the attempted annihilation of an entire race of people, heroically saved the lives of over a thousand Jews in his factories.

Times like war always bring out either the best or the worst in people. Somewhere along the line, Schindler realized what his country was doing. He realized his part in it and, in an act of repentance, used his considerable resources over the years to rescue Jews from the worst horrors of the Holocaust. He used not just his wealth in this saving effort but also his factory, which became a sort of sanctuary where Jewish workers could be protected. He deflected investigations with flattery and bribes, talking down or paying off Gestapo officers who noticed his behavior. Eventually, he went totally broke, having used his wealth to care for and protect his workers. Because of the turning of Schindler's heart, over 1,100 Jews escaped extermination and lived to tell the tale. Today, there are more than seven thousand descendants of the Schindler Jews.

Both of these stories story demonstrate the potentially unending fruits of true repentance, the vast possible effects brought about by the penitent actions of single souls. The power and magnitude of the act of repentance, so simple and pure, can reach infinite proportions and reap eternal consequences. And though Snape was a bully to Harry and Schindler himself remained a womanizer and an alcoholic, the changes wrought in them were enough to save the lives of thousands of innocent people. And to this day, they inspire further good and heroism in all who hear their stories.

I believe we, each of us, can do the same. For that is our purpose: to become saviors on Mount Zion. But what's needed first is change. Repentance.

Blessings of Repentance: Why?

Repentance begins with humility—the simple step of realizing and admitting we're wrong. Humility is generally brought about in one of two ways: the first, by being compelled to be humble—Snape, for instance, was forced into a scenario that necessitated a difficult choice; the second, being truly humble "because of the word" (Alma 32:14), or in other words because of one's own decision to change. This was Schindler's experience, gradually realizing the full gravity of the Nazi regime by opening his eyes over a period of time.

Alma the Younger illustrated both of these paths in his sermon to the poor and lowly of the Zoramites, who had been cast out of the synagogues because of their exceeding poverty and received ridicule and scorn. Alma rejoiced when he met them, "for he beheld that their afflictions had truly humbled them, and that they were in a preparation to hear the word" (Alma 32:6). He went on to tell them, "And now, because ye are compelled to be humble blessed are ye; for a man sometimes, if he is compelled to be humble, seeketh repentance; and now surely, whosoever repenteth shall find mercy; and he that findeth mercy and endureth to the end the same shall be saved" (verse 13). Alma then asked them a hypothetical question: "Do ye not suppose that they are more blessed who truly humble themselves because of the word?" (verse 14).

Perhaps Alma was thinking of his own father, Alma the Elder, when he said this. The first Alma lived and worked among the wicked priests of King Noah until he heard the words of the prophet Abinadi. Though no doubt each priest knew the truth of Abinadi's words, Alma alone responded to the Spirit's rousing cry; he alone received the word of God into his heart. Because of this, he repented and changed. He was not forced into it by poverty, tragedy, or hardship. He was not compelled to be humble. He chose it.

And in speaking of being compelled to be humble, perhaps Alma the Younger was thinking of himself. In spite of the righteousness of his father, Alma lived a life of rebellion in his youth. He fought against the Church with the sons of Mosiah and frustrated the work of the Lord's servants. They were an active stumbling block to the growth of God's kingdom. Until—as you're undoubtedly aware— God answered the prayers of Alma's father and sent an angel to speak words of damnation and warning to them. Over the next three days, Alma felt the pains of a damned soul; he was "racked with eternal torment," and his "soul was harrowed up to the greatest degree and racked with all [his] sins" (Alma 36:12). It was in this state of spiritual torture, of nothing but darkness and "inexpressible horror" (verse 14), that he remembered the words of his father, when he had spoken and prophesied of "one Jesus Christ, a Son of God," who would come "to atone for the sins of the world" (verse 17). In that darkness, Alma cried out to Jesus to have mercy on him, to save him. He cried out his willingness to repent and change.

In one glorious, miraculous instant, he was forgiven. In describing the experience to his son Helaman, Alma the Younger said, "There could be nothing so exquisite and so bitter as were my pains.

Yea, and again I say unto you, my son, that on the other hand, there can be nothing so exquisite and sweet as was my joy" (verse 21).

Alma's friends, the sons of Mosiah, who had persecuted the Church and sought to destroy it along with him, shared with others this experience of death and darkness raised to life and light. They too repented and came unto Christ. Ammon, who went on to become one of the greatest missionaries of the Book of Mormon, rhetorically asked his brethren, "Who could have supposed that our God would have been so merciful as to have snatched us from our awful, sinful, and polluted state? Behold, we went forth even in wrath, with mighty threatenings to destroy his church. Oh then, why did he not consign us to an awful destruction, yea, why did he not let the sword of his justice fall upon us, and doom us to eternal despair?" (Alma 26:17–19).

It's a good and important question. Why didn't He? Like with Oskar Schindler, the Lord had every right and reason to let them spiritually perish. They would have deserved it. They had grown up in the gospel, their father was king over the land, and their best friend's father was the high priest of the Church. They knew better. They rebelled anyway, and it took a miracle to set them straight. Schindler too was blessed with riches and resources, even as he participated in a society driven by evil, and *he* wasn't good.

So why them? Why were they blessed the way they were? Do you think the Lord would have sent that angel to the sons of Mosiah for their own sakes? If so, why hasn't He done so with every other sinner in the world?

And the opposite question could be asked too: Once we're at the point where we have truly repented, where mercy has claimed us, why doesn't Heavenly Father just take us back to His presence?

I found a potential answer to both these questions in a lesson I heard at a singles ward family home evening I once attended, and it's here we get to the crux of this chapter and the first real grasp on the sword. The sister giving the lesson began by saying that we regularly thank the Lord for our many blessings, such as having the gospel in our lives, being able to live in a free country, having a loving family, being financially comfortable, or any number of the wonderful and unique blessings God provides and affords us. But then she pointed out that we should not be merely thanking God for these things as if they are specifically and only for us, but that we should be asking God how we can use these blessings to further the work of the gospel and bless the lives of those around us.

In other words, we thank God for blessings by *using* them, not merely by enjoying them.

And the answer to those two earlier questions is one and the same. From Alma's accounting of his repentance to Helaman: "Yea, and from that time even until now, I have labored without ceasing, that I might bring souls unto repentance; that I might bring them to taste of the exceeding joy of which I did taste; that they might also be born of God, and be filled with the Holy Ghost" (Alma 36:24). God gave undeserved blessings to Oskar Schindler to be used as a means of saving over a thousand innocent lives, and He went to such lengths to save Alma and the sons of Mosiah because they were in a unique position to in turn share their experiences, faith, and newfound convictions—indeed their very salvation—with others so that those others too could taste of the exceeding joy of the fruit of the tree of life.

The Fruits of One Man's Repentance

Indeed, to this end Mormon documented the prodigious fruits of Alma's repentance, so numerous that they nearly constitute the whole rest of the Book of Mormon. They begin as Alma inherits the title of high priest and chief judge over the Nephites. Though he later dropped the latter office, he retained the former throughout his life, continually going out to preach to the various cities of the Nephite nation. After leading the Nephites against the rebellious Amlicites and personally slaying their leader Amlici, he cared for his people spiritually, as they felt the judgment of God and were "awakened to a remembrance of their duty" (Alma 4:3), eventually baptizing (in the words of Mormon) "about three thousand five hundred souls" (Alma 4:5). That is three thousand five hundred destinies altered—three thousand five hundred eternities changed.

And that was just the beginning. He continued his travels from city to city, bringing souls to Christ "throughout all the land" (Alma 8:5). He joined with Amulek, and together they confounded the wicked lawyer Zeezrom, who repented and, after being healed from a terrible fever, immediately joined them in their missionary work. As they traveled and preached, they gathered thousands more souls into the fold, establishing the Church throughout, insomuch that "the Lord did pour out his Spirit on all the face of the land" (Alma 16:16). Even after literally decades of missionary work, Alma "could not rest" and continued in the work of the Lord (Alma 43:1). Soon after going forth one last time, he disappeared, presumably being taken up by the Lord, death or translation being the only obstacles that could halt his zeal and prevent him from further proving his repentance with accompanying works.

Alma said to the people of Ammonihah, "I would that ye should humble yourselves before God, and bring forth fruit meet for repentance, that ye may . . . enter into that rest" (Alma 13:13). Surely the Lord took him up to grant him that same rest he promised them, the reward for a good and faithful servant who was worthy of his hire and who did in fact "bring forth fruit meet for [his] repentance."

But the fruits of his repentance did not stop there. His sons carried on his legacy, passing on the mantle of high priest and prophet down until the time Christ visited the Nephites. They magnified Alma's work exponentially and aided in thousands more joining the Church of God—even uniting the Nephite and Lamanite peoples. In one of the more significant missionary stories of the Book of Mormon, a Nephite dissenter even called to his fellow guards' minds the words of repentance preached to his people decades earlier by Alma, Amulek, and Zeezrom (see Helaman 5:41). Just think—the former wicked lawyer is mentioned by name! Were it not for Zeezrom's conversion, so far in the past at this point, that reunification of Nephites and Lamanites might not ever have occurred.

Alma's fruits stretched much further than the Nephites, for the sermons he delivered are canonized in the Book of Mormon, thus allowing him to speak as if from the dust to our day, two millennia later. His timeless words on faith, the teachings to his sons, the example of his life—all have served and do serve still to enlighten and edify millions of Latter-day Saints of our time and build up the kingdom of God, preparatory to the Second Coming of Christ.

Think back and consider what spawned this story, what brought about the repentance, conversion, and eternal salvation of tens, perhaps hundreds of thousands of souls, if not millions.

Alma said it directly: "For *because of the word which he has imparted unto me*, behold, many have been born of God, and have tasted as I have tasted, and have seen eye to eye as I have seen; therefore they do know of these things of which I have spoken, as I do know" (Alma 36:26; emphasis added).

All of that because the word was imparted to him, because he heard an angelic messenger, felt the desperate need to repent, and literally found Christ shining in the darkness. Everything sprung out of that moment, the conversion and repentance of a single man and his perpetually unsated desire to spread the word of Christ to others.

That is the power of just this one man's repentance.

Now, how can we apply this in our own lives? Clearly, repentance spawned from humility is the trigger that starts everything. That is the seed planted that can grow into a tree that has the potential to bear much fruit of light and life. Such fruit contains seeds that can bring forth their own likeness: more trees bearing more fruit bearing more seeds, and on and on. That is the concept of eternal lives.

The fruit, of course, represents salvation, the tangible love of God, which is offered to all, and the only requirement is repentance. At any point in our lives, we can decide to turn around and look to God and live. We will even be given this opportunity in the next life. Think of that mercy! God is willing to overlook an entire lifetime of sin and offer a new life with Him, if we only look. Look, and we can truly live again—all sin forgotten.

I don't think it's possible for us to comprehend the magnitude of that level of love. Perhaps only a parent can come close. Alma's repentance, after all, could not have been possible without the prayers of his mortal parents. That goes to show that even when we are in a state of rebellion and spiritual darkness, like Alma was, Heavenly Father's arm of mercy still reaches out, just waiting for us to grasp it. That defiance toward a supplicating hand sums up much of society right now. And that was exactly the situation of Severus Snape, Oskar Schindler, and Alma the Younger before the light intervened.

The Hero Doctrine

Do We Know What We Have?

Think about what Heavenly Father did for Alma. It could be said that "much [was] given" unto him (D&C 82:3). A miracle of miracles, in fact—the miracle of forgiveness, of repentance, of mercy after so much time rejecting and outwardly mocking the hand that stretched out to him. And yet we have all been given the same thing. The Atonement: the joy and stability of the gospel, the hope of salvation, and the potential for exaltation. Realize that we too have been given much, the greatest of all the gifts of God.

But having been given that gift, now comes the moment of truth, for the question arises: What are we going to do with it? What are we going to do with all our blessings? Will we stand upon the Rameumptom and thank God for being able to live in a free land, for being born in the Church, for knowing the Gospel, and for having a higher station in life than the rest of the people in the world? In the words of Moroni in his letter to Pahoran, "Do ye suppose that the Lord will still deliver us, while we sit upon our thrones and do not make use of the means which the Lord has provided for us?" (Alma 60: 21).

We have similar means provided for us by the Lord, and we *must* make use of them. We must not take for granted our gifts, abilities, talents, and skills. If we do, we are in danger of losing them, for they are not meant merely for our own delight or entertainment, but also the betterment of all those around us. They are a means, not an end unto themselves, and the Lord has provided them for us for His purposes.

The same goes for the Atonement. Christ's grace first works on a personal level; His sacrifice was for each of us individually. But then, as we internalize that grace, through the Spirit and through the offering of our wills unto God to serve others, it spreads so that its healing and restoring power may grow to an unimaginably grand and epic scale.

What a joy it is to be a part of that work. Can you imagine what a privilege it must have been for that angel who spoke to Alma and the sons of Mosiah to be chosen for that particular errand, knowing the ripple effect it would have on the Nephite and Lamanite nations?

We too can be on the Lord's errand. We too can be angels in this life as we produce fruit meet for repentance and serve our fellow human-kind by doing our best to bring them unto Christ.

But of course, it's not just a privilege—it's a responsibility. We are meant to be part of the work of the Atonement, and just as surely as the prophet receives revelation not for himself but the entire Church, we are commanded to use the light we've been given to illuminate the path for all. Hiding our talents in the earth or shielding the glow of our candles so that others may not benefit from its light—that is Satan's command, not God's.

We are meant to be easers of burdens, servants of our fellows and hence servants of the Lord. As King Benjamin pointed out in his masterful sermon, those are the same thing: in serving others, we serve God, because that's what He wants; that is His work. Spencer W. Kimball said, regarding service, "God does notice us, and he watches over us. But it is usually through another person that He meets our needs."[144] Could any knowledge be more ennobling, more inspiring? God needs us! We are His hands.[145] We can be the instruments by which He does His work.

Those who have been sealed in the house of the Lord have received all of the necessary saving ordinances. This means that their lives can and should become about everybody else. When our own salvation has been sealed, we must then turn around and help lift others. And in that service, we further secure our own salvation—a cycle that pushes onward, like the simple mechanics of riding a bicycle.

Jesus's words after washing the feet of His Apostles illustrate this great commandment: "Know ye what I have done to you? Ye call me Master and Lord: and ye say well; for so I am. If I then, your Lord and Master, have washed your feet; ye also ought to wash one another's feet. For I have given you an example, that ye should do as I have done to you" (John 13:12–15).

The Savior's question—"Know ye what I have done for you?"—is answered by His admonishment: If we do know and understand His gifts to us, then it is time to give to others what we have already been given. It is time to share with our neighbors the light and love we've felt from our Savior to help bring them to their own repentance and rebuild their lives in Christ.

What We Can Do

So how do we do this? It begins with us. As we live lives graced by repentance, we gradually take on the qualities of Christ, in particular kindness and compassion. As we change and repent, others notice and come to see us as sources of goodness, as an example of what the gospel does. President Gordon B. Hinckley said, "Your own constant self-improvement will become as a polar star to those with whom you associate. They will remember longer what they saw in you than what they heard from you. Your attitude, your point of view can make such a tremendous difference."[146]

As the progress deepens, our lives become testimonies of the Savior, similar to beacons on a hilltop. What we believe and what we know will be represented by our whole persons, in everything we do. Lives changed by true repentance transform one's core being into something else, something luminescent and beautiful. President Hinckley further said, "Let us live the gospel. Let it shine in our lives. Let it shine in our faces. Let it come through our actions."[147] The words that we say, the choices that we make, the way that we dress and carry ourselves—all in all, our very countenances will, or should, reflect the light that dwells inside.

Some time ago, I attended an endowment session in the temple with my good friend Joseph Harris. He had to go in a wheelchair because his body was too weak to stand and walk. It was a genuine struggle for him to complete the session. When it was over and he had passed into the celestial room, a brother in the temple told me that he was humbled because of the example my friend set for him in going to the temple despite being physically handicapped. The brother told me his resolve to attend the temple more often was strengthened. No doubt others in that room were also touched by my friend's example, and perhaps you might be too. In fact, I bring up his example in part so his life can affect even more than just those at the temple that day.

Being Christlike is not solely about our own standing with God, whether we choose right or wrong. It is also about how we affect our spiritual siblings—our friends, our neighbors, and even our enemies. It is about being a part of the Atonement and blessing the lives of others. When we take on Christlike attributes, we better not only ourselves but also those around us. And when we change, the world changes.

Remember, the quintessential Christlike attribute of love. Love is what drives our Savior and Heavenly Father. Shouldn't it be what drives us too? Christ told His Apostles, "This is my commandment, that ye love one another, as I have loved you. Greater love hath no man than this, that a man lay down his life for his friends" (John 15:12–13). Note that Christ literally did this in giving up His mortal life for all mankind, and we are commanded to love one another just as He loved us. Does He mean, then, that we too need to die for others? I'd suggest a more figurative but still substantial reading. What Christ asks is that we fully devote the rest of our lives to the welfare of others—to give the extent of our entire lives for their sake, as He gave Himself for us.

Ammon, the aforementioned son of Mosiah, demonstrated this principle perfectly. His repentance led him and his brethren to be "desirous that salvation should be declared to every creature" (Mosiah 28:3). Why? Because they knew the darkness that awaited those who rejected thee Savior, and "they could not bear that any human soul should perish; yea, even the very thoughts that any soul should endure endless torment did cause them to quake and tremble" (Mosiah 28:3). They knew what God and Jesus Christ had done for them, and, not content to sit back on their laurels and enjoy the blessing of salvation alone, they were compelled by their gratitude to share Christ's love and mercy with everyone they could. They answered the Lord's rousing cry.

With this eternal perspective in mind, Ammon and his brethren journeyed into the land of the Lamanites to proclaim the gospel. Soon after the brothers split up, Ammon was caught, imprisoned, and taken before the local king. The king, Lamoni, was curious at this, and when asked Ammon to explain his motivations in coming, Ammon stated simply, "Yea, I desire to dwell among this people for a time; yea, and perhaps until the day I die" (Alma 17:23). Then, without a word about his purpose to proclaim the gospel to them, he said, "I will be thy servant" (Alma 17:25).

And such he did, taking care of the king's flocks, defending them and his fellow servants against rampaging troublemakers, and even tending to the king's horses. He was literally willing to give up his life, the remainder of his days, in the service of the Lamanite king. This willingness to sacrifice ultimately put him and his brothers on the path to giving tens of thousands, if not *hundreds* of thousands, the hope for salvation and potential for exaltation. But it began with just a desire to serve in whatever way he could.

Did not Oskar Schindler do the same, giving his whole life and all he possessed, to save the Jews of his factory? And did his actions not lead to the blossoming of thousands more, as well as inspiration for millions since because of his story?

The Lord told Oliver Cowdery, "Verily, verily, I say unto you, even as you desire of me so it shall be unto you; and if you desire, you shall be the means of doing much good in this generation" (D&C 6:8). I believe that all of us who are blessed by forgiveness should share that exact same desire. We should all want to be the means of doing much good in our generation.

The Lord needs us to do His will and so offers us the same promise He gave to Oliver: If we truly desire, the opportunities to do good will be given. We will have chances to change lives, and in that we have chances to change the world.

After all, our works are what give form to faith. As the scriptures say, faith without works is dead (see James 2:26). Or as Hobbes from *Calvin and Hobbes* said, "I think our actions *show* what's in our hearts."[148] Our faith is demonstrated in the works we do. Faith is an expression of belief. If we don't act on our beliefs, if we don't employ the blessings we're given, then faith is dead. Those beliefs become mere vapors of thought; the blessings lose their savor. If we forget the ends for which they are given us, are we really thankful for them, even if we claim to be in our prayers?

President Gordon B. Hinckley said, "You are good. But it is not enough just to be good. You must be good for something. You must contribute good to the world. The world must be a better place for your presence."[149]

All We Can Do

However, some, despite their desires, just aren't equipped to contribute or fight the way others are. For many reasons, that may not be their fault. I understand this fact from personal experience. But if we can't serve on the front lines of this great battle, we should not feel unneeded or passed over.

If you have not been able to contribute to the Lord's work as directly or formally as others, remember that God consecrates all service done in His name and for His work, regardless of how successful you are. The fruits are anchored in your willingness to serve, for God judges based on your deepest desires, on what you *would* do if given the chance. What matters is what you put into it. I believe strongly that all those who earnestly strive to live the Lord's teachings, wherever they are and in whatever capacity they serve, can receive the same glory and blessings as those placed in more accessible stations of this life.

Sincerity is absolutely necessary in seeking to be a servant to the Lord. We must sincerely *want* to serve, to help, and even to change the world. That is how we verify if repentance is real—if it is, we will try, because it shows how much we appreciate what God has granted us. Elder Jeffrey R. Holland spoke to those needed elsewhere in this grand cause:

> To those of you who have served or are now serving, we thank you for the good you have done and for the lives you have touched. Bless you! We also recognize that there are some who have hoped all their lives to serve missions, but for health reasons or other impediments beyond their control, they cannot do so. We publicly and proudly salute this group. We know of your desires, and we applaud your devotion. You have our love and our admiration. You are "on the team" and you always will be, even as you are honorably excused from full-time service.[150]

When I first heard Elder Holland say those words in the priesthood session of the October 2011 general conference, I cried a little, there in the cultural hall. I cried because I felt he was speaking directly to me, for I suffer from a medical condition that prevented me from serving a full-time mission.

Others who have been given honorable release from serving full-time missions will testify that guilt can still enter in—guilt that you are not working as hard or sacrificing as much as full-time missionaries. Guilt that, somehow, you weren't worthy enough to go or as capable or as needed by the Lord for His cause. There's no easy answer to those feelings other than to pray and further develop your relationship with the Savior. He will tell you when your sacrifice, even if it's just your willingness to sacrifice, is acceptable. And He will tell you what you can do for His cause instead, through the subtle whisperings of the Spirit.

So that verdict does not excuse from other aspects of the work. Instead, it as an invitation to spend one's free time, even one's whole life, in service to God, in the ways He commands through priesthood leaders and personal revelation. Though this attitude is not something that can be lived perfectly immediately, it can gradually be accrued over time.

Even as our responsibilities for others may begin with our own family, this is not where they should end. Joseph Smith set the bar fairly high when he said, "A man filled with the love of God, is not content with blessing his family alone, but ranges through the whole world, anxious to bless the whole human race."[151]

Likewise, full-time missionaries should not count their service finished when they step onto that homebound plane. As Elder Jeffrey R. Holland reminded all of us who have made that baptismal covenant and renew it weekly with the sacrament, "we are all enlisted."[152] Our debt to God is never paid in full. This is a gospel of long-term commitment—even eternal commitment.

None are exempt from God-given duties—we all have stewardships. These duties and stewardships are varied and can often go beyond the basic, universal commandments. President Dieter F. Utchdorf taught in the October 2008 general conference, "Every priesthood holder stands at a unique place and has an important task that only he can perform."[153] The same is true for men and women alike. We receive these unique responsibilities through prayer, personal revelation, patriarchal blessings, or maybe a quiet thought whispered to us by the Spirit during Sunday School. As President Uchtdorf put it, it is our duty to "lift where we stand."[154] All members of the Church stand in different places and have unique offerings to consecrate to this all-encompassing work. So we must not be ashamed or perceive our current callings as being "lesser" than others'.

Do bear in mind that the Creator of the world washed His Apostles' feet, a lowly job if ever there was one. In this way, we are all commanded to be servants, and all who earnestly strive to live this way—giving our all for others—will be blessed the same as any other faithful servants who seems to have "higher" calls. Recall Christ's parable of the talents; what we give is always dependent on what we are first given.

The Sweetest Experience

There is only one way to properly attempt to repay our debts to the Savior: bringing souls unto Him that they may taste of the same exceeding joy you have tasted.

The Lord said in latter-day revelation that we "should be anxiously engaged in a good cause, and do many things of [our] own free will, and bring to pass much righteousness" (D&C 58:27). In other words, we don't have to wait to do good until we are asked. Blessed by forgiveness for their sins, the sons of Mosiah took nothing for granted and desired, of their own wills, to take the gospel to the Lamanites, risking and giving years of their lives and not knowing if they'd ever see their families or loved ones again. And look what service they were able to render unto so many souls.[155] See the works they did and know that we can do likewise.

In the end, what will be the fruits of *your* repentance? What will you choose to do with the means God has given you? What mission can you serve in the place and time the Lord has set you?

A life lived with piety and virtue is dead if lived in isolation. This was the sin of those who worshipped atop the Rameumptom. As Christ did, we too must live for the sakes of others. Oskar Schindler did that during the darkness of the Holocaust, when lights were needed most. Oskar Schindler, though not nearly a perfect man, did exactly what God put him on this earth to do. He fulfilled the mission he was given.

Outside of a full-time mission, God has a mission for you too. He has one for me, for all of us. Whereas Schindler saved mortal lives, we have a mission to save eternal lives. We have power, potential, and possibilities that right now we can't even fathom. We have blessings to be thankful for and use in creative, life-changing ways. We must not ever forget those blessings, nor take our gifts for granted. The Lord gives us them for His work. We repent so others can too. We can never know if even the briefest experience can cause cascades of change in a fellow struggling soul. We know what Alma did to attempt to repay his debt to the Lord. Let us go and do likewise. And if we reflect and find it necessary, let us repent of selfishness, and then make our own lives about others'.

President Thomas S. Monson said, "The sweetest experience in mortality is to know that our Heavenly Father has worked through us."[156] Our prophet invites us to taste that sweetness, just as Alma did, and dedicate our lives to God, making our wills malleable in His hands. Let us always remember, "Unto whom much is given much is required" (D&C 82:3), and go forth and produce fruit meet for repentance with the sword of the Spirit.

Chapter 8
The Work Is Not Yet Done

With a constantly beckoning finger, the Savior coaxes us to a certain place of ascension, of communion with the Almighty that brings us closer to Him. A place where we literally and directly do *His* work of eternity, where *our* hands become *His*, where we become His sword, and break spiritual chains, unlocking the gates of heaven and hell and allowing passage upward. Not just for us, but for all who have ever lived. Because the spirit world is not perpetually visible to us, it is easy to forget that the plight of the prisoners is real, and consequently that our obligation to help them is also real and, as we know, vital to our own salvation.

The Dark Knight Rises, the final installment of Christopher Nolan's Batman trilogy, paints a vivid picture of the hopeless condition of Hell's captives. Midway through the film, a broken and beaten Bruce Wayne is thrown into a prison at the bottom of an impossibly deep pit. His fellow prisoners, some who have been there years, even decades, try repeatedly to climb out, but fail and fall every time.

The idea of this prison is to induce true despair in its occupants, for, as the villain Bane explains to Bruce, true despair must include some form of hope that is never fulfilled, but constantly drawing upward. But if anyone can do it, Batman can, right? However, Bruce already suffered severe injuries that preclude any attempt to climb out of the pit. He lies broken at the bottom with several other prisoners, all whom live without hope of ever escaping, except for the nagging, taunting light at the top.

And so Bruce takes it upon himself to rise up, recover from his injuries, and train his body to be able to make the climb. After months of effort and failed attempts, he finally manages to make the ascent and, to the cheers of his former fellow inmates below, emerges into daylight and new life. On the edge of the pit is a rope. Before leaving to go save Gotham once more, he almost casually tosses the rope down, thus giving the prisoners who previously had no chance to escape on their own the opportunity to be free once again.

In Batman's rise from the pit, we also see the story of Christ and the Resurrection. Bruce Wayne takes on the role of the Savior, conquering that formerly unbeatable foe of death. As he completes his ascent and reaches the light, he throws the rope down behind him, opening the way for others to follow after, to be "resurrected" as He was. By making the heavenward climb first, both Bruce Wayne and Christ build a bridge to liberate the captives of darkness and despair.

This parable does not merely reflect Christ's role, however. It also describes the way each of us, as Latter-day Saints, can be like Christ, living as "saviours . . . on mount Zion" (Obadiah 1:21). In the temple, we can perform, by proxy, saving and exalting ordinances for our dead, thus giving them the opportunity to go where they hadn't been able to before, allowing the prisoners described by the prophet Alma to his son Corianton the opportunity to cross that bridge and enter paradise, into the presence of God. All we have to do is go first. Every time we work in the temple thereafter, we're throwing down another rope into that otherwise hopeless pit of despair.

This work of rescuing the captives of death and hell is a constant one. In *The Dark Knight*, Batman's work after defeating the Joker and taking the punishment for the fallen Harvey Dent did not end the Joker's effects; they merely halted them for a time. A massive "apostasy" soon took over Gotham as a result of problems roiling beneath the surface, like wolves among the flock. Likewise, the work of God was not totally finished after the performance of the Atonement. The Apostasy came to pass less than a century after Christ performed the Atonement, and the vast majority of souls are in serious peril to this day. God declared, "My work is not yet finished; neither shall it be until the end of man" (2 Nephi 29:9). "My work is not yet finished" should ring in our hearts as a call to action to hasten the work in our lives, as the Lord is hastening the work on a much larger scale. His work wasn't finished thousands of years ago when that verse was written, and it certainly is not yet finished today. It won't be until an era that He referred to "the end of man."

The House of the Lord

The sword of this work is wielded no more efficiently and profoundly than in the temple. It is, as we all know, the "house of the Lord." But do we ever think about what that title means? To me, it means that it should not be unexpected to see the Savior Himself walking the corridors of that building, where He "ministers personally."[157] As it is His House, that is His right and privilege. The temples is a place as holy as heaven—a tiny piece of celestial real estate plucked from the heavens above and lowered down to earth that we may bask in the loving light of our true home and prepare our minds and souls for that celestial state of being. The temple is the consummate place for preparation for the greater kingdom, for the presence of God, His angels, and His Son.

The following words from David O. McKay describe the incomparable significance of the temple, in particular the endowment: "I believe there are few, even temple workers, who comprehend the full meaning and power of the temple endowment. Seen for what it is, it is the step-by-step ascent into the Eternal Presence. If our young people could only glimpse it, it would be the most powerful spiritual motivation of their lives."[158]

The endowment ordinance is preparation for that crucial moment when it is our turn to enter into the literal presence of God. If you have questions about the temple, or even doubts, I would suggest that the next time you go through the endowment ceremony, try approaching it with this perspective in mind. The truths taught and covenants made in that house are essential to be known and kept, as they give us the capability to physically walk back to God's presence. And that is one important reason we should go back often: to memorize the words that are taught and treat them as the eternally sacred knowledge they are.

For it is a house of learning, where we, like Christ, move from grace to grace, degree by degree. It is a house of prayer, where we can be closer to God than at any other place. It is a house of revelation, where we can commune with God and receive answers to those prayerful supplications. It is a house of order, where we make covenants to order our lives after the pattern of the temple. All in all, it is a place where we feel love and a palpable peace.

As the light of the gospel grows, so too do the shadows of darkness it casts, demarcating the wheat and the tares as the sides grow more defined in our latter day. As the world grows stronger, darker, and more wicked, the Saints, through the temple, must shine all the more brightly. For when we go to that house of light, some of its illumination transfers to us, and, as Paul wrote, we become living temples in our own right, places where the Spirit can dwell, vessels that bear the Spirit of the Lord (see 1 Corinthians 3:16).

The temple as the house of the Lord gives further significance to the scriptural phrase "cut off from his presence" (Alma 37:13). To be in such a situation is to lose access to the special proximity to our God found in His House. Our highest goal should be to keep and be worthy of our temple recommends at all times, for this is to keep ourselves as close to God as possible. Having a recommend entails just about everything else that is required of us and shows that we are on the right track. But though we may remain at the necessary spiritual speed, what matters to God is whether we're decelerating or accelerating. If we find ourselves decelerating, we need to get to the temple, *fast*.

The temple can help replenish that which our souls lack. LDS scholar Truman Madsen explained that "the Jews speak of the temple as the navel of the earth, the very place that heaven brings nutriment to earth"[159] —the source of spiritual nourishment. The rise and return of temples is an emblem and result of the Restoration of God's Church. When the Saints were in Kirtland, a true, legitimate temple had not been seen on the earth for nearly two millennia, and the great blossoming of the gospel has occurred at least in part because of its return.

Likewise, it has also been said that the Apostasy occurred at least partly because of the dearth of temples—the line of spiritual rejuvenation that was cut off, along with the presence of the Lord. To apply that historical lesson to our modern day, the more work we do in the temple, the harder it'll be for the adversary to get us to veer onto paths of apostasy.

The Ancient Order of Things

Joseph Smith referred to the ceremonies, rites, and rituals of the temple as "the ancient order of things."[160] There is little record of temples in the earliest days of the human family. But we know that wherever the gospel has existed, there has been some form of the ordinances meant to help us return to God, whether that was in the grand and glorious temple of Solomon or just the humble second floor of Newel K. Whitney's store.

In fact, the work of preparing mankind to return to God's presence began at the moment humankind left God's presence. At the expulsion of Adam and Eve from the Garden, when they were "shut out from his presence" (Moses 5:4), the Lord almost immediately gave them commandments to uphold and principles to live. The most noteworthy commandment was to offer sacrifices of the firstlings of their flock to God. The ordinance of sacrifice was the primary ritual whereby the Lord's people would remember God and look forward to the sacrifice of the Son, in which they could gain second birth into a further preparatory state. Of these kinds of rituals, Joseph Smith proclaimed, "Being born again comes by the Spirit of God through ordinances,"[161] and these ordinances, throughout the history of the world, have always retained this purpose; the ceremonial reaching back to God has been performed for a long, long time.

These rituals have existed for millennia, but the complete temple experience—ushered in with the Nauvoo Temple and later with the temples in pioneer Utah—included not just work for one's self but also work for the dead. After receiving the blessings of the temple for themselves, the Saints were able to receive them by proxy for lost loved ones. The story goes (as Truman Madsen wrote it) that when this doctrine was first taught to the Saints at large, which was shortly before the Nauvoo Temple was completed, there was practically a stampede to the Mississippi River to perform baptisms for the dead. Brother Joseph put a stop to it, of course, saying that, as with every other aspect of the Lord's work, it had to be done "in order."[162] And yet, look at that sentiment and faith at the beginning of this holy work!

It has been nearly two centuries since that time, but the work is not yet done. The Kirtland Saints knew it was up to them to begin this dispensation, and we need to remember that it is our responsibility to carry on that work with that same conviction. Our hearts must be as theirs: touched, filled, and turned to their fathers by the Spirit of Elijah. Elijah represents the work of the dead; his spirit—as well as the priesthood keys he restored to us—catalyzes this concern, this desire to help our ancestors receive the ordinances of the temple. Think of how many on this earth who have died without hearing or knowing about the gospel. Can we even calculate such a number? *That* is the breadth of the work we must perform in this latter day.

The final words of the Old Testament in the Bible proclaim, "Behold, I will send you Elijah the prophet before the coming of the great and dreadful day of the Lord: And he shall turn the heart of the fathers to the children, and the heart of the children to their fathers, lest I come and smite the earth with a curse" (Malachi 4:5–6). These same words appear in the New Testament when an angel described to Zacharias the work his son, John the Baptist, would do in life. They were again quoted by the Savior when He visited the Nephites on the American continent. And they were rehearsed by the angel Moroni to Joseph Smith four times in one night in September 1823, doubtless to his puzzlement. From the repetition alone, we can surmise that those words must be essential to this dispensation.

And they are, for they contain the essence of the latter-day work. This is the day when every single aspect of God's work and glory is restored and being practiced in its fulness, for both the Saints of this dispensation and the children of God in every other age that has passed before it. This dispensation is meant as a "whole and complete and perfect union, and welding together of dispensations, and keys, and powers," that "glories should take place, and be revealed from the days of Adam even to the present time" (D&C 128:18). Scholars have even discovered similarities in the Kirtland dedicatory prayer to Old Testament texts and prayers that are connected to Solomon's temple of old.[163] All that was given to Saints anciently in the various dispensations has been restored here, including and especially the temple and all the saving and exalting ordinances therein.

That being said, some of the messages delivered in those ordinances have been tailored for our time. The endowment as it is presented in temples has changed a little over the years and, indeed, over the ages, adapting to fit the needs and weaknesses of society at various historical points so as to include "things that pertain to the dispensation of the fulness of times" (D&C 124:41). God adapts to the world, not to match their standards but to address their particular problems. Nephi reminded us that the Lord "speaketh unto men according to their language, unto their understanding" (2 Nephi 31:3). Times, customs, and even sins change. And though we live in the final dispensation before the Savior returns to the world, the work of God is not yet done.

Sacrifice

One thing that has never changed, however, is the sacrifice required at the hand of the Saints, especially when it concerns temples. Brother Truman Madsen wrote, "It is a characteristic fact that the Lord has commanded the sacrifice of temple building at the times when apparently our people were least able to build them; and the sacrifice has been immense."[164] Joseph Smith presented that sacrifice to the Lord early in his dedicatory prayer at Kirtland: "For thou knowest that we have done this work through great tribulation; and out of our poverty we have given of our substance to build a house to thy name, that the Son of Man might have a place to manifest himself to his people" (D&C 109:5). And as the Lord said, "After much tribulation come the blessings" (D&C 58:4). Never more was this true than in the fledgling days of the restored Church with the commandment to build the Kirtland Temple (D&C 94:1)—the first temple of this last dispensation—as the "first laborers in this last kingdom" (D&C 88:74).

That temple "cost more per capita than any other building in American religious history."[165] Joseph Smith himself helped out in the stone quarries, emulating the example of King Benjamin, who labored with his own hands for his own support. The builders of the temple were impoverished and barely getting by. Imagine that kind of sacrifice being asked of us in our day. To give all that we have away and use all of our free time doing extra work, straining, staining, and suffering? The dirtiness of that backbreaking labor makes them, I think, more clean than many of us today. They obeyed the law of consecration in a way we've never been asked to. Though we make covenants to that end in the temple, it seems that rarely do we actually offer to consecrate all of our resources to the Lord and His work, a requirement for our offering to be accepted and sanctified as the Saints of Kirtland were. It could not have been done without sweat, blood, and tears; that labor and sacrifice was an essential part, and it is from that work, that purging fire, that they—and we—are made perfect in Christ.

This trial of fire is one way the Lord has of preparing and purifying His people. Sometimes He does this harshly, in stark chastisement. For a while, the Lord condemned the Kirtland Saints for "a very grievous sin"—not building the temple (D&C 95:3). This might sound draconian until we remember what marvelous and eternity-changing works are done in the house of the Lord, and how magnificent and everlasting the blessings are that God could only dispense to the Saints through it for both the servants and the served.

The Lord's commandment to His people was for their sakes, not just for His. It was a matter of preparation for greater things. Contributing to the building of the temple back then was just as much a commandment as being worthy of a temple recommend is today. Both are acts of preparation for the endowment of power from on high. And in today's wicked, strife-filled world, our trials and challenges are generally more spiritual in nature, not temporal, like theirs.

However, it could be said that building the temple with the Saints' own money, labor, and perspiration is equivalent to our contemporary duty of attending the temple and performing the various ordinances for the dead. We do not get paid or thanked for it; it is done on our own time, and we are often asked to sacrifice precious time and energy to do so. Temples, especially those outside of Utah, can often require hours, sometimes even *days* of travel to attend. Our personal sacrifices of just a few hours' time pale in comparison—especially to the Kirtland Saints.

Without such an output of devotion, would the Saints' faith have been strong enough to withstand the persecution that would follow? How is it for us, whose trials are much less severe? Do we appreciate what we have? Perhaps the trials some of us have to work with are that we *don't* have such trials and are expected to learn, grow, and expand our souls without them.

The sacrifices of the Saints are all the more to be admired when we realize that they didn't understand what exactly the temple was all about. They didn't know of baptisms for the dead, the initiatories, the endowment, or the exalting power of temple sealings. They sacrificed without knowledge of what that sacrifice was for, just as Adam sacrificed the firstlings of his flock for many days without knowing the reason.

They did it because it was commanded of them, and only after it was finished did they come to know the full extent of what they were doing. Such is the Lord's pattern throughout the scriptures and our own lives. As mentioned earlier, "After much tribulation come the blessings" (D&C 58:4). Only after we step into the darkness is the light turned on. To put it another way, the Lord can only catch us once we've made a leap of faith. But today, we know why temples exist. So do we not stand in greater condemnation for lack of participation in a work that we actually understand? I fear that we might.

The Saints knew it was the will of the Lord, and so it was done. They believed Brother Joseph, even if, like Adam, they knew not the purpose their sacrifices. This sincerity of faith was shown in their attendance of the dedicatory services, and here all their faith was rewarded, all their labor paid, and all their prayers answered as they witnessed miracles and events that had been prophesied in the scriptures. They spoke in tongues, saw angels, and felt the burning Spirit that literally alighted on the dedicated house of the Lord. Christ Himself and the holders of the priesthood keys in ancient times visited and appeared to Joseph and Oliver Cowdery inside the veil. And as we learn from the Doctrine and Covenants, this was just "the beginning of the blessing which shall be poured out upon the heads of [Christ's] people" (D&C 110:10). The *beginning* of the blessing—the blessing being temple work and thus salvation and exaltation, both for the living and the dead—of temple work in our latter days.

Covenants

In doing the Lord's work, we invade Satan's territory where he once invaded God's. It was in the Garden of Eden, a place with startling similarities to the concept of the temple, that Lucifer vowed to destroy the work and glory of God. It is in the temple that we cancel out his sometimes stunningly effective achievements in this world by doing work for those in the next.

Like Bruce Wayne in that pit of despair, once we ourselves are saved, it becomes our duty to help save others. Our own ordinances are done only once, and every time afterward our efforts are expended in helping others make the same ascension Christ helped us make. Our lives, when consecrated and bent toward the work, can be lives of pure service. To be an instrument of God is perhaps the greatest honor we can receive in this life, prophets have said time and time again.

The Lord does not expect to do all the work Himself. He expects us to do it; He commands it, or, put in other words, offers us the privilege of doing it. He does this for a specific reason: the point of this world is to become like Him, do good, and ultimately become uncompelled, independent beings. As C. S. Lewis put it, "He leaves the creature to stand up on its own legs."[166]

To aid us in doing His work, the Lord gives us certain blessings and protections, particularly in the form of the sacred garments. While people of the world often mock the temple garments and those who wear them, we understand what they truly are, and I believe we have sinned if we forget about their function and purpose. It is meant to be a personal shield of protection to us as long as we are doing our work here upon the earth—a shield to keep us safe for as we wield the sword of justice in defense of truth and virtue.

The garments are also meant as emblems of remembrance that, when noticed, call our mind back to the covenants we made in the temple. The process of remaking covenants we have broken also cleanses us, just like the sacrament. This is why we are commanded to return to the temple often, not only to help save others but also to purify ourselves and reorient ourselves on the path of the straight and narrow.

Covenants are at the heart of temple work and can establish the most powerful connections in the world if enacted righteously, serving as both sword and shield. When we are obedient in keeping our covenants, Heavenly Father is compelled to action, to respond with His blessings. The empowering equation of covenant making has been offered freely by God to His children throughout all of time. The temple is the only place we can make the most solemn and significant of those covenants. We are washed as the garment is placed upon us, and it is only with clean hands that we can grasp the hand of God as He lifts us up into His presence.

One might ask why formal covenants are so necessary. Many have questioned the necessity of baptism into one particular religion, believing God just wants us to be good people and He'll sort everything out in the end. This is an understandable philosophy, but all the same, it is a philosophy of men, not of God. We hear the same thing about marriage—that it's just a piece of paper and people don't need it to know they love each other. Well, dear readers, this too is not of God. In God's kingdom, we make commitments that are recognized by witnesses, both mortal and angelic, to be recorded officially in the book of life and on the records of the Church forever after. Covenants are, among other things, a public declaration of truth and commitment to a cause.

It is a similar principle to saying prayers. Why say prayers if God already knows what we need? Because we have to show faith first. We have to ask, knock, and request of our own will and choice before God can pour down the treasures of heaven upon our heads in whatever form we need at a given time. Notice that God did not appear to Joseph Smith until after he asked, on his knees in prayer, and after his faith was tested by a satanic assault on his soul.

When we draw near unto God, He draws near unto us, and thus we are close enough to grasp hands with Him in covenant. It is up to us to make that step willingly, thereby showing our faith. Making a covenant—formally committing ourselves to staying close to God—gives Him an official reason to trust us and offer His blessings as a consequence. Those who are not committed enough to make covenants and deal with the subsequent consequences are those who are lukewarm about this important work, and therefore they too are not of God.

But why can't God just see what's in our hearts? Because our actions and commitments and, yes, covenants *show* what's in our hearts. And because without stark boundaries, there's too much wiggle room and space for self-delusion and deception. Are we really as good as we think we are? Without the iron rod to judge it by, it's hard to tell. Covenants hold us to a hard and specific standard from which we can either hold fast to or deviate. That standard remains straight so we can determine where we are in relation to God and know when we've left His presence. Chromatically speaking, if we lack a white foundation, it's easy to justify and rationalize gray behavior, even as we slip further and further into the black.

This danger also illustrates the need for absolute truth and plain and simple commandments to look to as we climb up the slippery slope of this world. Without truth, God, or covenants, we have no handholds to grip and will inevitably fall, with no strong reasons to remount that ascent.

We make covenants because "mine house is a house of order, saith the Lord God, and not a house of confusion" (D&C 132:8). Covenants keep us committed, and the covenants made in the temple are the supreme commitments; those who do not keep the covenants that they have made in the temple will be in Satan's power. We can either choose to obey and hearken to God's will and remain free or be made slaves to the whims of the devil. This is one of the reasons the temple is such a powerful place; what happens inside can either exalt with glory or condemn to damnation.

I believe God wants desperately to exalt. That is why He wants to help us honor the covenants we make with Him. That is why He allows us to return to the temple and remake covenants we've broken, to repent and recommit ourselves to Him. It's what we are given the opportunity to do every week in sacrament meeting. And that is the essence of His work, what He has promised to do in exchange for our good will—picking us up every time we fall and keeping us on the path to eternal life. The garments, and the covenants associated with them, helps us remember.

The whiteness of the garments represents the purity we are spiritually clothed in as a result of Christ's Atonement. Our human bodies are mortal; they get dirty and at times function improperly, and though our bodies may be cleaned and washed and administered to, they can never be truly cleansed or purified on their own. Thus, the white garments cover our spiritual nakedness, blanketing us with the purity of the Atonement.

Additionally, *if* we remain true to those covenants, the garments symbolically shield and protect us until we finish our work upon the earth. As I was told once in a priesthood blessing, that can be a long, long time, and it means that in this life we are perpetually on the Lord's errand, meant to be doing the His work. The garments remind us of this obligation. Elder Neal A. Maxwell once asked, "How much sin occurs because people momentarily forget who they really are?"[167] One could say that all sin happens because we forget what's right, who we are, and what we're meant to do. So remember the temple garments and do not forget—as we are so prone to do—that as long as we are alive, we have been called to do His work.

And for all of us here, still on the earth, that work is not yet done.

Other Reasons We Go

As important as it is to make covenants and participate in the work of the dead, there are more reasons we go to the temple. The Lord knew this, and so He described the temple before it was even built as several different things, including a "house of prayer," a "house of learning," and a "house of order" (D&C 88:119). Sometimes we go to just pray to Heavenly Father and feel close to Him. Sometimes we go to learn more of the mysteries of God through careful observation and contemplation of the endowment. And sometimes—perhaps most times—we go to receive answers to questions or solutions to problems that have been bothering us.

The house of the Lord often serves as a house of prayer. When giving directions for the building of the Kirtland Temple, the Lord said, "And let the lower part of the inner court be dedicated unto me for your sacrament offering, and for your preaching, and your fasting, and your praying, *and the offering up of your most holy desires unto me*, saith your Lord" (D&C 95:16; emphasis added). Even expressing our desires to the Lord can be an offering of righteousness! In simple terms, this equates to a prayer, which we can do anywhere. But I think a prayer in the temple has a different tinge to it, a more sacred significance. Though we may come to the temple seeking special blessings, I believe that there we won't seek answers for selfish reasons. They will be the desires of our hearts, our souls; they will be desires for spiritual gifts like increased faith, greater worthiness, the ability to share the gospel, or the desire to overcome a particular spiritual problem in our lives—in short, those sacred requests that, if granted, will bring us closer to our Heavenly Father. In the temple, we pray for others as much as for ourselves, if not more so. Adding names of struggling loved ones to the prayer roll to be prayed for by others at the altars of the temple is a way of praying by proxy—and proxy work is, as we know, one of the primary functions of God's holy house.

Personal prayer naturally leads to instruction. My friend Stephan Peers once said that if we want an answer from a spiritual source, first we pray about it; then, if that doesn't work, fast in addition to praying; if that doesn't work, get a priesthood blessing; and finally, if that isn't enough, go to the temple. I add my promise to those of others who have born testimony of the miraculous powers of the temple in telling you that if you go to the temple, you will receive an answer to your prayers, whatever they may be. It may take multiple visits to get the full answer; the answer may only be a promise of "peace in this world, and eternal life in the world to come" (D&C 59:23) or the promise of a heaven-sent miracle at some point in the future, but it will come. It will come in the form of the Spirit, who comforts, brings peace, and whispers to our souls to be still and know that the Lord is God.

The Lord has promised us, "If thou shalt ask, thou shalt receive revelation upon revelation, knowledge upon knowledge, that thou mayest know the mysteries and peaceable things—that which bringeth joy, that which bringeth life eternal" (D&C 42:61). I bear testimony of this principle directly. I have dutifully kept track and can say with absolute truthfulness that every single time I have gone to the temple seeking inspiration or revelation, I have received it—even when I've told God beforehand I am going there for other reasons. Even when seeking answers to trivial problems—like solutions to writer's block when I'm working on a story or essay—the Lord has answered my prayers. I testify that He cares, and He can and will help you with your personal difficulties. It is almost as if the temple itself cannot hold back from the truth of heaven, from inspiring and giving answers to those visiting its grounds. That is its power, the spiritual energy of the Lord's house and very presence.

But bear in mind, what you learn in the temple may not always be the revelation you want at that moment, but it is the revelation you need or will need for the future. Whatever it is, I promise you that you can receive an endless flow of inspiration when you faithfully attend His house of instruction.

And the miracle of it all is that you can go again and again to learn, for that is why it is there: to "seek learning, even by study and also by faith" (D&C 88:118). My stake president told me before my own endowment that during the ceremony I shouldn't focus necessarily on trying to get everything immediately, but more on what I was feeling throughout. After all, he pointed out, I have my entire life to return to the temple to learn more of what it's about and what it all means. I relay that same message: though we are meant to learn the secrets, mysteries, and sacred things of God in the temple, we shouldn't feel stressed about learning something brand new each time. While this is a worthy pursuit, remember that learning, while it should be regular, should not be rushed. Line upon line, precept by precept.

Truman Madsen reported of fellow gospel scholar Hugh Nibley in the temple—"Twice a month Ann and I go to the temple. We gain something each time. I hear people say: 'But it's the same thing. How can you stand the sheer repetition?' For the same reason that Hugh Nibley and his wife did. I used to watch him. He concentrated; he focused. It is never just 'the same thing.' This week there is greater depth of understanding; this week there is more of putting things together. In the temple Hugh Nibley was like a child on Christmas morning. So can we be."[168]

Now, it's easy for Brother Madsen to say that there's so much to it, but it's a much harder thing to actually discern more each time. I'm sure that for many of us, it feels repetitive and frustrating. But bear in mind what Brother Nibley and Madsen have done with their lives. They devoted themselves to studying the gospel, to researching sacred history and religious anthropology. Throughout their lives, they widened their perspective on the gospel and, as a result, have been led to even further light and knowledge than the ordinary soul who goes to the temple. This has taught me that the more we devote ourselves to this gospel and the search for the great truths of this world, the greater our understanding of the temple experience will be and the more we can learn from it. It won't come easily. We may have to even go outside the core temple experience and learn the greater context of the temple and its ordinances therein in God's plan. But in doing this, we seek out God and come to better know Him, which, as the Savior has told us, is the definition of eternal life. Even eternal lives.

We can go to the temple to pray, learn, be personally sanctified, and be cleansed from the grime of the world we live in. The temple ordinances thus contain the same power and promise as the sacrament. The rites and rituals we perform in the Church, especially those found in the temple, are what Brother Madsen called "the Lord's pattern of nourishment."[169] There, in His House, we receive spiritual replenishing after our time fighting against and working in the world. I might liken it to taking a spiritual nap, from which we emerge strengthened and refreshed.

Beyond fulfilling the bare essentials and receiving the core ordinances necessary for salvation, temple work is meant to gradually pull us along the Eternal Arc and transform us into beings like the Savior Himself. When we do work for the dead, our experiences can be like the Sunday School teacher who learns more through preparation of the lesson than those whom he or she teaches. In the temple, we assist in the salvation of ourselves and others and become more like Christ all at the same time. The work is all-encompassing, enlarging, and deeply personal, just like the Atonement. And our own work is not yet done, either.

So whatever the reason you attend the temple, let there *be* a reason. For though we are counseled to come to the temple often, we should not let it become something casual or without meaning. I believe there is danger in looking at temple trips with an air of "business as usual."

That is not to say we shouldn't go regularly and often; rather, we should treat every trip to the temple as a unique experience, one preceded by and occupied in prayerful purpose.

As in fasting, we cannot receive spiritual strength from the temple if we attend passively, as if we are merely working and adding numbers to the spreadsheets of the Lord's Church. This work isn't about numbers; it is about individuals. You can't make up for the loss of one person by gaining another; that is not how God views His children. So when you're waiting there in the temple, take some time to look at the names for those whose work you will be doing. They are not simply pieces of blue or pink paper; those are real people who once lived, people to whom you are tossing that rope down, enabling them to climb out of the pit to ascend into heaven if they so choose.

What is more, the Prophet Joseph Smith said that those on the other side of the veil, including our own ancestors and lost loved ones, "are not idle spectators."[170] The accounts of prophets as well as ordinary individuals testify that those souls have the opportunity to witness their own temple work being done from the other side of the veil. Some on this side have even been privileged to see them rejoicing. So even if you go to the temple by yourself, remember that you are surely never alone once you are inside.

A Great Web of Light and Love

While we know the Spirit of Elijah looks backward to our ancestors, it also looks forward to future generations. We also desire for them to be connected to us, sealed together eternally by the priesthood of God. And this is the note I'd like to end on: family.

Have you ever stopped to think about why the Church places such heavy emphasis on the family? Many other churches do, but ours sees something more, and it is even more important than merely being together forever. Family is the core social unit for this life, for eternity, and for the role and purpose God has been preparing us to achieve from His own beginnings as our Heavenly Father. The reason we so highly value family and marriage between a man and a woman is because that is how we become like Heavenly Father. It is the unit of the eternal social structure; it is in His very name: Creator, Progenitor, Steward, *Father*. And without a doubt, the canonized words of Eliza Snow in the beautiful hymn "O My Father" indicate the existence of our Heavenly Father's eternal partner in this His eternal work, without whom He Himself would be incomplete and unable to be our God and Father. The family unit is not just good or enjoyable—it is necessary, even essential.

In this life, the family unit is how God's children are organized and linked together. And make no mistake, our eternal salvation is not brought to pass individually; we ascend with our families. That means we must *sacrifice* for our ancestors and descendants, our families in both directions of time, as well as for those whose lives we influence and integrate with on a daily basis—those we live within our homes, the only place where the work of the temple can be matched or mirrored. These twin houses of holiness are the two most important places in the entire world: "Next to the temple, the home is the most sacred place on earth."[171]

Both in God's house and in our own, we are prepared for greater things. Children learn to be adults in one and adults learn to be like God in the other. In both, everyone prepares to be in God's presence via teaching and experience. Both God's house and our own houses lift telestial souls to the terrestrial, and then to the celestial. Both houses are places where we can commune with God privately and personally and are houses of the most important instruction and inspiration. The work in the home prepares all of us for celestial society and celestial stewardship, while the work in the temple prepares us to physically and spiritually enter into the presence of God.

In the temple, we learn that neither man nor woman is meant to live alone, that every king needs a queen and every priest a priestess, and vice versa.[172] We learn that the necessity and glory of eternal marriage, eternal love, and eternal lives are only possible through the temple and the sacred ordinances therein. This is the supernally sacred role the temple has in the Eternal Arc.

President Howard W. Hunter taught that the whole end of temple work is to bring together the family of God.[173] Ultimately, every child of God is meant to be sealed to every brother and sister—strands of light illuminating our identities, bridging our eternal arcs, and weaving into one grand web of light and love and priesthood power that connects every soul who ever lived and binds all of God's children together in a journey into forever. That is the grand goal and epic vision of temple work, but it is not yet done.

The Lord said in 2 Nephi 29:9, "My work is not yet finished; neither shall it be until the end of man." What is the end of man? It is the beginning of gods, the salvation and exaltation of God's family. It is the end goal of all the temple work we do. Every name and soul we do work for is one step closer toward that glorious end. It is God's chief purpose: eternal, celestial life for all of His spirit sons and daughters, transforming men and women into gods and goddesses. Eternal lives—the everlasting generations of gods. That is the end, the finishing, of His work.

At the end of a sealing session I once did with my wife, the temple sealer told us something simple and short, yet powerful and profound. He said to us, with a smile on his face, "Hurry back." I remember those words to this day.

Hurry back to the temple. Hurry back into God's presence. He wants you there, worthily in His house. The temple stands for our grand cause, something we cannot be apathetic about, something that should be returned to again and again and again.

So hurry back, for the work is not yet done.

Chapter 9
A New Call for Consecration

To gather in all of Heavenly Father's children, all of our gifts must consequently be consecrated. If you've seen the original 2002 *Spider-Man* movie, you no doubt know its quite clear but poignantly true theme, one that echoes across all superhero stories and indeed our own ordinary lives: "With great power comes great responsibility."[174]

Young Peter Parker was graced with extraordinary powers, and only after rebuke in the form of tragedy did he realize that he can't just use them for selfish reasons like to have fun, make money, or pursue his own general interests. His life was no longer his—it belonged to everybody. And so he had to use his new powers to help people, stop evil from spreading, and inspire good in others.

Christ said it originally: "For unto whomsoever much is given, of him shall be much required: and to whom men have committed much, of him they will ask the more" (Luke 12:48). We understand that we few who have the gospel—especially with our knowledge of God and the realities of this world—have the duty to share it; this is the duty of one who is handed the sword of the Spirit, and it must be wielded in defense of truth and virtue in whatever battlefield we stand—for our placements are many.

The Hero Doctrine

Here, I want to introduce a new way this idea can be applied, because the work of the sword can be accomplished in myriad ways. Our gifts stretch beyond repentance and spiritual knowledge; like Peter Parker, we as individuals possess unique gifts and personal potentials that all too many of us waste or fritter away on fruitless paths. What we don't often understand is how essential to our individual aspirations of godhood these particular blessings really are and how tragic it can be if we keep them to ourselves. There has never been a hero, super or mythic or everyday, who attained his or her heights by mere dalliance in the powers bestowed to them.

In that spirit, I want to share a few words on the parable of the talents. Three servants were each given a different amount of money by their master to go invest. The servant who was given five talents returned with five talents more. The second, who was given two, also returned with two more. To each of these servants, the master gave what is perhaps the highest praise our God could give any of us: "Well done, thou good and faithful servant: thou hast been faithful over a few things, I will make thee ruler over many things" (Matthew 25:21). But the third servant returned with a confession: he did not invest his talent, instead hiding it in the earth. The master issued a rebuking condemnation to this wicked and slothful servant and then proceeded to give his talent to the first, leaving this last servant with not just less than he started with, but nothing at all. Imagine the agony of such a judgment.

Historically speaking, these servants were not mere slaves, blindly and anonymously doing their master's will; in the system of the time, these servants had the ability to rise up and progress, earning money and reputation for themselves in addition to their master, who was a benevolent patron entrusting his own riches in the hands of the servants, making them temporary stewards of those riches.[175] The ones in the parable who used their talents and gained an increase were given larger stewardships, and thus an increase of glory. The steward who failed to even try lost his stewardship entirely and ended with less than he started.

Author Orson Scott Card pointed out something else in this parable. The benevolent master's plan did not only benefit the two good servants; that alone wouldn't be helpful to anyone else. No, the plan allowed the two faithful servants to invest their talents in others, which wouldn't just elevate themselves but also those in whom the servants had invested. The master's plan worked to increase not just his own wealth, but other participants in the same economy. The more talents a faithful servant generated, the greater the benefit to those around him. And if a faithless servant hid the talent from the world, it benefitted no one and was utterly wasted.[176]

At this time, we aren't commanded to live the financial aspect of the law of consecration, giving up all of our worldly resources to the Church. The law of tithing asks of us ten percent of our earnings, which, as we know, is the lower law, implemented because the early Saints weren't spiritually able to keep up with the higher law. But even if we were spiritually prepared to live such a law today, it would be nearly impossible to do so in this era, given the legal and financial complexity of the idea. So instead, we live tithing, though we are asked to voluntarily and privately contribute what surplus we have to the various charitable causes within the Church.

To put it a different way, think about missions. Young men are asked to give two years of total devotion to spreading the gospel, which is about ten percent of their age at that time in their lives. For two years, they consecrate everything they have toward the work, using and receiving consecrated funds according to their needs. Afterward, they are free to live as they choose for the remainder of their lives. This could be seen as another implementation of the law of tithing.

Though we aren't asked to give full-time service to missionary work after the completion of those two years, all of us are still asked to live the gospel wherever we are, in whatsoever place or situation we happen to find ourselves in. Bringing it back around, this is similar to what the law of consecration asks of us.

To synthesize these two ideas, it could be said that we are asked to give not just two years of our lives to the Lord, but the entirety of them. And this is my challenge to you. This is a new call for consecration, not just our financial and material goods, but our whole lives—all our time, talents, and everything else we have been blessed with by God.

The Hero Doctrine

Our Talents

Notice the title of the aforementioned parable: the parable of the *talents*. That is a curious name, isn't it? Talents. Seems rather fortuitous that the name of a monetary unit two thousand years ago turned out to mean something so applicable to our modern day—talents as skills or abilities. But it is, in fact, not fortuitous at all. The modern use of the word *talent* comes in part from this parable,[177] as something we have been given by our master, something that we can develop and gain increase in, and something we can use to expand our own souls and in turn expand the souls of those around us.

This word *talents* features prominently in the concept and covenant of consecration, as set forth in the temple; among our time and all that the Lord has blessed us, we pledge and consecrate our *talents* to the building up of the kingdom of God.

In the Topical Guide, the word *talent* is listed as synonymous with *gift*, implying anything given to us by our Creator. Paul listed many spiritual gifts in his letter to the Corinthians, and one of the final messages Moroni imparted at the end of the Book of Mormon is an expounding of spiritual gifts with the exhortation to "lay hold upon every good gift" (Moroni 10:30). Why? To do exactly as Moroni immediately impelled us to do in his final plea, with which he closes the Book of Mormon: call forth souls unto Christ. Our talents are not, therefore, something to be boasted of, but rather freely offered. They are not ours to bury beneath the earth, but rather held up as a guiding light, burning brightly that others may be warmed and comforted by its flame. They are given for us to change the world. That is how Christ operates—through servants, or instruments. We are His instruments, and our talents are in turn *our* instruments.

We are also meant to "seek . . . earnestly the best gifts," as said by the Lord says in the Doctrine and Covenants before adding, "Always remembering for what they are given" (D&C 46:8). And for what are they given? To do as we covenant in the house of the Lord—build up the Church and establish Zion.

One excellent definition of consecration, as it pertains to this particular message, is found in the Doctrine and Covenants:

And you are to be equal, or in other words, you are to have equal claims on the properties, for the benefit of managing the concerns of your stewardships, every man according to his wants and his needs, inasmuch as his wants are just—

And all this for the benefit of the church of the living God, *that every man may improve upon his talent, that every man may gain other talents, yea, even an hundred fold, to be cast into the Lord's storehouse,* to become the common property of the whole church—

Every man seeking the interest of his neighbor, *and doing all things with an eye single to the glory of God.* (D&C 82:17–19; emphasis added)

Simply put, the glory of God is the salvation and exaltation of His children. Our triumph is His, and His is ours. So when you read accounts of prophets—or even Christ Himself—giving the glory to God, remember, that means we're the real beneficiaries. We are all in this for each other, and God and Christ are in it for us.

Those verses, by the way, come from the same section of Doctrine and Covenants in which the Lord said, "To whom much is given much is required" (D&C 82:3), serving as a reminder that with the greatest gifts also comes the greatest responsibility. Elder Boyd K. Packer stated, "You who are gifted may not be more deserving, but you are much more responsible than the rest of us."[178] Certainly this was true of our exemplar, Jesus Christ, the greatest among all the children of God, who also had the greatest task to perform, and, in accomplishing that task, became the greatest and most profitable servant of our Father in Heaven.

The Apostle Peter, that great spiritual rock of a man, lived a consecrated life, but not at first. It took personal censure by the Savior to put him on that path after he had gone back to a life of mere fishing—and not of men. Elder Jeffrey R. Holland dramatized this moment in his October 2012 general conference address, illustrating the exchange between the resurrected Christ and His senior Apostle, in which He asked Peter three separate times, "Do you love me?" Peter answered in the affirmative all three times, but, as Elder Holland proposed, perhaps without fully understanding the question. So Elder Holland elaborated what Christ may have meant with the following response, in Elder Holland's words:

Then Peter, why are you here? Why are we back on this same shore, by these same nets, having this same conversation? . . . What I need, Peter, are disciples—and I need them forever. . . . Ours is not a feeble message. It is not a fleeting task. It is not hapless; it is not hopeless; it is not to be consigned to the ash heap of history. It is the work of Almighty God, and it is to change the world. So, Peter, for the second and presumably the last time, I am asking you to leave all this and to go teach and testify, labor and serve loyally until the day in which they will do to you exactly what they did to me.[179]

If we are not serious about this work, then we do not understand it. Peter, it seems, did not, even after traveling as the Savior's right hand throughout the three years of His ministry. But because of the Savior's gentle rebuke, he went on to devote his entire life to the work, even to, as we also covenant, the point of dying for it.

If we love Him, we will do as He asks, whatever it is. Just as good works show our inner faith, so does our willingness to give our lives to His work show the degree of love we have for Him in our hearts. Those of us who have been endowed have made a covenant to live consecrated lives, giving our all to the Savior. That *means* something.

Now, does such consecration mean we live as full-time missionaries? No. What it does mean is that we all have the opportunity to consecrate our lives, even in seemingly mundane circumstances. Brother Card wrote,

When the Consecrated Saint has to choose between job promotion and the needs of his or her family, the family wins. The Consecrated Saint does not look at co-workers as competitors or rivals, but rather as people engaged in a common effort, whom he will help whenever he can. The Consecrated Saint becomes a valued employee because he seeks not himself; instead, he works with others as Christ would have him work. Because *all* his time and talents—even his time at work, his time in the world—belong to Christ, and therefore must be used as Christ would have him use it.[180]

Distractions from the Work

There are many ways to consecrate ourselves, even in seemingly ordinary lives or times of life. But even then, it involves a quite extraordinary commitment, one that is often all too easy for Satan to shut down. Elder Holland, in another talk, referenced the story of the First Vision and how, before the sacred moment in which Joseph Smith saw Heavenly Father and Jesus Christ, a force of darkness overwhelmed him and attempted to bind his tongue so he could not utter a prayer at all. As Elder Holland went on to say, such does Satan wish to do with all of us who purport to be God's potential servants. If he can bind our tongues and get us to shut our mouths, he has succeeded not just in destroying us but part of God's work as well.[181]

Our tongues can be bound by many things, but perhaps no more significantly than distraction, laziness, idleness, or apathy. Distractions come in droves these days, emerging in many forms, but some primary examples might include potentially useful or by-themselves-ambiguous things like the Internet, television, phone apps, or video games. One game console uses, "Never Stop Playing," as its slogan in its advertisements. Is that a satanic slogan or what? If the adversary can get us to live our lives solely in virtual worlds, offering mere simulated growth in the form of illusory increase, then he has successfully debilitated our real growth so we cannot live like Heavenly Father and do the true work of this world.

But even good things, if obsessed over, can take us away from the fight. Any one thing taken to excess—be it school, work, or even hobbies—may eventually become something that takes us away from the gospel and from our true missions in life. If Satan can get us concentrated on or worried about something other than our Father's work, something other than our souls or our families, he can effectively neutralize any contribution we might have otherwise made.

I repeat that if we are not serious about this work, then we do not understand it. While it is true that we are all at different levels of spirituality and capability, walking along at different points on the path, all of us have the same infinite potential and are all thus charged with advancing our souls to fulfill that potential. If we are on the straight and narrow, honestly and sincerely attempting improvement in our spiritual lives, *that* is an essential part of living a consecrated life. After all, we must strengthen ourselves before we can strengthen others; but remember, if we are doing it sincerely, in strengthening ourselves we *are* strengthening others.

But if we seek not to share the blessings of our own gifts, then I believe we are under condemnation. Christ said, "With some I am not well pleased, for they will not open their mouths, but they hide the talent which I have given unto them," followed a few verses later with, "Thou shalt not idle away thy time, neither shalt thou bury thy talent that it may not be known" (D&C 60:2, 13). That is a commandment and, with it, a warning about wastefulness.

To truly live the gospel, we must be anxiously engaged in a good cause—not just in *a* good cause, but *the* good cause. It is not just avoiding doing bad things but also choosing to do good things; not just abstaining from transgression but also making the world a better place; and not just resisting temptation but also destroying sources of that temptation, dismantling Satan's strongholds.

Likewise, what is the point of an inoffensive movie if, in addition to having no inappropriate content, it contains no enriching material either? It is merely idleness and ambivalence, which the devil quickly capitalizes on. Even if he can't get us to actively lead lives of sin, he can still "be reasonably well-served"[182] by dangling a carrot in front of us and letting us pursue interesting wastes of time, while he in actuality is taking us farther away from the work and the mindset that drives our participation in it.

Time is precious, limited, and often wasted. The Lord watches to see what we do with that time, as well as what we do with our talents, and we will be judged by it in the hereafter. Of the Judgment, He revealed, "It is required of the Lord, at the hand of every steward, to render an account of his stewardship, both in time and in eternity. For he who is faithful and wise *in time* is accounted worthy to inherit the mansions prepared for him of my Father" (D&C 72:3–4; emphasis added). We are commissioned, therefore, to use our limited, precious time for important, life-changing work.

We may not see ourselves as extraordinary, but as ordinary people with ordinary skills. In reality, we are an extraordinary people, who have been blessed with higher knowledge and the commandment to change the world. And with commandments, God always provides the "means whereby [we may] accomplish" them (D&C 5:34). We are fifteen million out of nearly seven billion. That is *far* from ordinary. And so because we have the extraordinary gift of the gospel, it is imperative that we live extraordinary lives.

The great English scholar Arthur Henry King wrote, "Once we have been converted and have laid down at Christ's feet whatever talents and tools we may possess, we find ourselves able to take them up again and use them for the Church in his name and in the light of his countenance."[183]

In a few words, it is our duty to build the kingdom of God—an extraordinary yet humbling calling. If we don't do it, who will? This faith is not consigned to the ash heap of history. It is, in fact, the *culmination* of history, and we are the ones who will bring it about. We cannot afford to merely blend in, to watch passively from the sidelines. We who are blessed with extraordinary powers cannot afford to live ordinary lives.

The Realms of Art, Music, and Literature

Thus far I have spoken of talents and gifts in an abstract, vaguely defined manner. While I will now discuss them in a concrete fashion, please know that the tangible examples I am going to share are not the extent or limit of what consecration holds, but merely an area where I think certain of us can show more devotion. What I speak of are the realms of art, music, and literature, where very particular talents can see their greatest shine.

We all have spiritual instincts gained from our Heavenly Father— those parts of us that make us His offspring. As I previously said, I believe our deepest spiritual instinct is to create. This is Heavenly Father's most prominent role, as Father, Creator, and Designer of the universe, engineering the unending expanse of the cosmos all the way down to the tiniest strands of DNA in the tiniest insect. He is a builder of worlds and, more important, a builder of souls. He creates, and because He does, so do we.

That creation takes form in many different ways. Some paint, some sing, and some compose. The fingers of one grip a brush tightly, while others dance across ivory keys. We create constantly, whether in art or in civil matters. Plowing and planting fields is creating. Planning cities and structures is creating. Assembling a team that can accomplish great things is creating. Finding solutions to problems of all kinds is creating. Writing in a journal is creating. Establishing friendships and giving light to the lonely is creating. And in raising children and teaching them truth, we are helping in the creation of a soul, joined together with our Heavenly Father in the gradual process of creating a divine being. All of us have some level of innate desire to form order out of chaos and organize disparate parts into something new, whole, and beautiful.

But there is purpose to His creation as well, and so should there be in ours. Why did God create this universe, this galaxy, this solar system, this planet? So we could have a place to dwell and learn and be tested. He created all of it not to boast, but rather to further His work of exalting His children. His is the noblest creative act of all, for it is meant for others. He is trying to create gods, and He lets us be a part of that work if we choose to join Him in His work and glory. I can't help but believe He wants us to use our powers of creation, our deepest spiritual instinct, to help Him in that noblest of works.

That is the kind of consecration I call for today: a consecration of our arts—even our unconventional arts—and of all our creative gifts to the gospel, to the work of saving souls and building gods and comprehending Heavenly Father.

What are the spiritual possibilities with art, music, and literature? I immediately think of the Savior, who expressed doctrine with stories, with parables that not only taught but resonated with literary value. Those parables are the applied principles of our beliefs and can be seen as our theology made concrete and real. Most stories today are what my friend Ming Stephens once called "interesting wastes of time"—stories that make us keep reading, but they in the end leave us empty and unchanged. Such works may be entertaining in the moment, but the reader then moves on and someday perhaps even forgets what he or she even read it at all. But the power of art and media can be great if used properly.

BYU professor Wendy L. Watson said, regarding the effects of media, "When you interact with someone repeatedly over time, it changes you. That's why what you watch on TV or read or see in magazines is so critical. So watch what you watch. Be careful with whom or what you are interacting. These recurrent interactions change your cells. They change your soul. They change your countenance."[184]

This is the power Latter-day Saint artists can have. With our artistic abilities, we can change human beings—and in doing so, we can change the world. Orson Scott Card said about the artists of society, "We who learn to create artworks and share them with the audience, we *invent* the world. We put visions and music and stories into people's memories. Even when the audience for our works is small, they have received a priceless gift, for there is a place in their memories where, because of our work, all the people in that audience are the same. Sharing the shaped reality of art is the closest we come in this world to truly knowing what is inside another person's heart and mind. For a moment, as an audience, as a community, we are one."[185]

I once heard Jenny Oaks Baker, a famous violinist and daughter of Elder Dallin H. Oaks, at a concert about to play a piece from the film score of *Romeo and Juliet.* She expressed her love for those characters and revealed that, in her heart, she hoped those two characters could one day be sealed. Fictional characters receiving temple ordinances? Perhaps not true doctrine, but that's how real literature can be to us, that we'd want to see that happen. That's the power it can have on our hearts and minds.

Take a look at today's popular media and witness what the other side can do with that great power. Look at the degradation our culture has experienced without even being aware of it. One easy example is music and music award shows. Satan has bound that industry. Remember what music used to be? Now look at what popular music is: catchy but cheap, dirty and unrefined stuff that furthers the work of degeneration of our culture. Even popular music used to be about love, but these days you'll more often find songs celebrating not love, devotion, and commitment, but merely sex itself, without subtlety or nuance.

Those who are gifted with artistic talents can and must reject that process and reverse that spiritual entropy, at least within the hearts of those few souls within our realm of influence. That realm expands with the increased quality of our work, and as we advance in skill *and* spirituality, we will have a greater impact on the world around us.

You are promised by the Lord that "if thou wilt inquire, thou shalt know mysteries which are great and marvelous; therefore thou shalt exercise thy gift, that thou mayest find out mysteries, that thou mayest bring many to the knowledge of the truth" (D&C 6:11). One of our great early Saint artists, poet Eliza R. Snow, is most known today for the words to the hymn "O My Father." Consider the effect that single hymn and its introduction of our two heavenly parents has had on the Church and on investigators over the past 165 years—a poem written after searching the soul and finding out the mysteries of God by inquiry, just as we are taught to in the Doctrine and Covenants. Sister Snow certainly exercised her literary gift, and she has brought many to the knowledge of sacred truths. Through her careful ponderings and poetic meditations, the existence of heavenly parents is now an essential doctrine of our faith.

According to Elder Douglas L. Callister, President David O. McKay even called the masters of literature "the minor prophets."[186] Surely Sister Snow could be thought of in that way, a veritable prophetess. What else could be out there for spiritual artists to discover? What other mysteries are there waiting to be solved by thoughtful, faithful poets or novelists? What new understanding can be depicted in the arts that cannot be depicted any other way? What spiritual truth is there that can be delivered to a world that would otherwise reject religion at face value?

Please bear in mind, I am not asking us to resort to simple moralizing. That is not the kind of teaching I am talking about, both because it lacks art and grace and because it is not effective. I am, however, asking us to use our art to package our testimonies in new, creative, and subtle ways. Creative gifts can help the world understand our theological principles and finer points of doctrine. Through the great avenues of literature, through visual arts and music and film, we can depict our theology and principles and share them with the world in ways they'll understand.

The prophet Alma wrote, "For behold, the Lord doth grant unto all nations, of their own nation and tongue, to teach his word, yea, in wisdom" (Alma 29:8). I find it similarly imperative to use familiar language and elements the world might find reasonable to bridge the natural intellectual divide and convey spiritual ideas that a secular audience wouldn't be open to initially. Secular academics, for instance, would almost never be open to learning about the gospel if it were preached to them using traditional testimony verbiage. The gospel might need to be shared instead in the verbiage of academia, a translation work as necessary as anything learned in the MTC. Through art or academia, we can build our depictions block by block, reasonable premise after reasonable premise, until it culminates in the end with the natural illustration of a particular concept or teaching, and the otherwise close-minded reader can say something to the effect of, ". . . Oh. That makes sense."

I personally see a strict divide in the field of Mormon literature today. Mormon writers almost always write either secular books for a secular audience or Mormon books for a Mormon audience. I see comparatively few literary envoys from God's kingdom to the great and spacious building. Those who have tried have mostly ended up abandoning their goal as diplomats and claiming new citizenship in the realm they were supposed to preach to. I see almost no one taking the torch from the great modern LDS storyteller Orson Scott Card, with his *Worthing Saga* or Alvin Maker series or the Homecoming novels, all of which are in the vein of which I speak: taking Latter-day Saint concepts and ideas to a secular audience, these in particular draped in the clothing of science fiction.

LDS literary critic Karl Keller wrote, "When someone becomes capable of creating imaginative worlds where Mormon theological principles are concretely true, then we will have a writer of the stature of Flannery O'Connor. Because she was a Catholic, she said, she could not afford to be less than a good artist."[187] O'Connor was not a great writer *in spite* of her Catholicism, but rather *because* of it. Such, Keller argued, will be the case with the great LDS writers. Our faith should inform our art, and because we have that advantage spiritually, we have the potential to achieve even greater artistic heights, if we choose to pursue them.

This was the vision of greatness called for by Elder Orson F. Whitney, one of the Quorum of the Twelve at the time in 1888, when he spoke of a new age of Mormon literature and gave the following as his caveat to those starting out: "Above all things, we must be original. The Holy Ghost is the genius of 'Mormon' literature. . . . No pouring of new wine into old bottles. No patterning after the dead forms of antiquity. Our literature must live and breathe for itself. Our mission is diverse from all others; our literature must also be. . . . In God's name and by his help we will build up a literature whose top shall touch heaven."[188]

That is a heavy responsibility, and it has only been in the last few decades that we've seen this promise begin to be fulfilled. President Spencer W. Kimball, in his inspiring 1977 article "The Gospel Vision of the Arts," wrote,

> We are proud of the artistic heritage that the Church has brought to us from its earliest beginnings, but the full story of Mormonism has never yet been written nor painted nor sculpted nor spoken. It remains for inspired hearts and talented fingers *yet* to reveal themselves. They must be faithful, inspired, active Church members to give life and feeling and true perspective to a subject so worthy. Such masterpieces should run for months in every movie center, cover every part of the globe in the tongues of the people, written by great artists, purified by the best critics. . . . Our writers, our motion picture specialists, with the inspiration of heaven, should tomorrow be able to produce a masterpiece which would live forever. Our own talent, obsessed with dynamism from a cause, could put into such a story life and heartbeats and emotions and love and pathos, drama, suffering, fear, courage.[189]

That was 1977, but Mormon art and literature, as glistening as it is with talent these days, has not yet reached its full potential, the capacity for grand masters and legends that echo the works of yesteryear. President Kimball regretted that this hadn't happened and, in the article, repeated emphatically that there should be no reason for this, that the Miltons and Shakespeares and Beethovens and Michelangelos have not necessarily run dry in our modern age.

The reasons they haven't emerged, I believe, have very much to do with the victories of the adversary on the battlefield of our culture and the individual soul in his sinister quest to bind the tongues of the faithful.

One possible impediment pushed into our paths by Satan is the lack of doctrinal understanding in our youth, the field from which the next generation of great artists will have to emerge. LDS scholar and literary critic Eugene England wrote concerning Elder Whitney's call for Mormon literature and suggested some of our mightiest doctrines as fertile fodder for creative expression:

To fulfill this hope, of course, Mormon writers need some theological literacy. B. H. Roberts, whom some consider Mormonism's finest historian and theologian, provides an extensive overview in *The Truth, The Way, The Life* and a concise explication of what is most dramatic and unusual in Mormon thought in Joseph Smith, the Prophet-Teacher. Others could be added: Joseph Smith, of course, especially the King Follett Discourse (uncreated being and godlike potential); Doctrine and Covenants 88 and 93 (God's relation to nature and to human agency); 2 Nephi 2 (the doctrine of essential opposition in everything) and Alma 42 (how the Atonement works) from the Book of Mormon; Brigham Young's sermon, "The Organization and Development of Man" (our basic need for eternal progression).[190]

Understanding these concepts and being able to articulate them to those of the world in new and persuasive ways could be an incredible boon to the work of the gospel. These ideas are ripe to be portrayed in ways literary and fantastic, creative and powerful. Certainly Satan is working to prevent our understanding of these great and eternal concepts and is active day and night in his fight to suppress our souls and halt our pens in rational declaration of these noble truths. In doing so, he quashes both our potential and that of those we may have taught or influenced. He shows us an easier path, full of distractions, apathy, and even condescension of our own religion and the art it has inspired, calling such traditional art "kitsch" and "cliché" in comparison to the art of the world. Many artists may think they have more important things to write about, true art to express, and dealing with and even teaching gospel truths is didactic and artless.

This point, I confess, is not a straw man. As we seek to portray positive principles and explore theology, there is the possibility for overt didacticism, and our efforts can be taken as moralizing lectures. Karl Keller said of such well-meaning but ineffective stories, "The didactic sells the Church without making it very believable."[191]

Brother Eugene England explained further, "Most thinkers in this tradition have understood that the more directly literature teaches, the less delightful and persuasive it becomes. In contrast, a vivid and honest story, interesting and complex characters, powerful images, and affecting rhythms and sounds can often move the reader into new dimensions of moral understanding and religious experience."[192]

What does this mean for the goal of consecration of the arts? It means our writers have a fine line to walk between didacticism and depiction, between sermon preaching and subtle sharing. But successful balance and execution on the required multiple levels can bring forth the greatness Elder Whitney, President Kimball, and President Packer called for.

Though we are all under the obligation of taking our message to the world, there are many possible ways it can be done. A story doesn't have to be explicitly about church, God, or religion. It doesn't need to be shallowly couched in the context of direct doctrine. Christ's parables weren't. But neither do they have to reveal simple meanings in the end. After all, the best parables are the ones that work on multiple levels, both literary and spiritual, and carry implications loaded with meaning that aren't brought up outright, as the parable of the talents does. Theoretically, it should teach through a natural understanding of the story and the lifelike characters therein.

Remember Karl Keller's words: "Creating imaginative worlds where Mormon theological principles are concretely true." The worlds we create for our stories, for our art—and I don't just mean in fantasy or sci-fi texts; new worlds need to be created for literary, non-genre works too—should be built according to the spiritual laws of the gospel. This does not mean LDS cosmological laws but theological principles and spiritual laws as we understand them with consequences as real as gravity.

Orson Scott Card's Ender series takes place in a futuristic earth where Mormonism doesn't turn out to be true. And yet he is still able to promote ideas—ideas Card must hold dear to his heart—about family and marriage and how important those institutions are. Those books are not didactic in the slightest, and yet they still teach, instruct, and strike readers on a different plane.

With Elder Whitney, President Kimball, and President Packer, I again call to LDS artists to produce dual greatness: in the eyes of both the world and the Church. It is not an impossible line to toe, though no doubt it will be difficult. To this challenge, President Kimball said, "If we strive for perfection—the best and greatest—and are never satisfied with mediocrity, we can excel."[193] President Packer added, "Let the use of your gift be an expression of your devotion to Him who has given it to you."[194] The best art, even *true* art, will lead one to God, via one way or another.

And so I say, in whatever gifts you have, whatever talents you choose to develop, make sure the Lord has a reason to help you. Show Him what you'll do with His help, that you will use it to bring to pass much good in this generation (see Doctrine and Covenants 6:8). Consecrate your gifts to God, and you will see them bloom and bear fruit that could not have otherwise been born. Search deeply to understand why you might have the gifts that you have. Realize that He hasn't given such to you to merely gain the glories of the world—but if, in the process of developing it, you *do* gain the glories of the world, use that unique platform to share the gospel, proclaim truth, and live as an example of Christian principles. Show the world what the gospel of Jesus Christ can produce, what the fruits and effects of His word can be.

From my vantage point today, it seems that our faithful musicians are the latter-day equivalent of the Psalmist in using music to express sacred things. Look at the extraordinary example of David Archuleta, who is not only a popular singer in the eyes of the world or just a devout and unashamed Latter-day Saint. He declared implicitly and courageously that his faith is more important than his art by serving a mission in the midst of his fame, leaving the spotlight to blend in with all the other white shirts and ties out there preaching the gospel. Now that he's returned from his mission, he is one of the most public faces of the gospel, and I believe he has a long life of success and indirect proselytizing ahead of him.

In David Archuleta, we find someone who has used—and most certainly will use in the future—his God-given gifts and talents to share the gospel with the world. He is able to preserve both his artistic integrity and his devotion to the Lord's work, and in fact combine the two in using his talents for the benefits of the gospel. The pattern he has set should be emulated by every Latter-day Saint artist the world over: establishing ourselves in the eyes of the world, and then using that influence and stage to bear our testimony to them and share what is truly important in ways they'll listen.

Other examples include the burgeoning violinist Lindsey Stirling and rock-and-roll musician Brandon Flowers, who have participated in the inspired "I'm a Mormon" public relations campaign. In doing this, in sharing the fire of our testimonies from atop towers of fame, we can become beacons and cast our lights across the world entire.

Sometimes, however, our artists can lose track of what is truly important. Sometimes that light is even purposefully kept hidden beneath a bushel. To this concern, I want to remind you that your art is *never* more important than your faith. Devoting ourselves to the creations of our own hands instead of the hand of the true Creator is a sad mistake that is repeated often amongst greatest artists. President Packer said, "We find that there have marched through this grand parade of mortality men and women who were sublimely gifted, but who spent all, or most, in the world and for the world. And I repeat that they may well one day come to learn that 'many men struggle to reach the top of the ladder, only to find that it is leaning against the wrong wall.' "[195]

The Lord has said, "Behold, there are many called, but few are chosen. And why are they not chosen? Because their hearts are set so much upon the things of this world, and aspire to the honors of men" (D&C 121:34–35).

I'm reminded of the story of the play *Corianton* by B. H. Roberts, popular in the late nineteenth century in Utah. Others eventually took it to Broadway, but not before stripping it of the spiritual values that once defined it. It lasted only a week in New York, failing miserably because it tried merely to gain the glories of the world and not to add glory to God.

The Book of Mormon said of such cases, "And because of this their great wickedness, and their boastings in their own strength, they were left in their own strength; therefore they did not prosper, but were afflicted and smitten, and driven before the Lamanites, until they had lost possession of almost all their lands" (Helaman 4:13).

Those of us who have experienced time away from the presence of the Spirit can agree that we do not want to be left alone to our own strength. We need God in our lives, and for Him to be there—I repeat—we need to give Him a reason to help us. That reason will almost always be that we need His help to convey His messages to the world. In so doing, we have to keep our eye single to His glory, to the building up of Zion.

Think of the story of the lepers—only one came back to thank Christ for the miraculous healing. How many of us have received of the glorious bounties and blessings of the Atonement, in particular our own creative gifts, and then gone off to do our own stuff, what *we* want to do with them?

Remember the battle that rages around us, the battle we're supposed to be waging—what this whole scene on earth actually is. This isn't some game where we can bide our time and do whatever we want or "love" until we die. This is a *war*. And in a battle that will determine eternities, we must bear in mind what is truly important and wield our swords against the foe that would bind us down. As the rousing chorus of "The Battle Hymn of the Republic" resoundingly declares, "As He died to make men holy, let us live to make men free."[196]

That quest for true freedom is the battle, the epic war of this world. In war, we have allegiances. To whom or what are you loyal? For whom or what are you fighting? For what cause do you wield your sword? Do any of us want to tremble at the great Judgment Day of God and try to explain to Him that our own secular artistry was more important than spreading the gospel?

How you go about that missionary work is up to you. With your creative powers, you can find new, exciting, and subtle ways of repackaging gospel knowledge. Whether it be through allegory, drama, science fiction, or however else you think you can communicate the principles of the gospel, do it. The Lord has *commanded* that it should be done. Endowed members everywhere have covenanted to consecrate all of ourselves to this work.

How blessed are we? As pointed out previously, fifteen million out of nearly seven billion. Why are we so blessed to have the gospel? Because it isn't just a blessing or a privilege; it's a responsibility. We cannot go around saying, "Oh joy, I am saved!"—we must remember *why* we are saved and so be about our Father's business, else we not be worthy of our hire, and instead be wicked and slothful servants. And though I have spoken primarily of the creative arts, this commandment extends to all abilities, all professions, and all places in life.

There is work to do. The great and marvelous work is meant to be done by us, and we must do more than our best. For right now, we are not yet what we can be. Wherever we are, there is still distance to travel, relying all the while on the grace of the Savior to make our efforts sufficient. The whole idea of eternal progression is about *constantly improving* what our best can be. *Best* is not a rigid, inflexible goal; it is fluid—it rises and beckons us ever onward, inviting lifelong participation in the wondrous work. Christ has given us eternal life. Surely we can consecrate our mortal lives to Him.

I call out to the rising generation of the Church. I call out to them to become masters of their gifts, whatever they may be, and become champions of the Lord, using the sword He has given them to fight His fight, spread the gospel to the world, and bring souls unto Christ.

Go find what the Lord has given you. It is your duty to find it, develop it, use it to further the cause, and then receive the promised multiplicity of blessings promised to faithful stewards. In all the evolution of the temple endowment over the years, the covenant of consecration, though we think it a relic of the past, is still there—it still applies to all endowed Saints, and it will forever.

We need great thinkers to emerge. We need artists and intellectuals—coupled with a testimony of Christ—to arise out of obscurity and invest talents in the spiritual economy of the world. Let us make art, music, and literature that brings souls to Christ. Let us infuse our entertainment with edification and grace our paintings and plots with meaning. Let our art lead to truth, to God. Let us not spend our time critiquing the Brethren, and instead spend it supporting them, sustaining them, and joining them in the war against the rapidly spreading evil that is so pervasive in the world today. The Lord and His servants need allies, not critics—champions with their swords in hand, not spiritual pacifists.

What can we expect to tell God at the end about our time spent on earth when, in this brief but immensely important life, we purely pursue our personal passions and not the work that will last through eternity?

We must find ways to instead channel those passions as they are meant to be used: for the Lord! We must use them to enhance, further, and promote the work and lay a foundation of understanding in the people who are searching for the truth, preparing them to receive the gospel when they finally hear it. Let us be witnesses of God at all times, in all things, and in all places that we may be in and consecrate our time and talents to the work of Zion, that the kingdom of God may be built up on the earth.

Chapter 10
The Answer Lies above Us

"We've always defined ourselves by the ability to overcome the impossible. And we count these moments. These moments when we dare to aim higher, to break barriers, to reach for the stars, to make the unknown known. We count these moments as our proudest achievements. But we lost all that. Or perhaps we've just forgotten that we are still pioneers. And we've barely begun. And that our greatest accomplishments cannot be behind us, because our destiny lies above us."[197]—Cooper

"'Mormonism' is a religion of refinement. It reasons that every man has within him God-possibilities, that salvation is essentially development. It argues that every man is potentially a great man. And through an inspired system, it offers the most extensive facilities in all the world for every man to discover himself and his possibilities, to so live that he can stand on the summit of his life and look back upon a trail of accomplishment and not a slough of wasted energies. . . . Very few at most, and perhaps none of us will ever carve immortal names in the roll call of the great of the earth. Maybe none of us will achieve outside the narrow pale of our immediate surroundings. But this much is certain: happy will be the man or woman who has tapped some hidden resource and given it voice. To such a character will come the sweet satisfying feeling of strengthening powers, of having done something that has made life a little nobler. God has generously blessed us all with talent. . . . Catch the silent thrill of growth!"[198]—Gordon B. Hinckley

The Hero Doctrine

*Y*ou will find *that this chapter is a little different than the ones that came before it. In previous chapters, I introduced the parable at the beginning and then proceeded into the gospel discussion for the rest of the chapter, but here I'm going to follow the story in great detail all the way through the chapter. The film is so complex yet so brimming in truth and gospel parallels that it would be a disservice to merely look at one moment or even the general arc of the story like in previous chapters. I hope that this chapter will encourage you to look more closely at other works of literature and cinema to see the gospel parables. We have been counseled to seek words of wisdom out of the best books and films, and the details of these stories offer a plethora of gospel parallels.*

The scene is at the cliff-end of a seemingly endless cornfield. We see a father named Cooper teaching his daughter, Murph, how to pilot a drone. He holds her hand and guides her fingers on a laptop's touchpad. She is grinning from ear to ear, loving this personal attention and instruction from her father and beaming at his praise. "Nicely done," he says, approving of the use of her talents.[199]

The screenplay perceptibly tells us, "Murph is in heaven."

Indeed, Cooper's relationship with his daughter is the emotional center of *Interstellar* and nearly a perfect reflection of our own relationship with Father in Heaven. It illustrates the divine pattern of the heavenly order: a parent teaching his or her child how to become like him or her.

In earlier chapters, we have done a thorough digging into the nature and character of God and what He is trying to accomplish. What I desire to do now, at the close of this book, is interweave those truths into the other messages discussed on these pages. I want to clearly define the doctrines of the mirror, the sword, and the shield, and how they fuse together to form the overarching, cosmic context of life and the plan of salvation.

First, let me remind you of my terminology. By the mirror, I mean our true identities and our potential destinies, the path of the plan of salvation, and our beginnings and endings as literal children of our Heavenly Father. By the sword, I mean the work we are meant to do, or the things we are meant to accomplish with the gifts and tools God has given us. And by the shield, I mean the work that Christ does, or those truths that give us comfort in the face of sin and despair—whether through the faith we are called to keep in the face of unsolvable evil or the quintessential covering and recovering provided by the Atonement.

To get there, we have to start with the fundamental problem common to all ages and societies of human history: finitude. In this life, everything eventually ends. More important, *lives* end. Mixed up in the great soup of the universe, individual lives really don't matter. Oh, they might matter to us in the short term. I enjoy being with my wife, and baseball is a fine sport to watch. But fast forward a century or two, and most people won't even know you once existed, let alone your hobbies and personal pursuits. And if that's truly the end, then no matter what you do or who you are, any honest search for meaning or attempt at personal development will inevitably fail and dissolve into dust. Indeed, because of entropy both physical and spiritual, that dust is our only possible destination. Life, it seems, is fundamentally absurd, and terrestrial philosophies often only manage to kick up more dust.

So where can we turn? "The answer," *Interstellar* declares in one of its taglines, "lies above us."

Above us. Outside our own current place in and understanding of the world. Not just among the stars, but also in those truths that cold reason and mortal thinking cannot generate on their own. Helpless and doomed we remain if we rely only on what we can chart out, lost in the dust clouds as we are. But there exists a realm largely unexplored above those clouds, a realm many theorize about, though few have actually sought out.

Therefore, whether purposefully or not, *Interstellar* teaches its viewers the patterns of heaven, where to turn to for answers, and what some of those answers actually are. At its heart, the film, like the plan of salvation, is about the relationship between a parent and a child and how that child can someday stand as tall as his or her progenitors. It laments that we, as human beings, have forgotten our potential and identities. That, on this earth, we have barely begun, and that our destiny, like the infinite universe itself, lies above us.

Mirror: "It's like We've Forgotten Who We Are"

One of the most prominent images in the mind-bending, space voyage *Interstellar* is, ironically, dust—the same stuff we wipe off surfaces and get caked with after a day of hiking. In the world of the film, earth has been blanketed in clouds of the stuff, buffeted by dry storms straight out of *The Grapes of Wrath*, the consequence of a blight that has devoured most of the world's food supply. Dirt clouds periodically roll over the countryside, forcing everyone indoors. Dust invades their houses, fields, and even bodies, so pervasively that they have to set the table with upside-down plates to keep them clean until they eat. Multitudes have simply begun to die. Dust has essentially taken over the world—and, significantly, the denizens of earth have accepted it and seek to survive as long as they possibly can *in* it, rather than look for a way of rising *above* it.

In this world, children are taught that the moon landing of 1969 was an elaborate fraud, conducted as an opiate for the to make them think space travel was possible back in the twentieth century when it really wasn't. After hearing that his children are being taught this institutional complacency, Cooper laments to his father-in-law, "It's like we've forgotten who we are. We used to look up and wonder about our place in the stars. Now we just look down and worry about our place in the dirt."

Could there be a greater encapsulation of the latter days? While all mankind is fighting over things both temporal and temporary, squabbling over our fortunes and our empires of dirt, the true answers to life's mysteries lies outside the blinding dust in the reflection of the mirror found above. But this earthly dust is the only mirror seen by those of the world: the natural man, one with the dust—children of nature and nature alone who incapable of ever truly changing. They don't see what we see: the divine pedigree that draws us heavenward.

When Moses beheld the glory of God and of all His creations—including ourselves, the vision of God's glorified children—he commented afterward, when his "natural strength" had returned to him, "Now, for this cause I know that man is nothing, which thing I never had supposed" (Moses 1:10). In this scene, Moses witnessed the full height of God, the vast breadth of His achievements, and in comparison called us, God's children, "nothing." Similarly, elsewhere in the scriptures, we have been referred to as "less than the dust of the earth" (Helaman 12:7), because we disobey while even the dust obeys God's basic laws.

Though Moses learned that man is nothing, he did not forget his eternal worth to God. When Satan came to Moses directly after this experience, he tempted Moses, calling him "son of man" (Moses 1:12). Moses fired back at Satan with the high truth: "Who art thou? For behold, I am a son of God, in the similitude of his Only Begotten" (Moses 1:13).

Moses hadn't forgotten his true identity. Yes, in glory, we are far from God. But we are His children, still of the race of gods—a seed compared to a Redwood. The world argues that to deny our natures is to deny our true identities, and while this is correct in a way, the message ignores the inherent duality of man. Alongside our animal natures, we possess *divine* natures, and it is up to us to decide which we choose to embrace: the dust of the earth or the sky above.

The world generally scoffs at any such inherent divinity. So, in God's place, we worship ourselves, devote ourselves to our desires, and strive to fulfill our egos and appetites, ignoring the chains of the natural man that keep us shackled to a corrupt earth and content with mere telestial glory. Clinging to crude clay even as, like the blighted earth in *Interstellar*, it is actively working to pull us down.

In the film, we see a vision of the kind of being God wants us to become, the kind of being He already is. The characters' mission to find a new home in the heavens is possible only because some mysterious being or beings created a wormhole for the characters to travel through. Like us to God, Cooper finds himself infantile compared to these five-dimensional beings, who are capable of space and time manipulation and exist outside the realm of our perception. Describing this higher perspective, Amelia says, "To them, time may be just another physical dimension. To them, the past might be a canyon they can climb into and the future a mountain they can climb up." Through the creation of a tesseract (much like a Urim and Thummim), they have access to "infinite time, infinite space." The operator is drawn to whatever point in space and time, whatever truth he or she needs by the thoughts and intents of his or her heart. Time is seen not as a flat line, but, like the wormhole, a multi-dimensional sphere in its fulness and self-containment—or, as we might call it, *one eternal round.*

What a profound view, the perspective of Gods!

Amelia hastens to add, "But to *us*, it's not, okay?"

But while in the tesseract in the climax of the film, Cooper awakens to the truth: "Don't you get it yet? 'They' aren't '*beings*' . . . they're *us*, people who've evolved beyond the four dimensions we know."

Ordinary human beings who have transformed into superior beings, capable of transcending space and time. The kind of existence God Himself may dwell in, and the kind of life He is trying to give to His children.

Similar to how God wants a relationship with us so we can learn from Him, the deep connection Murph forms with her father proves crucial to the eventual saving of humankind. Essentially, Cooper must send out an incredibly complex and subtle message across space and time that contains information essential to the mission. But Murph as an adult is only able to recognize that there's a message at all because she feels her father's love associated with it. Only then is she able to decode it and use it to benefit mankind. Without the depth of that particular parent-child relationship, humanity would have died out, stuck in the poisonous dust of earth as they were. Without it, they would have died as nothing.

The same stakes apply today. Without becoming something, we will end as nothing.

Our culture and its people look into the mirror and see nothing but dust. And perhaps that is what we are right now. God formed man out of the dust of the earth, after all. But there is something we may not think about, which is that every speck of dust that comprises our bodies ultimately originated in space, in the stars—from interstellar dust itself.

It's like we've forgotten all that, who we are. Our true identities, like our destinies, have been lost among the clouds of dust when we should be looking to the clouds above.

Sword: "This Is No Time for Caution"

Facing the end of the world, the people we see in *Interstellar* are constantly on the move. Packed-up vans and loaded trucks are going every which way. Everyone is looking, desperately, for hope.

"What are they hoping to find?" one character asks.

"Survival," another answers.

Survival and shelter—both *against* and *amidst* the dust storms, a blatant contradiction. Though their search may be genuine, the failure lies in seeking to be saved while remaining in the mess that blinds and chokes them, because they see no other way. They grasp blindly for salvation and meaning in a world where there can be none, for death is no longer creeping over the earth—it is enveloping it.

But Cooper has a sense of what is truly needed. In a world where people are trying to survive while remaining stubbornly in their current state, Cooper understands the only way that survival is actually possible: change. People need to transform and transcend their usual barriers.

This change is the effect wrought by the work of the sword: the use of our gifts to convince others of the error of their ways and beckon them out of the dust and onto a higher plane, for the answers are only found above us, not amidst us.

"Shall [the Son of God] save his people in their sins?" Zeezrom once asked pompously of Amulek.

"I say unto you he shall not," Amulek answered plainly (Alma 11:34).

"See that ye remember these things," Zeezrom said, turning to the crowd, "for he said . . . the Son of God shall come, but he shall not save his people" (Alma 11:35).

Amulek countered, "Behold thou hast lied, for thou sayest that I spake as though I had authority to command God because I said he shall not save his people in their sins. And I say unto you again that he cannot save them in their sins; for I cannot deny his word, and he hath said that no unclean thing can inherit the kingdom of heaven; therefore, how can ye be saved, except ye inherit the kingdom of heaven? Therefore, ye cannot be saved in your sins" (verses 36–37). Or, to put it another way, only those who are willing to change can be redeemed.

But though Cooper has a sense of this truth, in the beginning of the film he has no way to act on it. All that is at hand is his farm and his family. Without further instruction, he is powerless to do anything but wax philosophical.

In this state, Cooper receives a message, this time more specific and brought to his attention by Murph. This message is literally written in the dust, shaped in code by what appear to be strange anomalies in earth's gravity, presumably manipulated by an unknown, invisible—but intelligent—force. While Cooper doesn't know the source of this message, he interprets it correctly and *acts* on it. They are coordinates that lead him to the secret headquarters of NASA. Here, he learns of a mysterious project that has been keep hidden from the world's eyes, begun when distortions in space-time appeared near Saturn: strange gravitational interactions from out-of-sight "beings" who seemed to have an interest in the human race.

"Tell me this is where you explain how you're going to save the world," Cooper says to the underground board of officials after first hearing of this.

"We're not meant to save the world," the project's leader, Professor Brand, tells him. "We're meant to *leave* it."

It is as if the earth is using the dust storms to chasten her children, to snap humanity out of its complacent ways. We are not meant to remain where we are born, embroiled in our sinful behaviors. We are meant to leave such things behind and take to loftier skies, to take (quite literally) to the heavens.

Professor Brand asks Cooper for his help with this mission. They need him to use his extensive former experience as a pilot to captain an expedition to find a new home for humanity. He'd have to leave his old life behind and take on a new role and do work he'd never done before, all with the purpose of taking mankind out of Earth's atmosphere to a new home on another world. Meanwhile, Professor Brand would remain on Earth to solve the problem of gravity; without a major mathematical solution, it would be impossible to send large masses of people into space. This twofold mission was the Lazarus Project.

"This world's a treasure, Donald," Cooper remarks afterward to his father-in-law. "But she's been telling us to leave for a while now." Then, he adds, so wonderfully, "Mankind was born on earth. It was never meant to die here."

No, it was not, we can agree emphatically. But sadly, so many of us are still languishing in the mire, lost and blind—many willingly so. Others, whether they know it or not, are indeed searching for the answer amidst the storms.

We, members of the restored Church of Jesus Christ, uniquely know the answer—that it lies not in the dust, but above—and we can help them find it. The sword of the Spirit cuts down enemies by converting them into allies. This process brings souls unto Christ, including our own, to be saved and exalted by Him. Using that sword and turning eyes heavenward is our duty, our work to do—and that work is not yet done.

Thus, the dust of these latter days chastens the Saints as much as it chastens the world, a stimulus to hasten the work and divide the wheat and the tares. Elder D. Todd Christofferson wrote, "In addition to stimulating our repentance, the very experience of enduring chastening can refine us and prepare us for greater spiritual privileges."[200] In my own life, there have been stretches where I was not permitted to hold a temple recommend because of struggles with addiction. Such a rebuke is not so much a rejection from Heavenly Father as simply a way of warning us sharply that we cannot stay in the dry dust of complacency any longer. It is the beckoning finger of God, urging us on to higher peaks—to act, work, and ascend, lest we fall.

From whatever avenue it comes, the Lord is ultimately going to bring us to that moment of decision, where we must choose what world we wish to live in by either action or inaction. Will we use the sword—our potential, talents, and gifts—for good? Or will we simply set such things aside and instead set our whole attention upon amusements while battle rages?

Though our work is not yet done, neither is Satan's, and unfortunately he is much more active in fulfilling his desires than many Saints are in fulfilling God's. The adversary has made these last days a spiritual battlefield, with real dangers, enemies, and consequences to every action and choice. We must be as vigilant in wielding our swords and shields as any weary warrior. We are, after all, a chosen generation—the best of the best, the prophets have told us—and we are marked and targeted because of it. And if my own experiences have taught me anything, it's that even the best of us can fall, returned missionary or not.

In *Interstellar*, this spiritual peril is made literal. With limited fuel, Cooper's team must choose between two potentially habitable planets, each of which was first discovered by a previous explorer: the planet found by Dr. Mann or that found by Dr. Edmunds. Mann's radio signal indicates that his planet is an ideal world, with a beautiful surface beneath a layer of frozen clouds, so they choose his. Earlier in the film, Amelia describes Mann as "the best of us," the most brilliant and courageous scientist at NASA, so down they go to Mann's base camp. After waking him from cryogenic hibernation, he immediately embraces Cooper, weeping as he has not seen a fellow human being in many years. He immediately begins to tell them about the surface of the planet—how wonderful it is, how perfectly it can support human life for as long as they need. At first, the mission crew members are encouraged and want to see the surface to know for themselves, so Mann takes Cooper on an investigatory hike.

Then the minor keys suddenly play. Out of the blue, Mann attacks Cooper and reveals a devastating truth as he attempts to hijack the ship so he can return to earth: the results were faked; his icy planet has no surface, no foundation, but he couldn't bear to be alone anymore. As Mann leaves Cooper to die, he begs Cooper not to judge him: "You were never tested like I was," he says pathetically.

Yes, Mann, the best of the best, the most intelligent and courageous, was indeed tested. And he failed, utterly. Mann's very name speaks the truth about his soul; he is the natural man: selfish, fallen, and full of fear, sending out unambiguous invitations to come to him and his planet and enticing us to follow him into the foundationless great and spacious building so he is not alone. Satan too is a coward and seeks to bring down the rest of God's children with him into outer darkness, which is the definition of lightless solitude.

Many of us have also been tested, and many have subsequently fallen, unable to handle the pressures of the mission. The same goes on all around us as Saints are beset by doubts and hard doctrines. These pressures, like a hot oven, rise and rise until not only does a former Saint turn away from the path, but he or she actively goes about destroying fellow souls, persuading others to fall with him and rebel against that which he or she once risked everything for.

I'm sure you know some who are like this. I know too many—hence this book.

Both Professor Brand and Dr. Mann make much of a particular poem by Dylan Thomas about our reaction to the notion of death. This poem is repeated several times in the film. The first three lines, as recited by several characters, are:

> Do not go gentle into that good night,
> Old age should burn and rave at close of day;
> Rage, rage against the dying of the light.[201]

When Professor Brand reads the poem, it seems to be intended as inspirational; the film is, after all, about fighting for survival in the face of a seemingly sealed fate. But as Mann quotes it, we see the other side of the coin: in stranding his fellow humans and hijacking their ship, he too is refusing to "go gentle into that good night." As Cooper's father-in-law says wisely to him back on earth, "Don't trust the right thing done for the wrong reason. The *why* of the thing? That's the foundation."

Dr. Mann does successfully hijack one of the expedition's ships, which he pilots up to their modular craft, the *Endurance*. His clumsy attempt to dock, however, fails, killing him and blasting apart one side of the *Endurance* and sending the ring-shaped craft spinning rapidly over the white planet. Cooper and Amelia watch in horror—the *Endurance* was their only method of continuing the mission or returning home.

Then, in what is quite arguably the most (unexpectedly) thrilling sequence in the entire film, Cooper, with his extensive piloting experience, moves his ship to dock the *Endurance* anyway. To do this, he must draw perfectly parallel with the *Endurance*, then rotate his ship at precisely the same speed as the modular craft's speed, enduring inhuman g-force while maneuvering an insanely intricate path to latch on.

"It's not possible!" Amelia tells him.

"No," he responds. "It's *necessary*." But even as he moves to do it, he is struck with sudden uncertainty.

That is when he is reminded, "Cooper, this is no time for caution." Cooper then grins and dives in.

Scottish theologian William Barclay wrote about the word the craft was named for: "Endurance is not just the ability to bear a hard thing, but to turn it into glory."[202]

We might call such a thing "endur[ing] . . . well" (D&C 121:8). Not just carrying the load, but running with it. Above the icy planet, Cooper had to endure incredible gravitational force *and* perform that perilous maneuver.

In our lives, we are tasked with not only resisting Satan's temptations—the pull of his dark gravity—but also working to turn the tides of the entire great spiritual battlefield we call the latter days. We must not only keep our own souls, but help save others'. That is the work of the sword we are called to wield in defense of truth and virtue.

We can either wield it or be lulled "gently into that good night." That is our burden, we Saints of the latter days. Given the state of the world, the flames that have spiritually swept over the culture, the blindness that obscures so many sacred truths to so many eyes, and the riotous celebration of the great and spacious building over the whole earth—given all this, and that we are fifteen million out of nearly seven *billion*—could it be any more apparent how much the Lord trusts us to deliver His message?

"Something brought you here," Professor Brand reminds Cooper, and all of us. "*They* chose you."

Cooper, the father, was chosen by those strange godlike beings. But in the end, he had to hand the work down to his offspring, the next generation—the last to survive on earth.

Our prophets are wise and are inspired by heaven. But they are not responsible for the work on the lines and in the trenches. As leaders, as generals, they teach and guide us, but we are the generation who must act and rise up in such a way as has never been done before in the history of the world.

"The major work of the world is not done by geniuses. It is done by ordinary people, with balance in their lives, who have learned to work in an extraordinary manner."[203] That's a prophet, Gordon B. Hinckley, speaking there.

Early in the film, Cooper gives Murph some basic instructions on a science experiment and leaves her to perform it for herself. She does, and it prepares her mind for the rest of her life, for the work she would go on to do to save the world.

Later that morning, Cooper is driving in his truck with Tom and Murph when the tire blows. After examining the tire, Cooper instructs Tom to get the spare.

"That *is* the spare," Tom replies.

"Okay, patch kit," Cooper says patiently.

"How am I supposed to patch it out here?" Tom protests.

"Figure it out. I'm not always going to be here to help you," Cooper responds.

The pressure of our day, with all our temptations and distractions, can be immense. When it comes time to dealing with such stresses, we are the ones who will have to decide what to do and how to do it. Our teachers and leaders will not be there; it is on us. God gives us those tasks to see what we do with them. Without that pressure, without the heat of battle, would we ever learn to fight? Would we ever work at anything? Would we ever desire to be like our Father?

"Such complicated data," the robot TARS says to Cooper as he seeks to communicate the necessary quantum information from the black hole across space and time to Murph. "To a child . . ."

"Not just any child," Cooper reminds TARS.

Indeed, Murph is not just any child—and it is because her father fulfilled his paternal responsibility and taught her everything he could in their short ten years together. In the same way, we are not just children of Heavenly Father—we, millions among billions, have the gospel.

"What if she never comes back to it?" TARS asks Cooper, referring to the watch, a relic Cooper left with Murph as a token of remembrance before he went into space. In this scene, Cooper is using it to communicate, manipulating the hands with time-distorting gravity from another dimension, like the spindles of the Liahona. The problem: Murph had cast it aside in a fit of anger at her absent father years earlier.

But Cooper does not doubt. "She will," he replies confidently. He trusts that she'll realize the connection, that she'll remember who her father is, that he loves her, and that he's there, somehow, even though she can't see him. She'll recognize it, even if her brother doesn't.

The expanse of the inexhaustible gospel and developing faith in it—complicated data indeed. But we too are given something like that watch. "This do in remembrance of me," the Savior told His disciples about the sacrament, that token of remembrance (Luke 22:19).

As bizarre as it seems, God has faith that we will remember Him, and listen and love Him and accomplish the tasks He asks of us. Just as Cooper lets his daughter do the work under his direction, so does God give us the responsibility of carrying out His will, relying on *us* to bring about *His* purposes. It is always shocking (to me, at least) how extensively He relies on imperfect people to further the cause of the gospel. Not just imperfect as in mostly righteous with a few slip-ups here and there, but people with serious flaws and sins in pasts both distant and near. Why? Because, like the layers of soil packed atop the seed, such burdens give rise to growth, and God is just as interested in cultivating our souls as He is in sharing the gospel to those who have not heard it before. We are the work, His work, as much as any other wandering soul out there, and in spreading His gospel, we are often the ones gaining in strength, finesse, discipline, and glory, which are qualities only obtained by acting with the possibility of failure.

But He provides exactly what we need to make it through—so often *only* what we need. When told to build a ship, Nephi asked God only where he might go to find ore so he could make tools.

In *Interstellar*, the mysterious beings who seem to be working behind the scenes gave humanity only the minimum help necessary to do the job of saving the world. They created the wormhole to the other galaxy and the tesseract that allowed Cooper to communicate

to his daughter. Everything else, every other effort, calculation, act of
courage, or bit of necessary cleverness came from the crew members
themselves.

Thus, it truly is we who are God's hands, asked to think as much
as to obey, and to do the best we can in whatever way we're capable.
Murph had to do exactly that as an adult. As she grew up, she con-
tributed to the Lazarus Project the only way she knew how—as a
scientist and mathematician, spending her whole life working with
Professor Brand at NASA to overcome the problem of gravity.

Staring at the chalkboard filled with mathematical formulations,
Murph has something of an epiphany. The reason they never found
their answer was because they were all drawn up with the same underlying assumption about time, specifically the mortal perspective of its
linear nature. As a result, "each iteration [became] an attempt to prove
its own proof." In other words, the only answers they discovered were
completely limited and only arrived back where they started. Murph
calls such thinking "nonsensical," which can be more broadly applied
to most of (if not all) the philosophies of men, as they assume a reality
limited to their own perceptions. With a similar ceiling on our own
minds, this world does indeed appear "nonsensical," and through it,
gravity cannot be conquered, nor can there be a saving net to catch
and retrieve humanity from death, which Professor Brand had promised Cooper.

Witnessed here are the failures of cold reason when it seeks to
imitate divine saving truths. Human reason is by no means a bad
thing, but to rely on it solely is folly. To receive *real* answers, we
must discard our telestial thinking and build instead on a celestial
foundation.

Though Murph's foundation was not totally firm, her intentions
were true and pure. And so after realizing the futility and limitations
of her life's work, she transitions into trying to save who and what
she can. She visits her stubborn older brother, Tom, who lives with
his wife and son at their dad's old farm, bringing along a doctor
friend of hers. While Tom is busy, the doctor looks over Tom's wife
and son. "They can't stay here," he says gravely, for the dust is poisoning their lungs.

But Tom arrives in the door. Murph and the doctor try to explain, but Tom throws a punch, knocking the doctor to the floor, resentful that Murph would try to change his ways and uproot him from the home he's known and the farm he's worked his entire life. He kicks his sister out of her old house, denying violently that his son is sick, that anything is wrong at all.

Like Tom, the people of the world abhor the idea that they are somehow broken, flawed, and in need of rehabilitation. They sing with pride of how they are "born this way," instructing the young to follow their passions and encouraging all to live solely for themselves, thus denying their divine natures. Then they turn around and blame religion for the world's problems.

The contradiction is almost humorous: the world doesn't need God's help, and yet if God or religion are ever invoked, it is in blame for the miseries of mankind. If God is real, why didn't He stop such-and-such disaster? Why didn't He do anything to save them? Why doesn't God want us to be happy all the time? Why me? Why now? Why all this?

As if the only function a Father would serve is to make sure we're all comfortable where we sit. Sadly, even many (supposedly) religious believers proclaim this and see no need to change, to transform. I'm sure you've heard their pronouncements before. "God loves every-body." "God created me this way." "God accepts everyone."

All those are truths in one way or another, but they are all spun by Satan to speciously substantiate the sinister story of stagnation as salvation—the narrative that God will save us *in* our sins, that we are good enough already and God makes no serious demands of His sentient creations. Problems are blamed on institutions or cosmic forces rather than unbridled human nature. In this name, they claim the banner of peace.

And aren't we supposed to be peaceful? Aren't we supposed to eschew violence and avoid contention?

Remember this truth: Peace and complacency are *not* the same thing. And what they advocate for is complacency, not peace. Complacency is Satan's counterfeit of peace. It tells us to stay right where we are because it's good enough already.

Even as their philosophies fail and the state of the world clearly continues to crumble, they insist the ideas and traditions of religion are irrational, out of touch, are based on limited understanding (the irony!), indicative of ignorance, and motivated by bigotry. Such insistences end the debate before it begins. Religious believers are just not worth talking to or reasoning with unless their conclusions, narrative, and God match the world's. These are the blinders put on people by the adversary.

As Murph yells to a stone-faced Tom, the earth—everything Tom holds onto—"is poisoning [his] family!" Satan too seeks to poison our families. His increased activity amidst the children of God is ultimately the spur that will propel us to choose, whether we're ready for such a time or not. Yes, there is urgency, for the day of repentance will not be here forever, and a lukewarm attitude toward the work of the gospel will not be enough for us to endure the fires of the latter days.

And so it is our responsibility to combat popular but foundationless philosophies, those false answers without a surface, and replace them with the truth that comes only from above. We must help our brothers and sisters see in God a distant mirror of who we really are. The natural man will never save humanity because it seeks to keep humanity precisely where it is. But when we consider the spiritual heritage we hail from, when we are able to look into that mirror—not a hand mirror or one you might find above a sink, but a great and towering mirror vast enough to hold the image of a god—and see who we really are, even *the children of a god*, the matter changes. The sky suddenly seems higher, the universe bigger. Our identities widen. Our potential is greater. And we understand the true stakes of this world and our purpose in it: to help the Savior bring to pass the image we see in that mirror for ourselves and for all of God's children.

The close of day is coming. We are rapidly approaching a point of no return similar to Cooper's with the spinning *Endurance*. We are in the last days and must soon make our choice where we wish to stand, which orbit we wish to ascend to, which sword we will wield. It is no time to nurture doubts or let distractions divide our attention. It is no time for complacency with lukewarm convictions.

In short, it is no time for caution.

Shield: "Dad, Can You Fix This?"

> Cooper: "You sent people out there looking for a new home?"
> Professor Brand: "The Lazarus missions."
> Cooper: "That sounds cheerful."
> Professor Brand: "Lazarus came back from the dead."
> Cooper: "Sure, but he had to die in the first place."

Sometimes our swords falter and our strength gives out. The gravitational forces of this world can be too much. We can become wounded spiritually, often from our own choices and mistakes in our battles with Satan's army. Or perhaps we see God's seeming absence from the fight and become bitter. Our faith fades and our love recedes, and we lose the will to care about God's work, if we believe He's there at all.

Murph was just ten years old when her father left to go into space and didn't fully understand. Even if she did understand it, her father's departure was beyond heartbreaking. She had no idea when she would see him again, if she ever would. He didn't know either. The only reassurance he could offer her was a wristwatch that matched his own. Time would move differently when he was out there, he explained. When he got back, they would compare the two.

In bitterness, Murph took the watch and threw it across the room. She refused to talk to him anymore. Cooper despaired that he had to leave her like this. Holding her one last time, he added one last tearful promise: "I love you forever, and I'm coming back."

But despite his promise, years pass and he does not. He doesn't even so much as respond to the many video messages sent from earth over the years—veritable prayers from children to a father. And the children don't understand why. They think he abandoned them, or that he is dead. Their faith in their father quickly crumbles. They resent him even though we, as the audience seeing Cooper's perspective, know he still cares about them more than anything and thinks about them constantly. Professor Brand even explains to Murph, "There are many reasons why communications are not getting through." Indeed, Cooper has been prevented by time distortions, hyper-sleep, the wormhole, and the lack of resources in their interstellar travel. The possibilities for

Cooper's silence are many, but such mean little to Murph in the face of so much uncertainty back on earth.

One of the film's most emotionally powerful scenes plays out when Cooper gets back from Dr. Miller's planet (the first planet visited, which caused fuel supplies to be diminished), where the gravity is so intense that an hour there is seven years on earth. Steeling himself, he sits down to watch the sequence of video messages sent while he was gone—over the two and a half or so decades of earth time. He weeps as he watches his son grow into a man on the screen, as Tom tells his father about his new wife and sons of his own. It is clear that Cooper's greatest emotions are invested in his children's progress, taking joy in his posterity. But sadly, almost all of the messages are from Tom; Murph has remained just as bitter at her father as when he left. It practically stabs him in the gut when Tom reports that he and Murph have decided to let him go, to cut him loose from their hearts because of his strange silence over such a long time.

However, Cooper does finally manage to send a message to Murph. But the situation is complicated, to say the least—in an artificial tesseract constructed by five-dimensional beings, Cooper, witnessing an infinity of iterations of one precise moment in space-time, uses gravity to manipulate the hands of the wristwatch he gave to Murph as a token of remembrance at their parting. This watch is then able to transmit the quantum data that would go on to save the world. Yes, complicated, limited, and intensely subtle—and based entirely on the medium of Murph's love for her father. Because of that love, she's able to sense that a message is being communicated, and then she concentrates and ponders and works out in her mind what that message is. As she feels that love somehow communicated across time and space, she is able to interpret it, even though there's no way for her to understand exactly how or why it is happening.

Though Heavenly Father is not actively prevented from sending us messages, His way of communicating is not always intuitive; it requires active learning, paying attention, and looking for patterns. And when we finally manage to find His messages, interpret them correctly, and speak back to God in return, the truths we receive, the love we feel, and the heavenly relief we gain are not generally understood by those standing on the outside. At one point, Tom cynically mocks Murph for seemingly "praying Dad comes back to save us all." How often are we mocked for relying on divine influence, life after death, spiritual salvation, or even that there is a divine purpose of some kind hidden from casual, mortal eyes? Just for believing in the power of prayer and the familial relationship we desire to have with God?

When Cooper is genuinely trying to interpret the message in the floor dust of Murph's bedroom in the beginning of the film, his father-in-law, Donald, softly derides, "You wanna clean that up when you've finished praying to it?"

But we see the value in the scriptures—those who are "speaking out of the dust" (Moroni 10:27). We know that God still loves us, even when wickedness reigns in the world and we experience pain, suffering, and loneliness. We know we can depend on Him, even when we cannot see Him, even when He appears to be silent.

That dependence is vastly important, for He is our ultimate shield. He is what protects us from the blows and buffetings of the adversary. He is what heals us when dust overtakes and the pull of Satan's gravity threatens to drag us down into misery and woe. When men and women realize the futility of their best theories—the devastating truth that, like Professor Brand's Lazarus Project—they then cannot offer true hope against the certainty of death and finitude.

"It was all a sham," Murph reports despondently in a video message to her father, clearly stricken and more bitter than ever. Her mentor had just admitted to lying to her all this time as he lay on his deathbed. No one on earth was going to be saved. Only those who had already been sent into interstellar travel would make it. "Did you leave us here to die?" she asks her father.

Murph has been betrayed twice over, now by her father and her mentor. And none of them, the men she looked up to and relied on, were ever coming back. They were leaving her and the rest of humanity to starve and suffocate, without any hope of continuance. Dr. Mann and Professor Brand, the best of the best, the false messiahs, had failed them.

Humanity was in a fix, all right. It could be said that people of earth had been caught in the gravity of a black hole, from which there is no escape. Within the black hole, "not enough *can* happen," or in other words, growth and progress are rendered theoretical concepts; the fate is sure.

The black hole in the film, called Gargantua, is shown as a gorgeous sequence of two intersecting discs of flowing light. It is beautiful, brilliant, and shining—on the surface.

The reality is something else, and here we see a familiar pattern to Satan's. That light, which is so breathtakingly beautiful, is actually constantly being sucked in, pulled into a literal outer darkness. However, because of relativity, it is impossible to see it. The light, in other words, is a lie, a monstrous lie. It is merely a symptom of that awful monster—death and hell.

In the film, it also holds the key to completing the mathematical calculations so necessary to humanity's survival. Buried deep within the black hole is data that would reconcile relativity with quantum mechanics. If they could get that data, they might be able to conquer gravity. Of course, the insurmountable problem is that nothing can escape a black hole. No human can endure it—no information could ever be relayed out. It is an absolute, an impossibility.

And yet, entering such a thing was also *necessary*. Faced with this dilemma, Cooper dives, and again with a grin. Perhaps not fearlessly, but willingly, unaware of what exactly he will experience, but knowing it will give them a chance to save the world. And, skipping a bit, it does. They find the data. By that miracle of communication mentioned previously a few times, he is able to send it in a way that transcends the usual boundaries of physics to earth, where his daughter is able to finish the equation and overcome the problem of gravity. Humanity can then be lifted up and off the decaying earth and into the stars, where they will find their next home.

Black holes are despair embodied, a darkness so thick not even light can escape. Gravity is so powerful it compacts massive stars into dots. Christ, it could be said, surmounted a spiritual black hole. Our Savior needed to know suffering at the lowest level of existence, where all is crushed into infinitesimally small points: the great cosmic winepress, which He trod alone, "yea, how hard to bear you know not" (D&C 19:15). He took the burden so we could fly free.

"Did you leave us here to die?" Murph pleads to her father. Our Father answers . . . no. While death takes all, Christ swallows up death. Without the Atonement, without that descent into the darkest abyss, all would be lost.

But it is not. The secret obtained at that literal heart of darkness, the depths of Gethsemane, allowed human beings to break free of earth's gravity and escape the otherwise unstoppable effects of the Fall. The natural man becomes a conquerable enemy. Death is no longer to be feared. Even sin is not to be feared, as we rely on the covering power of the Atonement.

I use that adjective *covering* on purpose. We are covered while we learn. We are covered while we are unsure. We make mistake and owe a debt, and we are covered by the Savior. When Cooper tries to teach Murph how to change gears in his truck, she makes mistakes, grinding the gears and earning derision from her brother. But Cooper expresses no anger—only patience as she learns.

Shortly after the stick shift lesson, Cooper spots a mysterious drone over his fields and immediately starts following it in the truck. They follow it right into the cornfields, where they drive into the unknown, blinded by the stalks, with the craft in the air as their only guide, forcing them to keep looking up in faith at the thing that can see all rather than trusting their own eyes with what's right in front of them. This sequence serves as an allegorical foreshadowing of Cooper's expedition into outer space, a practice ground wherein his potential mistakes are "covered" by the comparatively lower stakes.

The Atonement allows us to act in error and consequently learn too, sometimes the hard way, while we practice. It reassures us with a great safety net that lies below the workings of this world. While the stakes are always high, there is always a way back up to where we were before. When we fail and fall and flail in the dust, He is there to lift us up and out of it and to wash the dust from our faces, hands, and hearts. With the Atonement, Christ raises us out of telestial gravity and into a celestial orbit—as long as we are willing to jump and take that leap of faith.

In the beginning of the film, Murph brings a broken spacecraft model to her father. "Dad, can you fix this?" she asks.

That's the trust she had in him. Then she felt his departure and lost faith. But finally, after receiving the message in the wristwatch and feeling the love in his parting gift, she remembers, rejoices, and reignites her faith, shouting in delight to her soot-covered brother, "Dad's going to save us!" Her faith was renewed. Why?

"It's love, TARS," Cooper explains. "Love." That was the literal physical medium by which Cooper transmitted the data to his daughter—a semi-scientific proposal from Christopher Nolan I find mightily similar to the doctrine of the Light of Christ, or perhaps the Holy Ghost Himself.

Cooper's crewmate Amelia gives a brief speech on its mysteries earlier in the film when explaining her connection to Dr. Edmunds, a Lazarus scientist who is most likely dead: "Maybe [love] means *more*—something we can't understand, yet. Maybe it's some evidence, some artifact of higher dimensions that we can't consciously perceive." Divine love, as she points out, is not simply a matter of evolutionary utility, an irrational kind of love. As a real power, it goes beyond the capability of the five senses to comprehend things unquantifiable to lesser beings like us, but still at the core of what makes us human.

Cooper loved his daughter all along, but he eventually came to love the rest of mankind just as much. Thus he dove into the black hole and overcame the failure of evolution observed by Dr. Mann earlier in the film: "Evolution has yet to transcend that simple barrier—we can care deeply, selflessly for people we know, but our empathy rarely extends beyond our line of sight."

Such universal and absolute love was the foundation of the Atonement. Nothing else, not money or duty or even the intellectual need for the act, could have motivated Christ to undergo such a soul-mutilating experience. Not only love for God's children in the abstract, but as individuals, for each of us. He endured the environment of that spiritual, physical, and emotional black hole for *you* and, as I've come to discover so many times in my life, for *me* as well.

When the philosophy Murph professed and the human science she invested in fails, she remembers the feelings she experienced as a child, when the "ghost" sent those messages in the dust on her bedroom floor. Then, in the same room decades later, she feels the same thing. "It felt like . . . like a person," she says. "Trying to tell me something." She soon realizes it is her father, somehow, and suddenly it makes enough sense for her to continue the rest of the way in faith.

Such a remembrance of fatherly love and the message that father is trying to convey to her echoes Alma the Younger's experience during his three-day coma. As he was "racked with torment" and "harrowed up by the memory of [his] many sins" (Alma 36:17), he remembered the words of his father about Christ. Finally, he understood the words of God—because his father loved him.

We feel the same with our Heavenly Father, don't we? Once we know He loves us and can recognize that love's source, what He's trying to get across—whether through the scriptures, life events, whisperings from the Spirit, or any of the numerous ways He speaks—becomes so much easier to grasp and believe.

Like Amelia to Dr. Edmunds, we are drawn to that feeling. Even when reason demands we choose Dr. Mann's planet, there is a part of us that feels the gravity of God's transcendent love beckoning us in His direction. And when we discover the uncertain or even nonexistent foundations of mortal philosophies, the immortal love of God remains.

Yes, Cooper left his daughter behind. God parted from us when we were born—our spiritual death. But He did not leave us for something else, some unrelated errand. He left so that we could be saved. He crossed the room so we could follow Him to a greater place, so we, as His little children, could take our "first steps" into godhood, as humans once took their first steps on the moon.

So when He seems to have left us, when there seems to be no light in our lives, remember Cooper's promise as God's promise, and feel His loving arms encircling you: "I love you forever, and I'm coming back."

It takes another forty years, by Murph's count, but Cooper does it; he returns. After the miraculous success of their adventure, Cooper finds Murph on a spacecraft orbiting Saturn, a temporary stepping stone for mankind in their interstellar journey to Dr. Edmunds's planet. Murph, now in her eighties, is lying in a hospital bed, surrounded by children and grandchildren of her own. Cooper has hardly aged a day. But he knows it's her; she is wearing the watch.

"Nobody believed me," she says, "but I knew you'd come back."

"How?" the father asks his daughter.

"Because my dad promised me."

Cooper closes his eyes and tears slide down his cheeks and onto her hands, which he has pressed against his face.

Elder Jeffrey R. Holland said, "Heavenly promises are always kept."[204] So when we ask, "Dad, can you fix this?"—we know that He can. But we must truly will it ourselves and honestly desire His help, and then throw up that shield of faith and plant ourselves upon the firmest foundation. That foundation is not in the dirt. It, like the answer, lies above us.

Arise: "This World Was Never Enough for You"

"I've figured out the message. It's one word. Know what it is?"
—Ten-year-old Murph to her father, Cooper

If there was one word, just one that Heavenly Father could use to communicate His plan to His children here on earth, what do you think it might be? This word would have to encompass all of His commandments, as well as the reasons He has given them. It would have to imply the end goal, the grand purpose of our existence—as well as His. Entailed in this one word would be the relationship He has with us, the positioning of our respective roles, and the nature of the emotional bridge that connects us. In short, this one word would need to define both God and the measure of His creations.

Now, for a final verdict on *Interstellar*, we turn to a line spoken by adult Murph as she explains the failure of Professor Brand's mathematical calculations and theorems to save humanity: "His solution was correct," she says. "He'd had it for years."

"It's worthless?" asks her doctor friend.

She replies, "It's half the answer."

"How do you find the other half?" asks her friend.

The screenplay reads, "Murph points at the sky."

Interstellar, intentionally or unintentionally, does indeed have half the answer—Nolan has the correct philosophy. He seems to see the need for transformation and our potential for ascension. He does not actually provide the source of transformation, nor that ascension, but he knows it's more than just improved technology. For if history has taught us anything, it is the consistency of human nature across every age, regardless of levels of technology and power over the elements. Society will never truly change and will continue to be marred by human nature, mired in mortal dust, because science and other philosophies of men cannot turn back entropy of the soul. Science cannot change the heart—the foundation of all human society.

Those human causes, while perhaps noble in intent, promote a false (or at least incomplete) ascension. Many want to save the world, and from a variety of malignancies, but for the most part, they are swatting at symptoms and throwing money at problems in the hope they will go away while continuing to live the lifestyle of their choice and expecting others to change.

Here in the last days, where the influence of religion is waning drastically, are people happier than ever before? Are people *better* than ever before? Is civilization more refined? Are humans further away from their animal selves? Some surveys may list "personal happiness" at an all-time high. But such surveys—the only barometer we have to judge—are mere snapshots of pleasure in the moments of people's lives, asking about happiness relative to them. You might as well ask a heroin addict at the apex of his high.

The world can't answer such a question of happiness and betterment without resorting to standards of wealth and temporal success, because without a standard of truth, there can be no value judgments of any kind—no foundation. Progress without God is just *change*.

To truly *progress*, we have to change our hearts. Only religion, only the gospel, can do that consistently and permanently. As President Boyd K. Packer pointed out, "The study of the doctrines of the gospel will improve behavior quicker than talking about behavior will improve behavior."[205] You can't do it with politics, economics, entertainment, or ordinary educational settings. The Spirit must be present, for it is the strongest force on our hearts and wills.

The first half of the equation is us: human beings and all that we can do. But of course it's not enough. Though he was the best of the best, Dr. Mann's fear, selfishness, and limited vision broke the *Endurance*. Just as Cooper in the lander ship had to drastically alter his perspective and use every one of the lander's capabilities to align and dock with the *Endurance*, it takes an intense amount of discipline, skill, patience, humility, and faith to align our wills and "dock" with God's. Some say it is impossible to live a lifestyle that can be granted a temple recommend. They say it isn't feasible to even try to change our natures or live up to the expectations of an ornery and hateful God.

But *we* say it's necessary. Here, as the world ripens in iniquity, when everything counts the most, when the stakes have never been higher, and we are compelled to either strive forward or languish behind in the dust, we must rise and let the old ways fall behind us, for our destiny lies above us.

But even after all we contribute, it is still only half the answer.

"Well, we got this far on our brains," Amelia protests while they're in a desperate situation on Dr. Miller's planet. "Farther than any human in history."

"Well, not far enough," Cooper replies bitterly.

"Our brains" are not good enough. We cannot build our godhood on human knowledge alone. We need more. We need the mirror of Heavenly Father to remind us of who we are—our identities and potential—and the source of the power that allows us to reach it. That truth and power lie where Murph pointed: above us.

For the other half of that answer is Christ. He is who we need. His Atonement provides the launching power we require. His gospel provides the upward lift necessary to break our telestial orbit. Science or any given political or social cause are not sufficient for true salvation. They merely represent superficial fixes that try to mend outward manifestations while the foundation remains rotted and in need of ripping out and replacing.

And so we see the need for the Finisher's touch, that which truly lifts us above the clouds. Though Christ's suffering in Gethsemane would have been impossible for any mortal, flawed human to endure, God said to His perfect Son, "It's necessary"—and so it was done.

Thus, when our endurance inevitably fails, we are the broken, damaged ring module. We are the ones crippled by the ambitions and limitations of the natural man. We are the ones in need of external assistance, even divine intervention to repair and rehabilitate us. Christ seeks to join with us, enter our hearts, and become *at one* with us. His endurance in the Garden soothes our souls, washes our hands, and purifies our hearts of the dust that once enveloped and pervaded them. Our Redeemer endured what no human could to make us whole again and save us from the natural man.

And just as the music that plays during this docking scene is the most intense and thunderous of the entire epic score, so was Christ's moment in Gethsemane the most intense and thunderously triumphant of all human history.

The tears, the sins, the dust of the earth cannot keep us down if we let the Savior into our lives—and yet, even while the Lord does what He can do, the angels do what *they* can do, and the sealing power does what *it* can do, there is still a component for us to do what *we* can do.

And that is what the Hero Doctrine is all about: awakening to our duty and our potential, both essential halves to the great lifting up of our souls.

In the temple, that "step-by-step ascension into the Eternal Presence" fittingly deposits us in the celestial room. What quiet we hear there. It's similar to the stillness of space, the peace of the perspective above the planet, where all excess sound is absorbed. I hear that and almost feel it in *Interstellar* as the *Endurance* glides through the nothingness near Saturn.

"The earth looks amazing from here," Cooper comments when they first break earth's orbit, earlier in the film. "You can't see any of the dust."

Fast forward to the end. After humankind has been saved, Cooper is shown the temporary space station they are dwelling in while they prepare to travel into the wormhole. He learns they prepared a special place for him at the insistence of his now-famous daughter: an exact replica of his fields and farmhouse back on earth. He is able to sit on his porch and kick back a cold one, just like he used to, but totally distant from the dust and dirt that used to choke the world.

The robot TARS is curious about something. "Is this really what it was like?" he asks.

Cooper responds in the affirmative but adds, "I was never this clean, Slick."

What is heaven like? The scriptures answer, "That same sociality which exists among us here will exist among us there, only it will be coupled with eternal glory, which glory we do not now enjoy" (D&C 130:2).

"If there's an answer here on earth," Murph says, "it's back in that room."

That room, where she last saw her father as together they interpreted the message in the dust. Back in that home, where her family was still together. Something in that notion of family, that special love and parent-child relationship, held the key to understanding the secrets of the universe beyond.

We witness Cooper's tearful reunion with his daughter and see the joy he takes in his posterity. We feel the love emanating from both of them, the father reuniting with his child, seeing her with her own generations of children. Eternal lives, eternal progression—began on earth, and then cleansed from mortal dust by the Atonement before stretching on and on into the endless cosmos.

More than any metaphysical reality, this is the vision God has for us. This is what is dearest to His heart—His work and His glory.

And it is your work as much as His. So open your eyes and awake.

"Something seemed wrong about dreaming my life away," remarks one of the crew's scientists after revealing he decided to forego hypersleep while the rest of them go down to Dr. Miller's planet.

Something *does* seem wrong about that, doesn't it? What happens when an object doesn't move for a long period of time? What happens to a person who is not engaged in life and work?

They gather dust.

Too many have slept like Rip van Winkle as the world continues on, as souls in need of help continue to flounder and drown with no one to throw out a life preserver. Make no mistake: we are the rescue crew. Amelia passes out from the gravitational forces of the spinning spacecraft, leaving Cooper alone to complete the world-saving task. The Apostle Peter, Jesus's greatest earthly friend, fell asleep while the Savior atoned for the sins of the world. Rather than imitate Brand in the spinning *Endurance* and Peter in the Garden of Gethsemane, let us not doze off while the most important work of this world goes on around us. Let us not sleep through the Restoration. For "this is no time for caution."

Alma warned us, "And now, as I said unto you before, as ye have had so many witnesses, therefore, I beseech of you that ye do not procrastinate the day of your repentance until the end; for after this day of life, which is given us to prepare for eternity, behold, *if we do not improve our time while in this life, then cometh the night of darkness wherein there can be no labor performed*" (Alma 34:33; emphasis added).

Swallowed by the black hole, Cooper is put in a similar position where no labor can be performed, where all he can do is send out the most subtle of messages. The first he tries to send a message not to Murph, but rather to his former self. It is a message of warning. Thinking he is stuck beyond hope of escape in the center of a black hole and regretting the massive amounts of time he knows he's lost over the course of his expedition, Cooper sends out a single word to his old self: Stay.

When Cooper took control of the unmanned drone flying over the cornfields at the beginning of the film, Murph asked him, "Couldn't we just let it go? It's not hurting anyone."

A kind and nonjudgmental view, but one that almost satanically squanders potential. "Stay" is a message sent in weakness; a message sent in love, yes, but out of desperation, faithlessness. Fear. A message whose foundation was not solid, despite its good intentions.

"Stay where you are," the world might tell us about our place in the dust. "It's a good place. It's the right place for you to be. You won't be judged, and it will be easy. You won't have any problems. You won't be uncomfortable. It won't require any real effort. It's who you are, after all, and you can't change who you are. Stay."

Have you given any thought to that question mentioned at the beginning of this final section? The challenge was to think of one word God might use to sum up His whole plan, a single word to encompass His commandments to and communications with His children. A one-word message, like "stay," that God might choose if

He had only one word to deliver. I'll offer you a hint by reminding you that the name of Cooper's interstellar mission was Lazarus.

Earth, like Lazarus, was dead. What did Christ say to the dead? What did Christ say to those who were fallen? What *does* Christ say to all who are fallen?

He said it to the Nephites, "And he commanded them that they should arise and stand up upon their feet. And they arose up and stood upon their feet" (3 Nephi 20:2).

I believe that is the one word: *arise*.

Arise and achieve the stature, purity, and existence of God. Arise from sins, sleep, and suffocating dust. Arise, take up your sword and shield, do battle, and "reap while the day lasts" to wake up the world to the conflict of justice (D&C 6:3).

Cooper soon realizes that he is in possession of the answer they've been looking for. Understanding why the five-dimensional beings brought him to that moment, he proceeds to send a different message. It is data, the information Murph needs to take humanity to the stars. That is the explicit message. But, to me, the implied message is even more important: not "stay," but "come."

Do not fear pain, grief, and sin, God has told us. All will be experienced; we will be separated from our Father for almost our entire lives, but we will be changed and transformed, and humanity with us. We are commanded to use this knowledge gained from His sacrifice and rise to His station, to a higher plane of living. In other words, arise.

"Awake, and arise from the dust, O Jerusalem," Moroni implored in the close of the Book of Mormon (Moroni 10:31), echoing Lehi's cries to his slumbering sons. Remember your destiny, even as Satan whispers precisely the opposite to us through the world: Dust is who you truly are. Man is just another animal. But mere animals are not capable of ascending beyond this planet, this earthly state.

"Believe in yourself," President Hinckley counseled. "Believe in your capacity to do great and good and worthwhile things. Believe in the nature within you, the divine nature, that you are in very deed a son or daughter of the living God. There is something of divinity within you, something that stands high and tall and noble. *Get above the dirt and the filth of the earth and walk on a higher plane* with your heads up, believing in yourselves and in your capacity to act for good in the world and make a difference."[206]

Yes, we are made of dust. God said just that in Genesis. But don't forget the truth mentioned earlier, which is that same dust has its true origins in the stars, in the chemistry of the cosmos. And we can return to that refined, reorganized, extended, and expanded state as we reject the entropic advance of the world and turn to Christ. Ours is a cause of refinement and endless progress, not complacency or cowardly compromise.

In the film's final scene, Cooper, not content to sit on a space station biding his time, jumps into another spacecraft, off to further pioneer the endless expanse of the stars.

"This world was never enough for you, was it, Coop?" Donald observes to his son-in-law early in the film.

No, it was not. Nor can it be for us. Make no mistake, we too are still pioneers. Our spiritual forebears fought for their physical survival. In our time, we are fighting for our spiritual survival. And eternally speaking, we are all fighting for that kind of survival that is metaphysical transcendence, necessitated by the last days of this earth before the great burning. We are constantly forging through the cosmic wilderness, discovering untold territories in ourselves and taking our first steps into spaces we've never before been, into righteousness and exaltation we thought we never could attain.

At least, we are meant to. But as Cooper noted in the teaser trailer, we too often lose that sense. We forget that we've just barely begun, that our greatest accomplishments cannot be behind us. Our destiny lies above us, reflected in the mirror of our Heavenly Father.

Yes, you are a child of God. He loves you forever, and even if He seems distant, whether it's because of your own choices or the everyday storms of life, He promises He's coming back. So too must we, if we find ourselves lost or strayed from the path beaten by pioneers before us, say to Heavenly Father the same thing in prayer: "I love you forever, and I'm coming back." Because He wants us there, back where we were previously, but never before as clean. Even with setbacks, sins, doubts, falls, and failures—even when you hate yourself for your thoughts or actions—He does not hate you. He knows you better than you know yourself, and He loves you.

And He alone knows what you're capable of:

Everything.

A Rousing Cry

I write this because too many close friends and family members have broken my heart because of their decision to reject the gospel, leave the Church, and fight against it. I think it's only in those heartbreaking times that we discover just how deep love can be. In fact, that love and constant heartache I feel for them is precisely the love God feels. But, somehow, His love is even greater and is felt for every single one of us.

God has a unique and infinitely deep universe of love for every individual you see walking down the street, shopping at the store, or sitting in squalor and asking for change on the sidewalk—for every one of His children. Numbers are not His concern; the gain of one soul does not replace the loss of another. His children each have a story that matters to Him, and the length of the journey does not matter so much as the ending.

But we are not there yet. The journey is not yet complete. There is still time, still so much left to do. And the outlook is grim in some cases.

> There is no peace on earth. . . .
> For hate is strong,
> And mocks the song
> Of peace on earth, good-will to men."[207]

But "God is not dead, nor doth He sleep"![208] And neither can we "sleep through the Restoration." We are needed.

So wake up. Arise and be children of God. Throw up that shield of faith and wield that sword of justice in defense of truth and virtue like the hero you need to be, and the god or goddess you one day will become. You know your duty, so do it. Bring souls unto Christ—bring joy to the world.

Be His missionaries in this foreign field. Be His mirror, His sword and shield.

Endnotes

1. "Viva la Vida," *Viva la Vida or Death and All His Friends*, Coldplay (London, June 2008), CD.

2. *Journal of Discourses*, Vol. 16 (London: Latter-day Saints' Book Despot, 1854–86), 160.

3. Terryl and Fiona Givens, *The God Who Weeps* (Salt Lake City: Ensign Peak, 2012), 54.

4. Neal A. Maxwell, "The Pathway of Discipleship," *Ensign*, September 1998.

5. *Journal of Discourses*, 3:47.

6. Terryl and Fiona Givens, *The God Who Weeps*, 98.

7. Dallin H. Oaks, "The Challenge to Become," *Ensign*, November 2000, 32.

8. *The African Queen*, directed by John Huston (1951).

Endnotes

9. Boyd K. Packer "The Witness," *Ensign*, May 2014, 95.

10. C. S. Lewis, *The Weight of Glory* (New York: HarperOne, 2009).

11. Vaughn J. Featherstone, "The King's Son," *New Era*, November 1975.

12. J. K. Rowling, *The Prisoner of Azkaban* (New York: Scholastic, 1999), 385.

13. Ibid., 407.

14. Ibid.

15. Plato, *The Republic*, trans. Benjamin Jowett (New York: Vintage, 1991).

16. Ibid.

17. Neal A. Maxwell, *We Will Prove Them Herewith* (Salt Lake City: Deseret Book, 1982), 12.

18. Malcolm Muggeridge, *A Twentieth-Century Testimony* (Ann Arbor: Thomas Nelson Publishers, 1978).

19. "Scenes from an Italian Restaurant," *The Stranger*, Billy Joel (New York, September 1977), CD.

20. James E. Talmage, "Three Parables—The Unwise Bee, the Owl Express, and the Two Lamps," *Liahona*, February 2003.

21. Neal A. Maxwell, "The Inexhaustible Gospel" (Brigham Young University devotional, August 18, 1992, http://speeches.byu.edu/?act=viewitem&id=625).

22. Joseph Smith, *Teachings of the Prophet Joseph Smith* (Salt Lake City: Deseret Book, 1938), 343.

23. Terryl and Fiona Givens, *The God Who Weeps*, 117.

24. Quentin L. Cook, "The Doctrine of the Father," *Ensign*, February 2012.

25. Ibid.

26. J. Devn Cornish, "The Privilege of Prayer," *Ensign*, November 2011.

27. Neal A. Maxwell, "The Pathway of Discipleship."

28. Neal A. Maxwell, "All Hell Is Moved" (Brigham Young University devotional, November 8, 1977, http://speeches.byu.edu/?act=viewitem&id=1050).

29. See *The God Who Weeps* for a theodicy that describes this aspect of God in full.

30. Quentin L. Cook, "The Doctrine of the Father."

31. Neal A. Maxwell, "Called to Serve" (Brigham Young University devotional, March 27, 1994, http://speeches.byu.edu/?act=viewitem&id=398).

32. Neal A. Maxwell, "The Inexhaustible Gospel."

33. Ibid.

34. Boyd K. Packer, "The Play and the Plan," CES fireside for young adults, May 7, 1995, 1–2.

35. J. K. Rowling, *Harry Potter and the Chamber of Secrets* (New York: Scholastic, 1999), 333.

36. J. Devn Cornish, "The Privilege of Prayer"; emphasis added.

Endnotes

37. Neal A. Maxwell, "Called to Serve."

38. "Nearer, My God, to Thee," *Hymns*, no. 100.

39. Dieter F. Uchtdorf, "Why Do We Need Prophets?" *Ensign*, March 2012.

40. Neal A. Maxwell, "The Pathway of Discipleship."

41. William Marrion Branham, "The Good Shepherd of the Sheep."

42. "Dear to the Heart of the Shepherd," *Hymns*, no. 221.

43. Neal A. Maxwell, " 'Swallowed Up in the Will of the Father,' " *Ensign*, November 1996.

44. C. S. Lewis, *The Problem of Pain*, in *The Complete C. S. Lewis Signature Classics* (New York: HarperCollins, 2002).

45. Matthew Holland, "Wrong Roads and Revelations," *New Era*, July 2005.

46. Hugh Nibley, *Temple and Cosmos* (Salt Lake City: Deseret Book, 1992), 534.

47. *Evan Almighty*, directed by Tom Shadyac (2007).

48. *Journal of Discourses*, 9:292.

49. Neal A. Maxwell, "Sharing Insights from My Life" (Brigham Young University devotional, January 12, 1999, http://speeches.byu.edu/?act=viewitem&id=805).

50. It should be noted that we've been talking about God's dealings with us as individual children and that I have purposefully left temple ordinances, family history, and missionary work off the

list. Though of course these are ways of saving souls, I do wish to keep the discussion limited to how God works with His children in a more intimate sense, how we come to know Him as our Father in a personal way. It is, as Elder Maxwell called this world, "this constant shaping of souls . . . this strategic swirl of people and principles and tactical situations" that I am referring to. The question I seek to answer, therefore, is not about converting and baptizing, but in God's methods of building and refining the individual soul.

51. Neal A. Maxwell, "The Pathway of Discipleship."

52. Dieter F. Uchtdorf, "Lift Where You Stand," *Ensign*, November 2008.

53. Charles Duhigg, "With Time Running Short, Jobs Managed His Farewells," *New York Times*, October 6, 2011.

54. Edwin Markham, "Man-Making," in *Masterpieces of Religious Verse*, ed. James Dalton Morrison (New York: Joanna Cotler Books, 1948), 419.

55. J. K. Rowling, *Harry Potter and the Prisoner of Azkaban*, 410.

56. Joseph F. McConkie, Robert L. Millet, and Brent L. Top, *Doctrinal Commentary on the Book of Mormon* (Salt Lake City: Bookcraft, 1987–92).

57. *Shadowlands*, directed by Richard Attenborough (1993).

58. Ibid.

59. Jeffrey R. Holland, "Lessons from Liberty Jail" (Brigham Young University devotional, September 7, 2008, http://speeches.byu. edu/?act=viewitem&id=1798).

Endnotes

60. Ibid.

61. *Shadowlands*, directed by Richard Attenborough (1993).

62. Brad Wilcox, "His Grace Is Sufficient" (Brigham Young University devotional, July 12, 2011, https://speeches.byu.edu/talks/brad-wilcox_his-grace-is-sufficient/).

63. *Shadowlands*, directed by Richard Attenborough (1993).

64. "Be Still, My Soul," *Hymns*, no. 124.

65. Jeffrey R. Holland, "Lessons from Liberty Jail."

66. M. Louise Haskins, "The Gate of the Year," in *Masterpieces of Religious Verse*, 92.

67. William Shakespeare, *Hamlet*, 3.1.73 (references are to act, scene, and line).

68. Neal A. Maxwell, "The Holy Ghost: Glorifying Christ," *Ensign*, July 2002.

69. "Lindbergh Nightmare," *Time*, February 5, 1973, 35, as quoted in Neal A. Maxwell, "Enduring Well" *Ensign*, April 1997.

70. Ibid.

71. Jeffrey R. Holland, "Lessons from Liberty Jail."

72. Ibid.

73. "How Firm a Foundation," *Hymns*, no. 85.

74. "Nearer, My God, to Thee," *Hymns*, no. 100.

75. *Preach My Gospel: A Guide to Missionary Service* (2004).

76. Tad R. Callister, *The Infinite Atonement* (Salt Lake City: Deseret Book, 2000), 167.

77. Hugh Nibley, *Approaching Zion* (Salt Lake City: Deseret Book, 1989), 555.

78. Hugh Nibley, *Temple and Cosmos.*

79. Alfred Tennyson. *In Memoriam*, verse 54.

80. "Be Still, My Soul," *Hymns*, no. 124.

81. Neal A. Maxwell, "Such as Is Common to Man" (University of Utah Institute talk, October 5, 1980).

82. Tad R. Callister, *The Infinite Atonement*, 167.

83. Hugh Nibley, *Temple and Cosmos.*

84. "Fix You," *X&Y*, Coldplay (London, June 2005), CD.

85. Dallin H. Oaks, "Resurrection," *Ensign*, May 2000.

86. Neal A. Maxwell, *We Will Prove Them Herewith*, 12.

87. "If You Could Hie to Kolob," *Hymns*, no. 284.

88. Tad R. Callister, *The Infinite Atonement*, 169.

89. C. S. Lewis, *The Last Battle* (New York: Scholastic, 1956), 198.

90. Tad R. Callister, *The Infinite Atonement*, 170.

91. Ibid.

Endnotes

92. Neal A. Maxwell, "'According to the Desire of [Our] Hearts,'" *Ensign*, November 1996.

93. *The Empire Strikes Back*, directed by Irvin Kirshner (1980).

94. Dallin H. Oaks, "Resurrection," *Ensign*, May 2000.

95. Orson F. Whitney, in Conference Report, April 1929, 110.

96. Brigham Young, as quoted in Joseph Fielding Smith, *Doctrines of Salvation*, comp. Bruce R. McConkie, 3 vols. (1954–56), 2:90–91.

97. Alfred Tennyson, *In Memoriam*, verse 124.

98. William Shakespeare, *Hamlet*, 3.1.70 (references are to act, scene, and line).

99. John Donne, "Death Be Not Proud."

100. C. S. Lewis, *The Last Battle*, 172.

101. Neal A. Maxwell, "Such as Is Common to Man."

102. C. S. Lewis, *The Last Battle*, 194–95.

103. Ibid.

104. Ibid., 205–06.

105. Ibid., 210–11.

106. *Om Shanti Om*, directed by Farah Khan (2007).

107. *The Dark Knight*, directed by Christopher Nolan (2008).

108. Adam C. Olson, "What Am I Worth?" *Ensign*, September 2012.

109. *The Dark Knight*, directed by Christopher Nolan (2008).

110. Terryl and Fiona Givens, *The God Who Weeps*, 27.

111. "Be Still, My Soul," *Hymns*, no. 124.

112. Jeffrey R. Holland, "None Were with Him," *Ensign*, May 2009.

113. Neal A. Maxwell, "The Holy Ghost: Glorifying Christ."

114. Brad Wilcox, "His Grace Is Sufficient."

115. Joseph Smith, *Teachings of the Prophet Joseph Smith*, 240–41, 257.

116. Thomas S. Monson, "See Others as They May Become," *Ensign*, November 2012.

117. Jeffrey R. Holland, "None Were with Him."

118. Brad Wilcox, "His Grace Is Sufficient."

119. J. K. Rowling, *Harry Potter and the Deathly Hallows* (New York: Scholastic, 2007), 692.

120. Neal A. Maxwell, "Called to Serve."

121. J. K. Rowling, *Harry Potter and the Deathly Hallows*.

122. I'll keep that particular can of worms closed for now, but see Joseph Smith's *Lectures on Faith* for more on this.

123. Neal A. Maxwell, *Meek and Lowly* (Salt Lake City: Deseret Book, 1987), 6–7.

Endnotes

124. Neal A. Maxwell, *We Will Prove Them Herewith*, 3.

125. Darwin in particular is still at the center of religious conflict today, as his discoveries seem to directly contradict the origin of man that is depicted in the Bible. Darwin, though he was an ardent believer in his younger days and became less so as he studied the process of natural selection, never ceased in his wrestles with the existence of God, a grapple of agnosticism predicated on his research and own intuitions. But regardless of his personal beliefs, his scientific legacy has brought many since to reject the notion of God as Creator. So was his search for truth worth it? I, for one, think so. As I detail more thoroughly later, I suggest to the vacillating soul to wait before deciding if one side or the other in the debate of religion and science is truly and absolutely correct. After all, for many, Darwin's discoveries have inspired a grander view of God with a more expansive understanding of His creative ways. Though the theory of macro-evolution seems to contradict the story of Eden as the beginning of human existence, perhaps with time that discovery will be revealed as simply another stepping stone toward a greater truth that neither the Church nor science could have predicted or even understood at this moment in time.

126. Neal A. Maxwell, *We Will Prove Them Herewith*, 8.

127. Neal A. Maxwell, "Grounded, Rooted, Established, and Settled" (Brigham Young University devotional, September 15, 1981, http://speeches.byu.edu/?act=viewitem&id=910).

128. Brigham Young, *Discourses of Brigham Young*, comp. John A. Widtsoe (Salt Lake City: Deseret Book, 1954), 2.

129. Neal A. Maxwell, "The Inexhaustible Gospel," 224.

130. Of course, there is something to be said for the myriad ways the advent of medicine and technology have hastened the work

of the gospel. Truly, many of our advancements are inspired of heaven, meant for the sake of the work. And it is no coincidence that scientific advancements exploded exponentially around the time the Restoration began. Technology has aided and accelerated the work of the gospel in ways that were unthinkable before, and much of the missionary work we do depends on that technology. The scriptures and sermons of the Restoration surely relied on the invention of the printing press centuries previous, and in our time the Internet has changed the work as much as it has the world.

131. Neal A. Maxwell, *We Will Prove Them Herewith*, 16.

132. Spencer W. Kimball, "The Savior: The Center of Our Lives," *New Era*, April 1980.

133. Dennis B. Horne, ed., *An Apostle's Record: The Journals of Abraham H. Cannon* (Clearfield, Utah: Gnolaum Books, 2004), 229.

134. Neal A. Maxwell, *We Will Prove Them Herewith*, 17.

135. Neal A. Maxwell, "The Inexhaustible Gospel."

136. Jeffrey R. Holland, "'Lord, I Believe,'" *Ensign*, May 2013.

137. Gerald Lund, *Diving Signatures* (Salt Lake City: Deseret Book, 2010).

138. Terryl and Fiona Givens, *The God Who Weeps*, 9.

139. Jeffrey R. Holland, "Safety for the Soul," *Ensign*, November 2009.

140. Hugh Nibley, *Lehi in the Desert* (Salt Lake City: Deseret Book, 1988), 139.

Endnotes

141. Jeffrey R. Holland, "Safety for the Soul."

142. Neal A. Maxwell, "But for a Small Moment" (Brigham Young University devotional, September 1, 1974, http://speeches.byu.edu/?act=viewitem&id=1022).

143. J. K. Rowling, *Harry Potter and the Deathly Hallows*.

144. Spencer W. Kimball, "Small Acts of Service," *Ensign*, December 1974.

145. Dieter F. Uchtdorf, "You Are My Hands," *Ensign*, May 2010.

146. Gordon B. Hinckley, *Stand A Little Taller* (Salt Lake City: Deseret Book, 2001), 37.

147. Ibid., 32.

148. Bill Watterson, *Calvin and Hobbes* (Kansas City: Andrew McMeel Publishing, October 18, 1990).

149. Gordon B. Hinckley, "Stand Up for Truth" (Brigham Young University devotional, September 17, 1996, http://speeches.byu.edu/?act=viewitem&id=738).

150. Jeffrey R. Holland, "We Are All Enlisted," *Ensign*, November 2011.

151. Joseph Smith, *History of the Church* ed. B. H. Roberts, 7 vols. (Salt Lake City: The Church of Jesus Christ of Latter-day Saints, 1932–51), 4:227.

152. Jeffrey R. Holland, "We Are All Enlisted."

153. Dieter F. Uchtdorf, "Lift Where You Stand."

154. Ibid.

155. Read Alma 17–26 to see the fruits of their repentance.

156. Heidi Swinton, *To the Rescue: The Biography of Thomas S. Monson* (Salt Lake City: Deseret Book, 2010), 4.

157. Truman Madsen, *The Temple* (Salt Lake City: Deseret Book, 2008), 14.

158. Ibid., 24.

159. Ibid., 36–37.

160. John D. Charles, *Endowed from on High* (Springville: Cedar Fort, 2004), 29.

161. Joseph Smith, *Teachings of the Prophet Joseph Smith*, 162.

162. Truman Madsen, *The Temple*.

163. Ibid., 109.

164. Ibid., 3.

165. Ibid., 25.

166. C. S. Lewis, *The Screwtape Letters*, in *The Complete C. S. Lewis Signature Classics*, 207.

167. Neal A. Maxwell, "The Pathway of Discipleship."

168. Truman Madsen, *The Temple*, 42.

169. Ibid.

Endnotes

170. Ibid., 31.

171. Ibid., 96.

172. Ibid., 51.

173. Howard W. Hunter, *The Teachings of Howard W. Hunter*, ed. Clyde J. Williams (Salt Lake City: Bookcraft, 1997), 233.

174. *Spider-Man*, directed by Sam Raimi (2002).

175. Jennifer Glancy, "Slaves and Slavery in the Matthean Parables," *Journal of Biblical Literature* 119.1 (2000), 67–90.

176. Orson Scott Card, *A Storyteller in Zion* (Salt Lake City: Bookcraft, 1993).

177. Online Etymology Dictionary, http://www.etymonline.com/index.php?term=talent.

178. Boyd K. Packer, "The Arts and the Spirit of the Lord" (Brigham Young University devotional, February 1, 1976, http://speeches.byu.edu/?act=viewitem&id=380).

179. Jeffrey R. Holland, "The First Great Commandment," *Ensign*, November 2012.

180. Orson Scott Card, "Already Consecrated," *Nauvoo Times*, January 25, 2013.

181. Jeffrey R. Holland, "We Are All Enlisted."

182. Ibid.

183. Arthur Henry King, "A Testimony of My Conversion," *New Era*, February 1971.